Bright Underachievers

PUBLISHED FOR THE HORACE MANN–LINCOLN
INSTITUTE OF SCHOOL EXPERIMENTATION,
TALENTED YOUTH PROJECT

Bright Underachievers

STUDIES OF SCHOLASTIC UNDER-ACHIEVEMENT AMONG INTELLECTUALLY SUPERIOR HIGH SCHOOL STUDENTS

JANE BEASLEY RAPH, Professor of Education, Rutgers University ● MIRIAM L. GOLDBERG, Associate Professor of Psychology and Education, Teachers College, Columbia University ● A. HARRY PASSOW, Professor of Education, Teachers College, Columbia University

TEACHERS COLLEGE PRESS, Teachers College, Columbia University, New York, 1966

Manufactured in the United States of America

Foreword

When bright students do not do well scholastically, everyone feels the failure. The fact that an occasional bright dropout becomes a successful popular essayist, or dramatist, or businessman does not alter things, for it is the business of the school not only to offer learning, but to predict which students should undertake difficult advanced work and to expect a level of performance in accord with the prediction.

Very well—perhaps the expectation ought to be tempered. "Bright" means that at one time or another a child has shown examples of the kind of accomplishment schools exist to advocate; a "bright" underachiever has somehow managed to abort the schools' optimistic prediction, and incidentally to deny its most cherished values. No wonder teachers worry about underachievement.

The present study grows out of several years' close study of academically talented students. The Talented Youth Project of the Horace Mann–Lincoln Institute conducted studies and collected the literature of the field throughout the 1950's, publishing occasional summaries of its work; this study, like others from the Project, is thorough, based on an exhaustive review of the relevant scholarship—and, like the others, it demonstrates that simplistic answers to the question of the encouragement of bright students are, in the main, inadequate.

The studies provide insights into the behaviors, feelings, and aspirations of bright adolescents: those who achieve well and those who do poorly in school. But the major emphasis of the research was on the assessment of various remedial procedures intended to improve the underachievers' school performance.

The students studied by the Talented Youth Project staff are representative of thousands of their peers across the nation. The two high schools included in the study differed from each other geographically, socioeconomically, organizationally. Nevertheless, the students were similar in their views of themselves and in their teachers' views of them. Underachievement among bright students seems little affected by local conditions.

Studies of this kind, if they are attended to in our doctrinaire educational world, have an astringent effect. The students make simple-sounding demands on their teachers: that they know their subject matter, keep order, and accept the students as persons worth individual attention. But their demands on themselves are complex and contradictory. Possibly, if we can disentangle ourselves from our most cherished assumptions regarding academic expectations, in general, and the ability of the school to affect the academic progress of those who fail to act in accordance with the predictions made for them, we can seek new ways to listen to the children intelligently and help them cut through their confusions. It is to be hoped.

ARTHUR W. FOSHAY
Director, Horace Mann–Lincoln
Institute of School Experimentation

August, 1966

Acknowledgments

The authors are particularly appreciative of the fine cooperation and assistance given them by Walter Degnan, Principal of DeWitt Clinton High School in New York City, and Lloyd S. Michaels, Superintendent–Principal of Evanston Township High School, Evanston, Illinois. Without their support and that of their department chairmen, teachers, and students, the studies reported here could not have been completed.

The authors are also grateful to the staff members of the Horace Mann–Lincoln Institute of School Experimentation whose keen interest and thoughtful questions contributed richly to the research throughout its progress.

Dr. Abraham Tannenbaum, a member of the underachievement project during its inception, contributed freely of his wisdom and scholarliness. Dr. Paul Pimsleur, Mrs. Lois Appell Rothman, and Mrs. Aida Kashishian Price assisted in the statistical analyses. Mr. Nicholas Vecchione reviewed and criticized the manuscript. The tedious task of typing the manuscript was ably discharged by Miss Myrna Rosen.

JANE BEASLEY RAPH
MIRIAM L. GOLDBERG
A. HARRY PASSOW

August, 1966

Contents

Bright Underachievers

CHAPTER ONE

The problem of scholastic underachievement

THE INTELLECTUALLY GIFTED UNDERACHIEVER is an ubiquitous phenomenon, identifiable in all schools and at all academic levels; but he appears most frequently, stands out most markedly, and presents a most significant educational challenge at the secondary school level. He may appear in many guises—lazy, disinterested in school, bored, rebellious, unable to relate to teachers, or having difficulty with one or more subjects. Nonetheless, no matter what the appearance, he is generally a youngster who is not using his intellectual potential fully in meeting the academic demands of the school. As generally defined, the high-ability underachiever not only fails to reach the academic excellence which his outstanding ability suggests he is able to attain, but also is often found lagging behind the achievement level of students of average ability, or, at best, only managing to hold his own with them.

Recognition of academic underachievement as a serious psychological and social problem reflects the values of a culture which attempts to look beyond performance to potential; maintains a prolonged compulsory system of education; seeks to nurture and develop diversity of abilities within and among individuals; and concerns itself with the maximum development of the individual as well as his contribution to society. John Gardner (1961), in his book, *Excellence*, states the challenge as follows:

1

"Our society cannot achieve greatness unless individuals at many levels of ability accept the need for high standards of performance and strive to achieve those standards within the limits possible for them. . . . the fact that large numbers of American boys and girls fail to attain their full development must weigh heavily on our national conscience" (p. 131).

Definition of Underachievement

The broadest definition of underachievement among the more able would refer to all those who, for whatever reasons, fail to develop their potentialities maximally. Only if it were possible to assess potential with sufficient accuracy to enable prediction of performance for all individuals would such a definition become operationally meaningful. Assessments now made by intelligence and aptitude tests predict intellectual behavior from samples of performance at a given time. Since the sampling is, in all cases, from the universe of learned behavior, the assumptions are made that, in general, all children of a given age have been exposed to more or less comparable learning opportunities and, therefore, differences in aptitude test scores reflect differences in individual abilities to take advantage of the learning opportunities generally available. For groups which have been deprived of exposure to many facets of the learning environment familiar to the general population, aptitude test scores, although predictive of performance under continued cultural deprivation, provide scant indication of how such a group might function if brought into contact with enriched cultural experiences. In the absence of any evidence to indicate that innate intellectual ability or other talents are to be expected in one ethnic or racial group more often than in another, it might be assumed that there are potentially gifted people in all groups, who, at present, have not been identified. For instance, one large group of potentially able underachievers remains hidden within the mass of culturally disadvantaged people in American society. To discover these underachievers requires experimentation with varied social and educational modifications, now just beginning in some urban centers.

A somewhat narrower definition of underachievement refers to all those individuals who demonstrate well above average intellectual or academic ability on intelligence and aptitude tests but fail to develop their abilities. This definition includes all those who rank in the upper third of the population in ability, but who do not graduate from high school, do not go on to college, or drop out of college before completing their studies, thus failing to acquire the academic preparation needed for the high level jobs they are potentially able to fill. A study undertaken for the National Science Foundation and reported by Bridgman (1960) estimated that, in the top 30 per cent of high school graduates, 55 per cent of the boys and 70 per cent of the girls do not complete college. The greater part of the attrition occurred after students had entered college. The actual number of young persons in the top third of the population who did not complete college is quantitatively a serious talent waste. Even more serious, qualitatively, is the failure of about half of those in the top 10 per cent in ability to prepare themselves for the high level pursuits of which they are capable.

Several criteria need to be considered when identifying underachievers in the top 10 per cent in intellectual ability: (1) From a societal point of view, the group would include all those in the top 10 per cent in ability who fail to complete a course of academic preparation which would enable them to enter the professional or managerial vocations. (2) From an educational point of view, it would include all those students who score in the top decile (or beyond 1.5 standard deviations above the mean) on tests of intelligence and academic aptitude but whose academic performance is at or below the median (or mean) for the general age group. Within this group two distinct subgroups can be identified: (a) Those students who rank high on IQ tests but low on both teacher grades and standardized tests of achievement. (b) Those students who score high on both intelligence and standardized achievement tests, but whose school grades are low. Within this latter subgroup there are some who receive consistently low ratings in all or most school subjects and some who receive poor grades in only one or two subjects.

History of the Study of Bright Underachievers

Following advances made in the measurement of intelligence in this country during and after World War I, Volume I of the *Genetic Studies of Genius* by Terman and his Stanford University associates (1925) furnished us with a core of scientific knowledge about persons with superior intellectual endowment. Their findings pointed conclusively to the generally superior physical, emotional, and social characteristics of intellectually gifted children, serving to dispel gradually "the widespread notion that . . . precocity is pathological" (Terman and Oden, 1947, p. 452). At about the same time Hollingworth (1926) and Conklin (1931), using Terman's work as a springboard, began to raise questions of a clinical and educational nature, the answers to which would help explain why, in spite of this apparent all-round superior endowment, many able young persons failed to achieved scholastically at a satisfactory level. Hollingworth studied the social adjustment of the highly gifted and the effects of special school programs upon these students' scholastic achievement, while Conklin turned to an investigation of the relationship between certain psychiatric factors and school success.

Terman's follow-up studies of his subjects (1947) provided much of the current impetus for recognition and study of the problem of underachievement among the academically gifted. Average academic grades obtained in college by 1,003 of his subjects with IQ scores above 135 were examined. Of the 849 subjects who were graduated from college, 20 per cent made an average college grade of C or lower, while of the 154 who dropped out of college after two years, 34 per cent made an average grade of C or lower. Of the men who entered college, 7.7 per cent failed.

When comparing the 150 men in the sample who had been *most successful* in their occupations with the 150 *least successful*, Terman found that 90 per cent of the first group had been graduated from college, while only 37 per cent of the second group finished college. Only 7.2 per cent of the group of 125 graduates who later were rated *most successful* vocationally made an average of C or lower in college; in contrast, of the 52 graduates who were rated the *least successful* vocationally, 31 per cent made an average of C or lower in college. Other differences between the two groups showed the most successful subjects to have had greater breadth of interests, stronger educational traditions in their families, and more positive trait ratings in the areas of emotional stability, social adjustment, and drive to achieve. The two groups differed most widely in the following traits: persistence in the accomplishment of ends, integration toward goals, self-confidence, and freedom from inferiority feelings.

The nature of these findings by Terman (1925) was to foreshadow considerable continuing attention to the problem of underachievement among the academically superior during the decades following World War II. Terman's commitment to the seriousness of the talent loss is reflected in his own words: "Circumstances (which) affect the fruition of human talent are questions of such transcendent importance that they should be investigated by every method that promises the slightest reduction of our ignorance" (Preface). It is undoubtedly true, as noted by Kreuter (1962), that the bulk of Terman's work stressed the potential of the gifted for social adaptation, moral stamina, and attainment of leadership positions to the neglect of such factors as the social value of genius and the importance of the economic and political attitudes of these persons. Nevertheless, later events redirected attention to the importance of wise use of talent in our society and to the information Terman and his associates had made available. Scientific and technical manpower shortages created by World War II, the need to meet the Soviet military threat, and an ensuing critical examination of educational aims, problems, and programs by an aroused public and a thoughtful segment of professional educators stimulated anew interest in the gifted. The Rockefeller Panel's *The Pursuit of Excellence: Education and the Future of America* (1958), for example, dealt with the critical need to make better use of achievement at all levels in a rapidly changing and increasingly complex society.

> The cultivation of excellence, the pursuit of achievement for its own sake, is a latent force in any society. . . . Intellectual excellence has not always ranked high in the scale of values of Americans generally; but with our rising educational level and increasing prominence of intellectual pursuits, there are signs that this evaluation is changing. The desirability of such a change cannot be too strongly stressed. . . . a nation only achieves the kind of greatness it seeks and understands. Only if we value intellectual excellence shall we have it. (p. 46)

The widespread use of tests of intelligence, achievement, and aptitude, the higher school-leaving age (as compared with the post World War I period), and the greater competition for admission to college also served to set in bold relief the discrepancy which frequently exists between intellect and achievement.

Incidence of Underachievement

The need for attention to the problem of talent waste was stated as follows in a report by the Fund for the Advancement of Education (1957):

> Despite the great strides made by American education over the last 50 years, we are still far-short of the goal of enabling and encouraging every young person to develop to his full potential. The resulting waste of rich human resources is enormous, and is deeply rooted in our educational system, right down to the earliest grades. We must therefore attack the long-run problems of talent supply primarily through our schools and colleges. (Foreword)

Alter (1953), in a study of 1,162 students living in a high-ranking socioeconomic area, found a total of 74, or 7 per cent, of a suburban junior-senior high school with scores of 130 IQ and above on the California Test of Mental Maturity (CTMM). Among the 45 young persons in senior high school, 19, or 42 per cent, were underachievers, and of these, 3, or 6 per cent, were severe underachievers. Ritter and Thome (1954), investigating two graduating classes of a county high school in California, found that only 35 per cent of the students won a grade-point rank as high as their IQ-score rank. On the college level, too, substantial numbers of superior students have been observed as functioning below academic capacity. Wedemeyer's study (1953) in a large western college revealed that fully 22 per cent of the students ranking in the 98th and 99th percentile in intelligence could be regarded as nonachievers. A study of 4,900 "bright" high school students conducted in New York City in the Talent Preservation Project (Krugman, 1960) reports that, when halfway through high school, 54 per cent of the boys and 33 per cent of the girls had scholastic averages which were already so low that their admission to college was in doubt. These students represented the high-ability populations of their classes (selected from a total population of 50,000) in 39 academic high schools; and of the 4,900, only 20 per cent were able to complete the first three terms of senior high school without faltering at some point by receiving grades below 85.

Holland and Austin (1962) called attention to figures which indicate that almost all of the top 5 per cent of high school graduates now go on to college, but that a much more significant loss occurs among those who rank in the next 5 per cent of ability. Here, the loss is about one out of ten for boys and one out of five for girls. At the same time Holland criticized surveys of talent loss where loss is defined only as the proportion of high-aptitude high school students who do *not* attend college. Even if the validity of the aptitude measure employed is accepted, the conception that failure of bright students to go on to college is a clear-cut indication of underachievement has several shortcomings. Such an index, in the first place, is restricted to high school seniors. Secondly, the preoccupation with financial problems as a reason for not attending college means that such factors as being a woman, a member of a minority group, or a person with physical or mental illness are overlooked. Thirdly, it is not yet known if failure to attend college inevitably constitutes a talent loss to the nation.

In the entire picture of failure to achieve, the differential figures between men and women raise certain issues regarding sex roles and academic learning. Although more males than females demonstrate scholastic underachievement throughout school, the preponderance is reversed in the college, graduate, and postgraduate years. Drews (1957), noting that the incidence of underachievers in her group of 150 high-ability high school students was low, found that most of the boys were planning on college careers. Wastage was great among girls, who, although achieving well in high school, often looked upon high school as terminal education. High school boys studied by Pierce and Bowman (1960) showed greater *unconscious* need for achievement as measured by projective devices than did girls. The authors attributed this result to the tendency of society to evaluate a boy largely on the basis of his personal achievement. Girls, in contrast, revealed more *conscious* concern with regard to achievement values, an outcome inferred by the investigators to be indicative of conformity patterns employed by girls as a means of maintaining approving personal relationships. It was concluded that sex differences in motivation in this study were a function of adaptive responses to differing cultural expectations for boys and girls.

However one focuses on the problem of loss to society of high-level ability, there are sufficient wasted human resources of an exceptional type to point to a critical need for making better use of our talented generations of young persons (Wolfle, 1960). Better use calls for approaches on many fronts—encouragement of talent, examination of social factors which influence development of potentially high ability, early identification and remediation of school achievement problems, and systematic study of possible antecedents of poor academic performance.

Characteristics of Research in Underachievement

Investigations related to underachievement have been many and varied and have subjected the problem to a thoroughgoing analysis from many points of view. In the articles reviewed for these studies, popularity of the topic as a subject for research is demonstrated by the increase in the number of studies of underachievement reported in the literature—from 8 in the decade of the 1930's to 146 in the 1950's. Trends in the educational level at which studies of underachievement have been undertaken are shown in Table I-1. The direction has been from an almost total emphasis on poor scholastic performance at the college level to an increasing number of studies undertaken at the high school and junior high school level, and a growing

Table I-1. The Number of Research Studies on Scholastic Underachievement Published from 1923 to 1962 by Decades according to Educational Level of Subjects Studied[a]

| | | Educational Levels | | | | |
Decade	Elementary	Junior High	High	College	More Than One Level	Total
1923–1932	2	0	1	2	1	6
1933–1942	2	0	2	4	0	8
1943–1952	1	2	1	17	2	23
1953–1962	16	16	51	50	13	146
Total	21	18	55	73	16	183

[a] Thirteen 1963–1964 studies reported in these studies include eight at the high school level, four at the college level, and one other.

number of studies now being conducted in the elementary grades.

Trends in the nature of the variables studied reveal no clear-cut pattern. From Terman's beginning work to the present, studies have contained descriptions of various underachieving samples selected from different grade levels. Personality traits, self-evaluations, attitudes, interests, and social adjustment of high-, normal-, and overachieving groups have been compared. Additional studies have been concerned with causative factors. In this connection, home and family relationships, socioeconomic backgrounds, educational and cultural levels of families, and achievement motivation have received attention, as have students' study habits, vocational aspirations, and extra-curricular activities.

Questions Regarding the Concept of Underachievement

Before results of these studies are reviewed, it may be well to consider some pertinent questions currently being directed at the entire concept of underachievement. From the perspective of almost forty years of persistent effort to identify, explain, and ameliorate lowered scholastic performance, the researcher today can see vast improvement in the theoretical framework of studies, the methods of sample selection, and the techniques of assessment. Certain problems remain.

If by underachievement is meant achievement below some standard expected or predicted on the basis of IQ scores, then the validity of using IQ scores for predicting overall school performance and performance in particular school subjects must be examined. Any study purporting to determine the "why's" of unfulfilled promise must assume, a priori, that it is dealing with a group of students whose capacity for school work clearly exceeds performance. The burden of proof in designating the students as underachievers rests upon the researcher. He must have confidence in his predictors, in what is being predicted, and in the comparability of the samples he identifies to study.

Measurement errors in the use of IQ scores as predictors

In regard to measurement errors, the following questions should be raised:

1. How logical is it to assume that IQ scores are immune to the effects of the nonintellective factors which are frequently hypothesized to be inhibiting good school performance such as personal, social, or motivational influences?
2. To what extent can a single measure of intelligence predict performance accurately? Can giftedness be defined on the basis of one IQ measure? Where there is a time gap between the IQ score and the achievement score, is attention given to the possible changes in intellectual functioning which have been shown to occur within even a short period of time (Bayley, 1955)?
3. Where a discrepancy score between intelligence and performance is used as a criterion measure for underachievement, have the errors attributable to lowered reliability of the difference scores of the two tests been considered? Has the tendency of scores to gravitate toward the mean, which may place a student two standard deviations above the mean on an IQ test, but only one standard deviation above the mean on an achievement test, been considered, for example, as account-

ing in part for the apparent unsatisfactory academic performance?

4. Since it is known that IQ scores have better predictive value in such areas as English literature and language than in mathematics or foreign language, is a low grade in a particular subject matter area likely to reflect an expected unevenness in the prophetic power of the IQ test rather than bona fide underachievement?

Validity of achievement measures

The validity of the various achievement criteria also needs to be examined:

1. Although teacher grades have been commonly employed as a criterion measure of scholastic underachievement, can the fact be ignored that such grades are influenced by teacher personality, bias, experience, and special interests, or by student attitudes, behavior, and work habits?
2. When total scores on achievement test batteries are used as a criterion measure of achievement, do these totals blur the presence of specific underachievement in one subject or superior achievement in another area?
3. When grade-point average (GPA), class rank, and battery mean scores on achievement tests are used as measures of achievement, can such criteria cloud the important fact of achievement quite commensurate with capacity in certain academic areas (Mitchell, 1963)?
4. Even if failure by a bright youngster in one specific subject such as French or Spanish occurs, is it justifiable to label him an underachiever when intelligence plus ability in English have been shown to account for only 20 per cent of the variance in foreign language achievement, leaving 80 per cent of the variance unexplained (Pimsleur, 1962)?

Criterion heterogeneity

Thorndike (1963) calls attention to the importance of not only avoiding errors of measurement as far as possible, but also eliminating criterion heterogeneity. Criterion heterogeneity is the extent to which a criterion score of either aptitude or achievement changes its nature and meaning from one person to another. To reduce heterogeneity two avenues are open. Either a very large, randomly selected sample is needed in order to "wash out" the effects of differences in sex, schools, socioeconomic factors, curricula, and teachers, or research analyses should be carried on within subgroups that are homogeneous with respect to the variables thought to be significant determinants of criterion scores. This latter suggests that a researcher could justify predicting tenth grade mathematics grades within a group of tenth graders in the College Preparatory Program of High School X which is being taught by Teacher Y. These predictors could then be pooled with those from other homogeneous groups if there were need to increase the size of the experimental population.

Special research issues

Research designs, in retrospect, also raise many provocative questions regarding the frameworks in which they are cast:

1. Underachievement, once its presence is determined, becomes frozen, so to speak, in a research model, and may obscure, except in the rare longitudinal type study, a view of its dynamic qualities. Should there be established, as Fliegler (1957) suggests, a typological distinction within the classification of underachievement which would make possible a differentiation between the long-term and the situational underachiever?

2. Maladjustment finds many ways of expressing itself. With reference to achievement, one student may defensively overcompensate for felt deficiencies through intensive concentration on his studies; another may dwell at such length on the problems he feels that he pays no attention to his studies, or finds himself unable to concentrate on them. Both students are likely to "fool" the predictions which academic ability tests have for them, but in opposite directions (Hoyt & Norman, 1954).

3. Should a closer look be taken at the value system which in the present day places tremendous weight on one aspect of talent, namely that of scholastic achievement, to the exclusion, all too often, of recognition of talented performance in music,

writing, technical skill, social leadership, and even "follower-ship" (Wolfle, 1960)?

4. Should there be concern about the extent to which the value patterns of the high achiever seem to be highly correlated in study after study with the values of the teachers who give the high marks (Battle, 1957; Getzels & Jackson, 1962; Michael, Jones, & Trembly, 1959; Reed, 1955) suggesting a type of conformity in our potentially creative students?

5. How can the study of the causative factors associated with the underachievers' commonly expressed lack of interest in or negative attitudes toward academic achievement be approached? Should teachers, teaching methods, and content material be scrutinized more closely?

6. Despite some clear-cut differences among groups of high and low achievers, is there not a danger in viewing the constellation of adjectives describing the two groups as representing a typical "underachiever" or "overachiever," because the with-in-group variance is soon overlooked or even completely forgotten? A constellation of adjectives leading to a generalized profile, according to Cooley (1962), may be merely a summary of a summary, and may not describe any one student.

Thorndike (1961) interprets the search for answers to the kinds of questions raised in an attempt to account for the dissonance between ability and achievement as follows:

> Probably the most common type of research on "underachievement" is that which looks for facts or factors associated with that "underachievement." What this means is that we are looking for facts associated with the discrepancies between predicted and observed achievement, that is, with that part of achievement that is not already predicted by the variables or team of variables with which we are currently working. We are looking for predictors of the unpredicted residual of achievement. . . . The end result of finding factors associated with underachievement can be expected to be the incorporation of those factors into our prediction, with resulting increase in predictive accuracy and disappearance of part of the underachievement. (p. 5)

It is probably justifiable to conclude that regardless of how much of the discrepancy between prediction and achievement may be due to errors of measurement, to statistical artifacts, and to inadequate research designs, a part of the dissonance in all likelihood resides within the social and psychological makeup of the individual and the nature of the school he attends. It is with these latter factors in mind that the inquiries to be described here were addressed.

The Talented Youth Project's Studies
of Underachievement

Two investigations were carried out cooperatively by the staff of the Talented Youth Project, Teachers College, Columbia University and by members of the staff of the Evanston Township High School, Evanston, Illinois, and the DeWitt Clinton High School, The Bronx, New York.

Purposes

At the time these two studies were conceived, there were few studies dealing with the underachiever's phenomenological frame of reference, and even fewer attempting to provide planned intervention within the school and to assess the effectiveness of a particular provision or series of provisions.

The purposes of these two studies, accordingly, were: (1) to penetrate beneath the outward manifestations of the behavior of high school underachievers to their own perceptions of themselves, their abilities, personal characteristics, and aspirations, as well as to their perceptions of their academic life, satisfactions and dissatisfactions with school provisions, faculty attitudes, and parental interests and pressures; and (2) to experiment with specific curricular and administrative modifications in the high school situation which might serve to raise the achievement level of underachieving high ability students.

Limitations

The first study was conceived of as descriptive in nature. In view of the difficulty of determining to what extent the self-concept is responsible for achievement status and to what extent it may itself result from a sense of esteem or inadequacy engendered by high or low achievement, no attempt was made to seek causative relationships. The intent was to gain understanding of how the gifted underachiever, compared with the gifted high achiever as well as with the general population, views himself, his present abilities, characteristics, and competencies, and also to discover what kind of a person he wishes to be. From such data it would then be possible to assess differences in extent of satisfaction or dissatisfaction with his own status.

Similarly, information on attitudes toward home and school and other background material was gathered to shed light on factors related to underachievement rather than to explain the cause of underachievement. However, some of the factors disclosed were found to be operative throughout the lives of the students and warrant hypothesizing, at least, so that they may provide some leads to the etiology of underachievement.

The second study sought also to obtain descriptive material regarding the self-concepts associated with achievement patterns, but in addition undertook to study some specific administrative modifications within the school which might ameliorate scholastic underachievement. These experimental studies were concerned with studying such characteristics of underachievers as could be identified readily in a school setting and with testing only such special provisions for them as could be carried out in any large high school, utilizing generally available personnel and facilities. With respect to the remedial modifications undertaken within the school, therefore, no attempt was made to experiment with procedures which would require the services of psychologists, psychiatrists, or other specialists.

Both studies originated at a time when there was great impetus in education to understand and to alter the direction of low academic productivity on the part of numbers of potentially able students. It was also a time when many of the pitfalls of identification procedures, statistical analyses, and research design were not clearly understood or defined with respect to school underachievement patterns. These studies, along with many others, have helped to clarify what should be done in any investigation of poor academic performance in the superior intellectual group —especially with reference to procedures to be used in definition, selection of samples, development of measurement devices, utilization of standardized test results, and approaches to remediation and evaluation. These valuable lessons about research methods may be considered almost as important to the investigators as the outcomes of the studies themselves.

CHAPTER TWO

Review of the literature
on scholastic underachievement

THE TYPICAL BRIGHT UNDERACHIEVER has been subjected to such a plethora of definitions, descriptions, and analyses that the information we have about him is at one and the same time so encompassing and so detailed as to make virtually impossible any thumbnail sketch.

First, we might ask at what age scholastic underachievement begins to manifest itself. It has generally been noted that junior high school is the point at which the problem of underachievement becomes obvious (Goldberg, 1959) and that the incidence increases throughout the high school years. Shaw and McCuen (1960) selected two comparable groups of high school male and female achievers and underachievers whose intelligence test scores placed them in the upper 25 per cent of the population and whose grade point averages in grades nine, ten, and eleven placed them clearly above, or below, the mean of their class. The investigators then examined the academic records for each student from grades one through eleven. Grade-point averages for each grade, and mean GPA for each group at each grade level was calculated. A significant difference in the two groups of boys was noted beginning at the third grade level. The difference increased in significance at each grade level up to grade ten where it decreased somewhat in the males. The decline noted in tenth and eleventh grades was due primarily to a drop in the

17

mean GPA of the achievers rather than a rise in grades of under-achievers. Shaw concluded that the predisposition for under-achievement is present in males when they enter school. Fe-males appear to do better in the first five grades, with the drop beginning in grade six. This well-conceived, retrospective in-vestigation suggests the chronicity of underachievement and the need for looking for its predisposing factors much earlier than the high school and college years. Nash (1964) noted a greater proportion of underachievers in the eighth than in the ninth grade. Barrett (1957) found an underachievement pattern pres-ent by grade five in his intensive study of a small number of gifted underachievers. D'Heurle (1959) also identified academic underachieving behavior in a gifted group of third graders.

We might also look for clues regarding the underachiever's make-up by comparing him with his achieving counterpart and assuming that failures of the former make him somehow different. This conclusion cannot be safely drawn in most instances, ex-cept as it pertains specifically to the underachiever's not qualify-ing scholastically either via school marks or test performance for scholarships, acceptance at certain institutions of higher learn-ing, and the like. Suffice it to say that at the present time there is considerably more data available on the achiever than on the underachiever. For example, findings by Holland and Stalnaker (1958) on the 1956 National Merit Scholarship winners were as follows: geographical distribution follows national popula-tion trends; 74 per cent had attended large high schools; mean College Board Entrance Examination scores were well within the top 2 per cent for the high school graduating population except for women in mathematics; the greatest number (85 per cent) were from small families, and over 70 per cent were first-born; a preponderance of males (73 per cent) planned a science or related career; the majority were drawn from high socioeco-nomic groups; sex differences in values and goals were evident in the greater concern of the males with practical and self-cen-tered values in contrast to the prominence of interest in marriage and family life on the part of females.

Such results raise many provocative questions about the equally intellectually able group whose performance bars them from the successful group of achievers. One might ask to what extent membership in a middle or upper socioeconomic strata has resulted in rebellion against school standards when young persons were pressured to achieve by achieving parents, or to what extent membership in a lower strata has caused less motivation for academic excellence when parents themselves lack any positive orientation toward education. Our educational system is confronted with a problem of values regarding learning which is in sharp contrast to that of an earlier generation. Musselman (1942), in a study of 297 bright Baltimore high school students, brought to light certain personality and home background factors related to underachievement which are supported by current research. But his findings also showed that in that era the lag between promise and performance of superior pupils of foreign extraction was less than that for pupils of native extraction and that pupils whose parents and grandparents came from foreign countries consistently exceeded the mean achievement ratio of pupils whose parents and grandparents were born in the United States. By contrast, today a large portion of school dropouts occurs among the immigrants in our urban areas, as in the Spanish population of New York City, and among the rural migrants to the city, particularly the Negro groups. Equally important is the apparent extrinsic motivation for grades chiefly as a means of admission to higher education, better paying jobs, and higher income brackets on the part of the middle class students. Intrinsic interest in learning for its own sake, an interest ascribed to the earlier generations of the foreign born, appears to be no longer as strong an element in any student group today.

Issues pertinent to membership in a minority group, sex identification, or affiliation with particular ethnic, religious, or cultural values may well be the real barriers to successful academic performance (Strodtbeck, 1958). Further, the effects on achievement of attending a small high school, of being the second or third child in a family, or of being a member of a large family should be considered.

Boyce (1956) distinguished certain identifiable factors which appeared to determine over- and underachievement in a group of freshman liberal arts students at the University of Wisconsin. Through the use of a completed information blank, the Strong Vocational Interest Inventory, the Minnesota Multiphasic Personality Inventory (MMPI), and the Cooperative English Test, it was found that the overachievers had a foreign born parent or parents; were nonresidents of the state; lived in private residences at school; considered their study habits efficient or average; felt handicapped by lack of reading skill; had lived most of their lives in cities; devoted more hours to study than others; and had more deviate Depression scores on the MMPI. The underachievers had more deviate Hypomania scores on the MMPI, and had fathers engaged in professions and business, with more formal education. Hopkins and associates (1958) compared failures among students at University College, London, with an equal number of graduates who had entered at the same time. Failures had fathers in top business and professional groups; had more illness; chose the university for social reasons; chose subjects of study because of parental pressures; had decided on a career early in childhood; and had few friends of the opposite sex.

Gowan (1960) formulated some broad trends which seemed to be crucial to talent fruition, and which reflected existing research pertinent to the topic. These were environment and parents; consonance of parental and individual values; parental involvement in task demands; cathexis of satisfactions from libido to superego areas; purpose, motivation, inspiration, morale; self-confidence, self-acceptance, positive self-concept; anti-authoritarian behavior; interest-maturity; early strong set on industry tasks; positive personality integration; breakaway from home; peer socialization; and economic or vocational adjustment.

Personality Adjustment

In an academic setting where satisfactory school achievement is regarded as expected behavior, particularly for those students who are intellectually superior, it has been hypothesized by a number of investigators that underachievement must be related to factors indicative of personal and social difficulty. A number of studies suggest a relationship between personality adjustment and school performance.

Evidence supporting a relationship
between adjustment and achievement

College subjects. Assum and Levy (1947) examined the records of two groups of 70 underachieving college students—one group designated as the maladjusted group on the basis of their seeking solutions for their problems at the university's counseling center and completing counseling within a one-year period; and the other, a random group matched for sex and date of entrance into college, and not seen for counseling. When a comparison was made of scholastic aptitude scores on the American Council on Education Psychological Examination for College Freshman (ACE) and certain college reading and writing test scores, no differences appeared between the two groups. However, on ratings of comprehensive examinations covering the work of the school year in a given course, the maladjusted group received significantly lower scores. In other words, although the ACE total score predicted later achievement very poorly, personal adjustment did seem to bear a relationship to academic performance. Gough (1949) bears this out in a review he made of certain of the studies (Altus, 1948; Brown, 1947; Owens, 1949) of nonintellectual factors related to collegiate academic underachievement, wherein it was found that lack of maladjustment and the presence of adequate personal and social orientations pertained to better achievement. Stagner (1933) notes in his study of 250 freshman men with whom he used the Berneuter Personality Inventory that personality factors had a marked influence on the correlation of aptitude and achievement. Extreme personality trends seemed to counterbalance advantages on aptitude.

Altus (1948), who compared two equated groups of psychology students, collegiate achievers and nonachievers, on the MMPI, found a trend of greater maladjustment on nine clinical scales in nonachieving students. When sixty items on which the equated groups showed a difference of five points or more were administered to a new group of students, there was a correlation of .39 with psychology term grades indicating that particular items were of some use in predicting level of achievement. Hoyt and Norman (1954) selected two groups of freshman college students designated "maladjusted" and "normal" according to MMPI scores to test the hypothesis that maladjustment significantly affects college achievement by producing both over- and underachievement. The Ohio State University Psychological test predicted grades more accurately for freshman men with normal MMPI profiles than for those with very deviant profiles. The relationship between predictability and adjustment was less clear when the ACE results obtained for admission purposes were used as the measure of aptitude. Here MMPI profiles did not differ according to grades earned. A study by Monroe (1945) showed that the Inspection Rorschach Technique adjustment rating was much more successful than the ACE in predicting academic failure of 36 failing students at Sarah Lawrence College. Out of 348 entering freshmen who were tested, 34 out of the 36 failing students had been rated as relatively maladjusted by the Inspection Rorschach, whereas the ACE did not discriminate among them at all.

Darley (1937) sought to find a relation among the variables of ability and adjustment, ability and attitudes, achievement and adjustment, and achievement and attitudes. He compared 326 college men and 217 college women on scores from the Minnesota Scale for the Survey of Opinions, the Bell Adjustment Inventory, and the Minnesota Inventory of Social Attitudes, with scores from the ACE and the Minnesota College Aptitude Test. He noted that measured maladjustment or radicalism may depress achievement below the level to be expected from ability unless affected by some counter-stimulant. Weigand (1957) compared a group of students admitted to college on probation because of poor high school performance with another group similar in scores on standardized tests of scholastic aptitude and achievement but succeeding in their school work. He found the successful students more adaptive than the unsuccessful ones not only in academic life but in personal relations as well. Although both groups faced similar scholastic and social problems, the underachievers took less initiative in attempting to alleviate their disadvantageous situations. Centi (1962) studied the 32 lowest and 32 highest ranking full-time students enrolled during the 1955–56 school year in an urban day-session group of a university's School of Education. Sixteen subjects were selected from each of the four levels—freshman, sophomore, junior, and senior— on the basis of their first semester grade-point average. The subjects were chosen at random from the ten highest ranking and ten lowest ranking students in each level. Results of scores on the MMPI and the College Inventory of Academic Adjustment indicated that the highest ranking students tended to be better adjusted than the lowest ranking students.

Berger (1956), who administered the Rotter Incomplete Sentence Blank, the Yale Educational Aptitude Test Battery, and the ACE to an incoming freshman college group of men and women in a large mid-western university, followed the academic performance of his subjects for four years. In a review of the entrance scores of these students with their academic performance, it was concluded that students with high intellectual ability and an adequate personality adjustment achieved higher academic performance than did those students who showed signs of emotional maladjustment. Horrall (1957) compared high- and low-achieving college freshmen whose scores on the ACE were at or above the 94th percentile. Various projective tests were used in the study, including the Thematic Apperception Test (TAT) and the Rorschach. Results indicated that deep-seated personality problems were strongly associated with academic underachievement among these gifted students.

Senior and junior high school subjects. Terman's (1947) C group, selected on the basis of unsuccessful occupational achievement, had a history of academic underachievement apparent to a marked degree in high school. His evidence pointed to less overall personality stability and to the presence of more disturbing conflicts in the C group as compared with the group which was regarded as successful in achievement. Similarly Nason (1958), on a variety of paper and pencil tests, student check sheets, and peer and teacher ratings, found some indication that superior high school students with high achievement were better adjusted than students with low achievement records, but differences were not significant statistically on total adjustment scores.

Pierce's (1961a) study of the top 30 per cent in intellectual ability of tenth- and twelfth-grade students showed a significantly better adjustment on the part of the high-achieving boys and girls as measured by the California Psychological Inventory (CPI) than was true for the low achievers. In a comparative depth study involving 32 high-ability junior high school students, 16 achievers and 16 underachievers, Barrett (1957) found that the achievers came considerably closer to their counselor's conception of the well-integrated personality. Achievers were better accepted by their peers, excelled in feelings of self-worth, and appeared more rational in their approach to solving personal difficulties. Feelings of inadequacy could be found in both groups of students, but whereas these emotions seemed to act as motivating forces among achievers the nonachievers were seen as tending to withdraw from competitive situations. De Hirsch (1963), in a clinical study of adolescents with marked scholastic difficulties, concluded that in spite of superficial similarity in symptomatology, the young students fell into two main categories. In one group the academic dysfunction was related to ego impairment and was a manifestation of a severe character disorder, indicating primary learning disabilities. In the other group the difficulty was secondary to residual language deficiencies. Psychological problems as well as school dysfunction were the result rather than the cause in this second group.

Elementary school subjects. Leibman (1954), who studied all fifth graders in one large elementary school on the Winnetka Scale for Rating School Behavior and Attitudes, the California Test of Personality, the Rogers Test of Personality Adjustment, and the Rorschach found in general that children who rated better in personal and social adjustment achieved more adequately.

Evidence not supporting a relationship between adjustment and achievement

The evidence from the above findings, although indicative of slight group differences on various measures of adjustment, is insufficient to conclude that differences in adjustment are a major factor in scholastic achievement, especially since other studies fail to differentiate the underachiever group from the normal- or overachieving population on personal adjustment scores. As indicated in the following studies, the heterogeneity which apparently exists within and among groups of various achievement levels would seem to negate the adjustment factor as the sole or most important basis for differences in scholastic functioning. In many investigations either underachievers could not be differentiated from achievers on adjustment measures, or profiles actually favored underachievers.

College subjects. Griffiths (1945) examined the relationship existing between scholastic achievement and personality of male college students as measured by the Bell Adjustment Inventory. He found that men in school difficulties or on academic probation were not much inferior in personal adjustment scores to men of superior college ability; that men with brilliant school records were no better adjusted in personality than men of lowest academic achievement; and that men with unsatisfactory emotional adjustment scores tended toward higher grades than men of excellent adjustment scores. He also found no great difference in personality scores between men in the lowest and highest deciles of college ability as measured by the Ohio State University Psychological Test.

Morgan (1952), using the MMPI to compare achieving and nonachieving college students of high ability, found that profile patterns in both groups were heterogeneous and that there was no clear relationship between scholastic achievement and profiles. Owens and Johnson (1949), using the MMPI, the Minnesota Personality Scale, and a personal checklist, concluded that neurotic or psychotic forms of adjustment were not prominently associated with the scholastic underachievement of their subjects. Dowd (1952) likewise found that achievers and nonachievers in college, selected from a group of 80 students who scored in the highest decile of their class in scholastic aptitude as measured by the ACE, could not be differentiated on such pencil-and-paper personality tests as the MMPI, the Bernreuter Personality Inventory, and the Bell Adjustment Inventory. More recently, Quinn (1957) made further use of the MMPI, selecting from it a number of items to form a nonintellective achievement scale designed to predict academic success among college freshmen. Results showed the predictive value to be weak. The conclusion drawn by Quinn was that the MMPI personality characteristics sometimes found in past research to differentiate between under- and overachievers could actually be ascribed to the influence of intelligence.

While paper-and-pencil type tests may account for some of the lack of differentiation between adjustment of achievers and non-achievers, projective measures have failed also, in large measure, to differentiate between the two groups. Findings from five Rorschach studies (Cronbach, 1950; Leibman, 1954; Pearlman, 1952; Ryan, 1951; Sharpe, 1954) did not separate under-, over-, and nonachievers on total adjustment scores. Monroe (1945), who found on Rorschach adjustment ratings prevalence of mal-adjustment in failing students, did not state to what extent she found indications of such maladjustment in students who did not fail. However, when Montalto (1946) applied group Rorschach techniques to the problem of achievement in college, she found in her sample of ninety women equated on the basis of ACE scores that, while the achievers possessed more signs of adjustment than the nonachievers, the achievers had a neurotic trend in personality makeup which seemed to be a pertinent factor contributing to their academic success. Montalto did, however, evolve a pattern of five signs of academic achievement in the Rorschach which correlated highly with grade-point averages when intelligence scores were held constant. Steinzor (1944) compared in detail the Rorschach responses of two equated groups of liberal arts students at Ohio State University, both in the 85th centile or better on the Ohio State University Psychological Test, one group having average course marks of B+ or above, the other of C— or below. Achievers differed from the nonachievers on eight Rorschach signs. The nonachievers seemed on the whole to be less well-adjusted. However, some individuals in the successful group also showed signs of severe maladjustment.

High school subjects. Conklin (1931), making a detailed clinical study of gifted students who failed in two or more high school subjects, concluded that 50 per cent of both the failed and nonfailed students would be considered atypical according to social and psychiatric study.

McGuire (1962), in a summary of his own research pertaining to the secondary school and by Peck pertaining to the university level, discussed a complex distribution of types of personalities in student bodies at all levels of achievement. Rejection by peers was reported to induce intense self-centered desires, conflicting emotions, hostility, etc. These feelings seemed to result in withdrawal, academic difficulty, lack of creativity, and low productivity, according to the investigators.

The inconclusive and somewhat contradictory evidence on the relationship of total adjustment to achievement may be due to the problems inherent in assessing personality functioning and to the types of instruments and inventories available, as well as to the varying definitions of underachievement. Or it may be a spurious notion indeed that adequate school performance necessarily correlates with the commonly accepted standards of good adjustment. Gough's (1955) view that the use of scale scores from instruments which were devised for use in other prediction problems, often clinical and with no intended relationship to variables relevant to academic achievement, may account for the lack of clarifying evidence here. Stagner (1933) suggested in the light of the lack of linear relationship between objective measures of personality and either academic aptitude or academic achievement that personality, in all likelihood, influences achievement in an indirect way by affecting the degree to which use is made of the individual's potentialities.

Other methodological approaches, particularly more precise statistical procedures, hold promise for more refined definitions and measurement of personality variables. Saunders (1956) contrasted the use of analysis of covariance for studying situations in which the degree or mode of predictability is thought to vary as a function of membership in one or another of distinct homogeneous groups with the method of the "moderated multiple regression equation." He proposed that the latter method is ap-

plicable to the case in which the basic parameter is not membership in some group, but score on some continuous variable. He
discussed a number of situations of potential practical significance
to variables frequently examined in studies of underachievement
such as degree of insight, degree of emotional stability, and the
like. Of relevance then to the previous discussion of the relationship of adjustment to school performance is the possibility that
the element of degree in the variable studied has not always been
adequately dealt with in the commonly used methods of analysis
applied to distinct groups.

Stephenson (1953) discussed the Q-technique measurement
method of discovering complex facts of an inferential nature
about a phenomenon such as school performance. He illustrated
his rationale by the results obtained on a 70-statement questionnaire on study habits applied to three small, known college groups
of men and women, clearly differentiated with respect to successful and unsuccessful school histories. One factor array which
emerged (b), that of *self-sufficiency, independence,* and *individ-
ualism,* was related to underachievement, while another factor
(c), that of *pleasantness, serious-mindedness, responsibility,* and
conscientiousness, was related to overachievement. Stephenson
pursued further through a number of examples the measurement
approaches now at our command for understanding the relationship which exists between the factors of a person's self notions
and his more socialized personality. Such research designs open
up possibilities for study which promise greater clarity in the
future regarding relationships between personality adjustment
and achievement.

Personality Traits

The fact that total adjustment measures do not seem to furnish
a substantial explanation for underachievement suggests the need
to study some of the components of personality which might
influence positively or negatively the learner's behavior in school.
The variety of studies directed toward the identification of personality correlates of underachievement, and, by comparison,
achievement, and even so-called overachievement, represents a

large bulk of the research undertaken to account for discrepancies between predicted and actual school achievement in bright students.

Investigations have utilized case studies such as Hollingworth made in the 1930's, analysis of contrasting groups, the factor analytic studies of Gough and McGuire, descriptive categorizations, such as those made of National Merit Scholarship winners over a period of years, and a few longitudinal studies such as those of Terman and that of D'Heurle and associates at the University School in Chicago. Although final conclusions cannot be drawn because of this very diversity of experimental design, the complexity of the underachievement phenomenon itself, the widely divergent identification criteria applied from study to study, and the familiar limitations of personality assessment, there are a number of specific characteristics upon which different research studies appear to agree.

While it is difficult to ascertain whether we are considering a cause or an effect relationship, we can say with some degree of assurance that the underachiever is more likely to be a boy than a girl and to have poorer work habits and study skills than his achieving peer; he is also likely to be somewhat impulsive, to lack independence and initiative with respect to school work, to have more negative attitudes toward himself and others, and to resist assuming responsibility for his own behavior. For a more detailed delineation of personal dimensions, the following studies have yielded some useful information.

College subjects. Rust and Ryan (1953), by means of the group Rorschach, Strong Vocational Interest Blank, and a questionnaire eliciting information about family situations from a college population of high, under-, and overachievers equated for general predicted grade score but different in academic performance, obtained support for the hypothesis that a relationship exists between positive deviation from the general predicted grade score and superego strength; i.e., the degree to which certain moral and social values are accepted may be the factor responsible for persistence favorable to making good grades. Burgess (1953) administered a battery of projective and standard personality and interest inventories (Rorschach, TAT, Rosenzweig Picture Frustration Study, MMPI, Bernreuter Personality Inventory, Strong Vocational Interest Blank, College Inventory of Academic Adjustment) to 20 underachieving and 20 overachieving engineering students whose first semester grades deviated most below and most above a predictive index of grades. The sample studied was selected from a class of 492 freshman engineering students. Results showed the underachievers were less intellectually adaptive and showed less intellectual control and repression of emotional reactivity. They showed easy, labile affectivity, were more dependent in their attitudes toward others, had weak motivation for academic achievement, and saw their own environment as desirable. Morgan (1952) studied a somewhat similar group of 40 achievers and 30 nonachievers selected from 132 college sophomores. These students were at or above the 90th percentile on the ACE and had either obtained honor grades (achievers), or their grades had fallen below the mean average of the freshman class (nonachievers). The achievers scored higher than nonachievers on the MMPI scales designed to measure dominance, social responsibility, and intellectual efficiency, while more nonachievers than achievers had profile elevation on scales referring to psychopathic characteristics and profile low points on paranoid traits. Altus (1948) found in his sample of psychology students that the nonachievers on the MMPI showed greater femininity, immaturity, fearlessness, self-assertiveness, and manic tendencies than the achieving group. Terman's (1947) subjects, their wives, and their parents showed high agreement in rating the vocationally successful group far higher than the unsuccessful group on perseverance, self-confidence, and integration toward goals.

Holland (1960) investigated the validity of the Sixteen Personality Factor Questionnaire, the National Merit Student Survey, and the Vocational Preference Inventory administered to 641 boys and 311 girls drawn from 7,500 finalists in the National Merit Scholarship competition. Predictive validities of the Scholastic Aptitude Test and high school rank were also tested. The students were attending 277 different institutions. Nonintellectual variables such as superego, persistence, and deferred gratification were found useful in predicting and understanding the academic achiever. McKenzie (1961), defining deviant scholastic achievement in terms of discrepancy between measured ability and grade-point average, attempted to develop MMPI scales predictive of achievement. Seven scales resulted from an item analysis comparing various combinations of student groups which differed in ability (low, average, and high) and achievement (low, normal, and over). The only scale revealing differences which held up in a cross-validation test was between the normal- and underachieving groups. His findings suggested that underachievers tended to externalize conflict, to be impulsive, to lack long range goals, and to depend for guidance on the standards of others. Hostility seemed to play an important role with this group.

Gebhart (1958), who studied the relationship of the Edwards Personality Preference Schedule scores to over- and underachievement in college freshmen, found that overachievers in his sample showed greater drive to compete (*Achievement*) and to organize or plan (*Order*), and greater intellectual curiosity (*Intraception*), while the underachievers showed greater need for variety (*Change*), and higher social motivation (*Affiliation*). Middleton and Guthrie (1959) sought to delineate personality syndromes among 50 high- and low-achieving college students, also using Murray's need system. A factor analysis yielded five factors characteristic of high achievers and four characteristic of low achievers. The factors interpreted indicated that achievement of high grades is motivated by needs for power, by resentment, by dependence, by needs for social acceptance, and by aggressive denial of social feeling; low achievement by pleasure-seeking, extraversion, denial of normal social shortcomings, and preoccupation with power. Clark (1953), in a study of nonintellective factors on the MMPI related to grade achievement of female college students, found that poor grades were *not* related to any specific syndrome measured by the MMPI, but that a selected group of items could distinguish achievers from nonachievers. He proposed that the entire range of scores be used in setting up the achieving versus the nonachieving dichotomy instead of the upper and lower quartiles only, and that motivation, interests, and study habits be considered. Winkelman

(1963), in a study of male sophomores in a college of engineering, using the California Psychological Inventory (CPI), GPA, and ACE scores, found no profile patterns or scale scores on the CPI which differentiated underachievers from average or overachievers.

High school and junior high school subjects. Since no single factor seemed to differentiate adequately between high and underachievers, Nason (1958) approached the problem through studying the discriminatory power of the summation of various factors. The patterns of circumstances which he measured on high school students included personality adjustment, pupil's and parent's level of academic aspiration, pupil and parental choice of a future vocation, and pupil's reported source of inspiration. He found that among bright students positive status on all of the circumstances assured membership in the top quintile on achievement, but that no single factor was a better discriminant than any other. However, low scores on the personality test, if accompanied by high scores on the other factors, did *not* militate against high achievement. In general, the patterns of circumstances associated with different quintiles appeared to vary only in the *number* of circumstances *missing* from a complete pattern. Pierce (1961a), comparing 52 high achievers with 52 low achievers in grades ten and twelve on several instruments, found that high achievers showed more favorable personality characteristics, reflected greater independence, and had mothers that supported independence. On a similarly selected type sample of high school students, Morrow and Wilson (1961b), using self-administering individual questionnaires, reported no significant differences in self-described general social and emotional adjustment between bright high-achieving and underachieving high school boys. More underachievers, however, described themselves as restless, impulsive, and irresponsible, and as belonging to cliques whose values were discrepant with those fostered by the school.

Shaw and Black (1960) pursued some of the qualitative dimensions of hostility in two groups of high school boys. The achievers had a GPA above the mean for the junior and senior classes, while the GPA of the underachievers was below the mean. Both groups had IQ's of 113 or higher on the SRA Primary Mental Abilities test. Analysis of response to the Rosensweig Picture-Frustration Study revealed only one statistically significant category: The achievers tended to deny aggressively any responsibility for the offense with which they were charged, while the underachievers admitted their guilt, but tended to claim that circumstances beyond their control were responsible for whatever happened. Their findings suggest that underachievers are individuals who feel that some uncontrollable factors in their environment are in large part responsible for what happens to them and who are probably less capable of directly attacking the barriers which stand in the way.

From a total of 275 eleventh graders with IQ's above 120 in a San Mateo, California, high school, Stoner (1957) selected the 35 highest and 35 lowest performers in percentile scores on the Iowa High School Content Examination, and then matched by intelligence 19 representatives of each group. He found that even with intelligence thus held constant, the high and low achievers differed significantly on 5 out of 17 scales of the California Psychological Inventory: dominance, socialization, intellectual efficiency, psychological interests, and flexibility.

Carter (1961) analyzed data obtained by means of the Stanford Achievement Tests, the Henmon-Nelson Tests of Mental Ability, and the California Study Methods Survey on 725 seventh and eighth graders. His findings suggest, as one would expect, that the overachievers made more use of study techniques associated with superior scholarship. They were more systematic in doing their work and showed a higher degree of intellectual curiosity. In addition, they were happier in school, had more self-confidence, and exhibited better morale. Blackman's (1955) group of 15 underachieving readers in eighth and ninth grades was found by projective measures (Rorschach and TAT) to differ in an unfavorable direction from matched high and overachievers in behavior immaturity, emotional instability, feelings of inadequacy, and in attitudes concerning physical defects. The underachievers displayed a somewhat greater capacity to respond to emotional and environmental stimuli; their emotional responses were indicative of more impulsivity and immaturity than was true for the other groups.

Elementary school subjects. Kurtz and Swenson (1951), in a descriptive study of 40 over- and underachievers in grades four to seven, using reports, ratings, and observations, generalized that the underachievers appeared less happy, more unstable, and had greater feelings of inferiority. Lewis (1940, 1941) studied one group of 1,078 children whose educational age was one year or more in excess of mental age and one group of 756 children whose educational age was one year or less below mental age in the fourth to the eighth year of school. On the basis of teacher ratings, statistically reliable differences were found between the two groups in dependability, originality, self-reliance, and investigativeness, favoring the accelerated group. Walsh (1956), using a study of projective doll play with 20 boys designated as low achievers in reading, seven to eleven years, with IQ's between 120 and 146, matched with a control group of normal achievers in reading, found the low achievers consistently differed from adequate achievers in portraying the boy doll as restricted in actions, unable to express his feelings appropriately and adequately, being criticized, rejected, or isolated, and acting defensively through compliance, evasion, or negativism.

Haggard (1957) and D'Heurle and associates (1959) have been engaged since 1950 in a longitudinal study of 76 gifted children at the University of Chicago Laboratory School. This investigation is distinguished by several commendable features: (1) it attempts to understand the complex of factors associated with patterns of academic achievement, that is, the sets of relationships among socialization pressures, developing personality structure, the ways in which the child learns to direct and utilize his energies toward valued goals in the world as he sees it, and the degree of proficiency in the skills necessary to achieve in different academic areas; (2) it views achievement in a more differentiated sense in that analysis has been made of components associated not only with high general achievement but also with achievement in arithmetic, reading, and spelling; (3) the study utilizes multiple tests, group and individual, for assessing mental ability and personality as well as teacher observations.

Results reported for third grade children showed the high general achievers to be characterized by traits representing exposure and responsiveness to cultural influences. Conformity and acceptance of parental values seemed to give them a high degree of security and confidence in their relations to parents and other adults. Achievers showed independence, self-confidence, effective work habits, and active social participation. Some evidence was present, also, of inner strain in living up to adult expectations, well-developed superegos, strong guilt feelings, and concern with problems of discipline and control. Other results suggested that high arithmetic achievers were more outwardly oriented and spontaneous in their behavior, while the high reading achievers were more inwardly bent, more anxious, and less confident, albeit more imaginative, spontaneous, and original in their fantasy life. The spelling achievers yielded a picture of less activeness and spontaneity, and more compulsive reactions, with a mental approach somewhat concrete and stereotyped. Of 45 per cent of these same third-grade subjects studied when they were in seventh grade, the high achievers had retained a high degree of mental flexibility and spontaneity, particularly in their ability to manipulate abstract symbols. Noted also was an increase in antagonistic attitudes of achievers toward adults from third to seventh grade, an increase in anxiety level, and some corresponding decreases in intellectual originality and creativity. There was some tendency also for more aggression and competitiveness.

The studies cited above each suggest the presence of certain traits which can be said to differentiate particular underachiever groups from high achiever groups. Taken collectively, these investigations are so widely diverse in their findings, their definitions of underachievement, the instruments used, and the ages studied that no generalizations can be made about characteristics of personality which might be associated with academic performance. However, each study in its way can be said to form a link in the chain of evidence that the personality is a stable configuration of dynamic processes reflected and expressed in many diverse behaviors.

Self-Ratings

The theory of self has formed the basis for a growing number of studies attempting to determine what relationship, if any, exists between bright students' perceptions of themselves and their abilities and the utilization of such abilities. In the largest number of studies, Rogers' (1959) definition of self has been used: The self is "that organized, consistent, conceptual Gestalt composed of perceptions of the characteristics of the 'I' or 'me' and the perceptions of the relationships of the 'I' or 'me' to others and to various aspects of life, together with the values attached to these perceptions" (p. 200).

Matire (1956) examined the relationship between the self-concept and differences in strength and generality of achievement motivation on a small, "casually" selected college sample. His general findings suggested that high need-Achievement was motivated by a discrepancy between self-ratings and self-ideals. Payne and Farquhar (1962) assumed that a student's self-concept is a functionally limiting or facilitating factor which interacts with motivation in academic achievement. The investigators constructed and employed a 119-item instrument (the Word Rating List) on which students rated their own personality traits as they thought the teachers would. Four factors in males and two in females differentiated between underachieving and overachieving eleventh grade high school students. A multiple scalogram analysis yielded dimensions which, when interpreted, suggested that male students perceived high achievement to be associated with ambition in learning subject matter required for securing grades, conformity to socially acceptable types of classroom behavior, motivation for mastery of material, and conformity to teacher-sanctioned behavior. Dimensions for females, when interpreted, indicated that high-achieving female students carry out tasks promptly, and are motivated by competition where mastery of subject matter is of primary concern. Borislow

(1962) obtained several measures of general and self-evaluations, and goals from four groups of college freshmen before and after their first semester. He divided the sample into achievers and underachievers on the basis of GPA and Scholastic Aptitude Test (SAT) scores and college intentions expressed on the Student Behavior Description. His fiindings did not support general self-evaluation based on a global concept of personality, as exemplified by Rogers, as being a factor in academic achievement. Borislow suggested the usefulness of a more specific self-evaluation related to student role rather than the whole person.

Brookover and his associates (1962) studied the relationship between self-concept of ability and achievement, both generally and in specific school subjects, with over one thousand junior high students. Findings analyzed to date have substantiated the relationship between self-concept of ability and actual achievement; have shown that self-concept of ability is differentiated along subject matter lines by the student; and have indicated that correlations do exist between the student's self-attitudes and his perception of the attitudes and evaluations held by certain persons who are important to him. While the investigators were cognizant of their inability to draw conclusions about whether self-concept accounts for achievement, or whether achievement accounts for self-concept, they presented evidence that self-concept is relatively stable even in the face of contradictory evaluation by teachers. In their sample, self-concepts of ability and IQ were positively related (.46), and significant correlations between self-concepts of ability and achievement (for boys and girls) remained when the effect of IQ was controlled for statistically. There was a positive relationship between the self-concept of ability in a given subject and performance in that subject.

Fink (1962) formed 44 pairs of ninth-grade achievers and underachievers matched by sex and IQ (20 pairs of boys, 24 pairs of girls). Information on each child, derived from personality inventories, projective instruments and autobiographical data was presented to three psychologists, each of whom, independently and without knowledge of the pupils' achievement status, rated the child's self-concept as "adequate" or "inadequate." Of the boys, those rated as having an inadequate self-concept by the psychologists were more likely to be underachievers; those rated adequate in self-concept were more likely to be achievers. The relationship between self-concept and achievement did not hold for girls, however.

The finding that underachievement is related to an inadequate self-concept of ability is further supported by several studies. Mitchell (1959), in a study of 100 female subjects enrolled in an educational psychology class, analyzed goal-setting patterns of self-acceptant and self-rejectant underachievers. The self-acceptant underachiever led all four groups in overestimation of future accomplishment. The self-rejectant underachiever was least motivated of all the groups, had the highest anxiety score, and expressed feelings of being "no good at all." Measures used included the Bills Index of Adjustment and Values and the Taylor Manifest Anxiety Scale. Achievement level was determined on the basis of discrepancy scores between grade average and ACE for one semester. Shaw, Edson, and Bell (1960) and Shaw and Grubb (1958), employing the Sarbin Adjective Check List as a measure of self-concept, found in a comparison of a group of underachieving male and female high school students with a comparable group of achieving students that differences in self-concept did discriminate between high and underachievers and, particularly, that male underachievers seemed to have more negative feelings about themselves than did equally bright achieving boys. The researchers further suggested that, as a group, the underachievers, especially boys, were more hostile than bright high achievers and that the hostility did not have its genesis in the educational framework, but was brought by the child to school.

Kehas (1963) selected three groups from a high school senior class, achievers and over- and underachievers with respect to the individual's own class, through an efficient multiple regression procedure for each grade in school. The most important variable that differentiated the three groups was the way in which students experienced themselves in the school situation. Total adjustment for his subjects as measured by the self-ideal correlation (self-concept) was not an important correlate of achievement in any general, group sense. Differences involving individual adjectives seemed to center around intellectual, task-oriented material, and a personal-social constellation. Nash's (1964) findings in a study of self-perceptions of 370 students in the entire seventh and eighth grades of a middle-class community reflect a similar trend, namely, that on an inventory of 115 self-perception items constructed on an a priori basis the most consistent themes related to achievement patterns were those pertaining directly to school and school tasks. There were wide differences, however, between the items which distinguished achievement for each grade, for each sex, and for the achievement classification used. Items distinguishing achievers and underachievers included perceptions of importance of peer relationships and family interrelationships, nonconformity and competitiveness, and satisfaction with self.

Self-concept has been a central feature of underachievement theory and research, and a most viable one. It also has accounted for some rather superficial approaches to the problem. Hopefully, current critiques of the theory may have some influence on the quality of conceptualizations and empirical research to come. Crowne and Stephens (1961) see self-acceptance as having promise for becoming an increasingly attractive focus of interest in both formal and informal psychological theory. They note, however, in their article containing a critique of methodology employed in self-acceptance and self-evaluative behavior, that in spite of the considerable volume of research, there is a very small amount of understanding of self-acceptance and its relationship to other personality variables. They list several crucial psychometric and methodological principles which have been neglected in the work to date: unsupported assumption of equivalency of assessment procedures; absence of any clear construct-level definition of variables; failure to construct tests in accord with principles of representative sampling; questions concerning the social desirability factor in self-report tests; absence of data concerning generality of self-acceptance; implication of difference between phenomenological approach to self-acceptance and a behavioristic approach to self-evaluative behavior. Strong and Feder (1961) have done a careful review of the more than 15 different instruments which have been used to measure some form of an individual's concept of himself. They regard the self-concept approach to personality adjustment as one that is productive of meaningful reflections on total personality organization, and as a highly promising diagnostic device in its apparently reliable objectification of what has heretofore been considered to be projective. Shaw (1961) views the self-concept as one of the most promising aspects of the personality of underachievers yet studied. Kehas (1963) proposes a note of caution in the uncritical adoption and extension of an appealing psychological construct, saying that the house of self-concept has to be put in order before we can look to it for valuable information.

Social Behavior and Attitudes

The relationship of poor social adjustment to high achievement

It has been hypothesized that social modes of adjustment might be related to achievement—that the high achiever is likely to be an isolate with few friends and little social adaptability and, conversely, the underachiever is likely to be socially outgoing.

College subjects. The theme of introversion applied to the high and overachiever is substantiated by several studies using several instruments. Altus (1948) and Owens and Johnson (1949), employing the MMPI scale, found normal or high achievers gave more introverted responses, the underachievers more extraverted responses. Stagner (1933) pointed to evidence in the literature and from the Bernreuter Personality Inventory that in a college population those with high scores on introversion received proportionately higher marks than did those with high scores on extraversion. Gough (1949) noted in a review of previous studies using the MMPI that social extraversion among other items had been found predictive of underachievement. On his own scales, constructed on MMPI items to determine whether a set of items could be isolated which would constitute reliable predictors of honor-point ratios independently of intelligence, he did not find any of them reliable in differentiating between achieving and nonachieving groups.

Holland (1959), in studying the usefulness of the California Psychological Inventory and the Scholastic Aptitude Test for prediction of college grades, drew on a sample of exceptionally talented freshmen attending 291 colleges and universities. In scale terms, his findings suggested that high achievers were unsociable, lacked poise and self-confidence, were self-deprecating and inflexible, and minimized worries and complaints, but were conscientious and responsible. In contrast, the low achievers were poised and socially skillful, flexible, admitted worries and complaints, had less intense superego qualities, were impulsive, and possessed less motivation for academic achievement. His results tend to confirm Gough's (1955) theory that achievement and underachievement among gifted persons is a specific facet of the general problem of socialization. Holland noted, in conclusion, that at a high level of scholastic aptitude, personality variables may yield validity coefficients which are two to three times as great as those obtained using aptitude measures alone.

Davie (1961), in a comparison of 345 students with GPA of 80 or more with 485 students having a GPA of less than 80, confirmed the unsociable quality of high achievers found by Holland. Davie noted greater self-initiated intellectual activity with postcollege plans for graduate school in medicine or law as characteristic of the achieving group. He suggested the possibility that the high achiever in college was encountering the increasing importance of heterosexual relationships and was facing the necessity of reconciling a great many internal impulses with external pressures which were subjectively meaningful and objectively important for his present and future welfare. Accordingly, the young student appeared to be using intelligence as a defense against immaturity, but to the benefit of his academic record. In another study, Knaak (1957) drew comparisons (based on school records, personal interviews, and responses to a questionnaire) between a group of 44 freshman women on academic probation and another group of 35 freshman women with minimum grade averages of A— in a large university. He found that whereas the successful students rated higher in seriousness and reflectiveness on the Guilford-Zimmerman Temperament Survey, the probation group appeared to be more successful in the area of relationships with people. On self-ratings used with college students Young and Estabrooks (1934) found a tendency for the studious college student to see himself as unsocial. Burgess (1953), employing both projective means and paper-and-pencil inventories (Rorschach, TAT, Rosensweig, MMPI, Strong, Bernreuter, and College Inventory of Academic Adjustment) with college engineering students, saw the underachievers as establishing rapport in social situations more easily than the overachievers. Roe (1952) noted that many of the scientists she studied had quite specific and fairly strong feelings of isolation when they were children. Duff and Siegel (1960) found a negative relationship between academic ability and degree of participation in physical, social, and heterosexual activities in a group of college freshmen.

Senior and junior high school subjects. Robinowitz (1956), using self-ratings, found the high school overachiever gave a number of ambivalent responses in the area of peer acceptance, indicating uncertainty about his relationships. Bresee (1957) compared 44 achievers and 33 underachievers in high school on a variety of personality measures. Students in both groups had IQ's greater than one standard deviation above the mean. Those with school grade averages of B+ or better were designated as achievers, those with school grades of D or worse as underachievers. Results showed the underachievers to be more hostile and extrapunitive than the achievers. The achieving group aimed toward more remote goals requiring higher level training, and also identified more closely with friends, family, and the community, and rated higher on altruism. Blackman (1955) concluded from Rorschach responses of eighth and ninth graders that overachievers were primarily introversive, underachievers extratensive. Clarks (1962) studied the personnel data cards of 94 underachievers in the Independence, Missouri, junior high schools. Contrary to his expectations, he found that 81 per cent of the underachievers lived with both parents and 64 per cent perceived themselves as well-liked by their peers. One might conjecture from this evidence that underachievers are socially oriented and socially active to such an extent that this interest takes precedence over academic pursuits and, conversely, that high and overachievers function more comfortably in the scholastic realm than they do in the social area.

The relationship of poor social adjustment to low achievement

A contrasting picture to that of the introverted, unsocial achiever was first proposed by Terman (1947), who called attention to the superior social adjustment of his successful achievers over that of his unsuccessful ones. Many later studies have lent support to Terman's conclusions.

College subjects. Hall and Gaeddert (1960) reported a study demonstrating the importance of social skills in success at school. Evaluating 93 college students by subscores on the ACE, grade average, an interview score, and by The Friendship Rating Scale developed at the University of Nebraska, they were able to determine the power of the separate variables in predicting grade average at school. It was found that although neither the Rating Scale nor the interview score correlated with the ACE scores, the measures did contribute significantly to the prediction of school achievement (while the ACE scores did not). The results suggest that academic success is based not only on intellectual skills but also on certain abilities to deal with people socially. Holland (1961), in an analysis of the relationship between three criteria of academic and creative performance and 72 personal, demographic, and parental variables in a sample of talented adolescents confirmed a relationship between academic achievers and persevering, sociable, responsible attitudes.

In another study by Shaw and Brown (1957) of personality characteristics, groups of low- and high-achieving college freshmen were compared. All subjects scored above the 75th percentile on the ACE test, but one group rated below the mean and the other group was in the upper quartile of the freshman class in overall GPA. Results showed no significant differences on the Allport-Vernon-Lindzey Study of Values or the Bell Adjustment Inventory. However, real differences in favor of the achievers were found on the Economic and Social Scales of the Bell Preference

Inventory. The differences were interpreted as indications that the underachievers harbored attitudes of hostility and hypercriticalness toward people in general and feelings of resentment toward their parents for denying them the material things of life. These results were partly confirmed by Shaw and Grubb (1958) in their comparison of gifted achievers and underachievers in high school. Utilizing the Bell Preference Inventory, along with the Guilford-Zimmerman Temperament Survey, the Cook Hostility Scale, and a measure of authoritarianism, the researchers noted that for the males only there were significant differences between achievers and underachievers on all instruments except the measure of authoritarianism, with the underachievers showing greater tendencies toward hostility in every case.

Senior and junior high school subjects. Nason (1958) found no differences in social adjustment between high- and low-achieving boys. He did obtain evidence that high-achieving girls scored significantly higher on teacher and peer rating scales in school and community relations than did underachieving girls. Armstrong (1955), on the basis of the Kuder Preference Record, teacher ratings, and interviews of secondary school normal and underachievers, confirmed Nason's findings showing that underachieving girls in her study were significantly different in not being chosen for positions of responsibility as often as were normally achieving girls. Bishton (1957) investigated differences in academic achievement among intellectually superior eighth graders on the Mental Health Analysis, the Ohio Youth Survey Needs, the California Achievement Battery, and a general information sheet. From a factor analysis, 16 orthogonal factors emerged. Factor VIII was interpreted as meaning that close peer relationships and affinity for social activities are associated with high achievement. Dealing with an age group similar to that studied by Bishton, Layton (1951) found, from school records and in interviews, apparent poor social adjustment to be related to school failure at the ninth grade level. Bonney (1959) compared two groups of eighth graders, students whose grade-point averages at school sharply exceeded expectation as indicated by their scores on standard achievement tests, and students whose achievement test scores were considerably higher than would be indicated by their school grades. Through the use of pupil reaction questionnaires and teacher ratings it was shown that the high-achieving, low test group was found *not* to be made up of social isolates.

Elementary school subjects. Granzow (1954) obtained teacher ratings of elementary under-, normal-, and overachievers in reading and found the first group to be poorly adjusted to school rules and procedures and not well accepted by peers. Kurtz and Swenson (1951), using reports, ratings, and observations, concluded that underachievers in a large population, grades four to seven, had fewer friends, and their friends had attitudes toward school which were less favorable than were those of the more plentiful friends of the overachievers. M. Williams (1958) studied the effects of acceptance on scholastic performance in elementary school children from suburban Connecticut whose IQ scores were 130 or more as derived from the California Test of Mental Maturity. Academic performance was measured by the Stanford and Metropolitan tests, social performance by the California Test of Personality, and extent of acceptance by the Classroom Social Distance Scale. Academic performance was more highly correlated with acceptance extended *to* the group (.58) than to acceptance extended *by* the group (.22). Total performance (academic and social) and total acceptance (extended *by* and *to* the group) showed the most pronounced relationships.

The relationship of peer attitudes to achievement

For adolescents, the importance of liking and being liked by peers tends to exceed that of doing well in school. Such attitudes have been thought responsible in many instances for poor scholastic achievement. Coleman's (1961) study of nine public high schools of varying size and rural-urban composition supported the hypothesis that in general the peer culture in these schools was not particularly interested in outstanding academic attainment. When requirements for membership in the leading crowd were studied, good grades or being smart in school ranked sixth out of eight criteria, and only 12 per cent of the boys and girls viewed school success as important. Coleman contended that the indifference of the adolescent culture toward academic success was related to the individual competitive nature of school achievement rewards. He suggested that academic pursuits be placed on an interschool competitive basis, much as athletic events, thus enlisting the group spirit of the teenager in putting his best ability forward for the sake of the school rather than in competition with other members of his group. He further proposed that if the kudos paid to the athletic star and the high level of interest shown by adolescents in the athletic endeavors of their school were viewed as an expression of identification with the group, then the introduction of interscholastic competition in academic matters would raise the interest in and prestige of educational endeavors in the minds of high school students.

Tannenbaum (1962) investigated peer attitudes toward academic brilliance among adolescents. He asked students to attribute various personal characteristics to brilliant and average students, who might or might not be overly studious and who might or might not be athletic. He also investigated the relationship between the students' responses and their own intellectual and socioeconomic status. He found that the characters described as brilliant, highly studious, nonathletic ranked the lowest. In fact, the four students described as athletic surpassed the four described as nonathletic, regardless of the accompanying characteristics (brilliant and studious). Studiousness was viewed as a handicap, especially by the girls, and brilliance, though viewed as desirable when accompanied by limited studiousness and by athletic ability, became a handicap when associated with a high degree of studiousness and a lack of athletic prowess. No significant differences in ratings were associated with the intelligence or socioeconomic status of the respondents.

Morrow's (1961) previously cited study on a comparison of bright high-achieving and underachieving high school boys concluded on a note not unlike that of Tannenbaum and Coleman, namely, that underachievement seems to be a form of individual asociality anchored in peer-clique asociality. His underachieving group, to illustrate, described themselves as belonging to cliques with negative attitudes to school achievement, opposition to authority, and restless and excitement-seeking interests.

The relationship of social orientation and behavior to achievement is clearly contradictory, some of the evidence implying that a certain gregariousness characterizes achievement, other evidence suggesting that isolation is an accompanying component. The discrepancies may be due in part to the diversity and vagueness of concepts studied, wherein social behaviors may mean getting along agreeably with others (Terman), being chosen for positions of leadership (Nason and Armstrong), or extratensive behavior (Altus, Owens, Gough, and Blackman). Of even greater relevance is the unexplored question of how particular social modes of behavior are interrelated with scholastic achievement.

Home Backgrounds and Family Relationships

The search for explanation of the phenomenon of underachievement has led to an examination of the education and occupational status of the families of achievers and underachievers, an appraisal of interpersonal relationships within the family, and an analysis of family attitudes regarding child-rearing practices. Investigations have also been made of family attitudes toward learning in general, and toward learning on the part of their offspring. More recently, the focus has shifted to more subtle dimensions of family life such as extent of parental dominance, power balance within the family, ethnic values, and early independence training. The expected and rather obvious circumstances have been largely substantiated, namely, that students with a record of successful academic achievement tend to come from the higher socioeconomic and educational backgrounds, and from homes where there has been emphasis on cultural pursuits. Early attention to these factors in the decade of the 1940's by Dearborn (1949) and Gough (1946) tends to support the assertion that there is a significantly positive moderate correlation between academic success and socioeconomic status, cultural factors, and occupational levels of parents.

Educational level

In regard to educational level of parents Ratchick (1953) found among his higher achievers in the eleventh and twelfth grades that significantly more of the mothers had graduated from college than among the underachievers. Pearlman's (1952) intellectually superior college freshmen designated as scholastic achievers with mean grade index of B+ were more likely to come from families where the fathers had undertaken studies beyond baccalaureate levels and the mothers had a high school level education than were the underachievers. Terman (1947) showed that in his successful group the proportion whose fathers had graduated from college was three times that in his unsuccessful group. Regensburg (1931), contrasting an educationally successful group with a matched group of educational failures found that parents of the successful group had more educational advantages than did the parents of the failing group. Shaw and Brown (1957) likewise noted a tendency among the parents of achievers to have carried heavier academic loads than did the parents of equally able nonachievers.

These conclusions were also confirmed by Granzow (1954) who found, in a comparative study of levels of achievement in reading, that parents of the underachievers in reading had had fewer educational advantages than parents of normal achievers. Roe (1952) saw some indications that parents of the scientists she studied tended to be better educated than average and that the father more often tended to be a professional man.

A few studies reported no difference in respect to education of parents of achievers and underachievers (Blackman, 1955; McQuary, 1953). Comparing two small groups of junior high school students about equal in academic potential but differing sharply in school achievement, Ford (1956) found relatively little difference in the occupational distribution of the fathers of the two groups, in the educational backgrounds of either fathers or mothers, or in the aspirations toward further schooling expressed by the members of the two groups.

Occupational status

Occupational distribution parallels educational trends. Terman (1947) showed 38 per cent of the fathers of his successful group were in the professional class, while only 18.5 per cent of the fathers of the unsuccessful group were in that category. Lewis (1941) found the group he designated as accelerated had fathers in the higher vocational and socioeconomic classifications. E. Williams (1957), in a study of 911 fifth graders in Scranton, Pennsylvania, found that levels of parental occupation seemed to be associated with ability and accomplishment at school. Regensburg's (1931) school failure group had more fathers in semiprofessional, business, semiskilled, and common labor occupations than the school achievers, whose fathers were more often in the professional group. Using National Merit Scholarship awards as an index of achievement, a 1956 National Merit Scholarship Corporation report indicates that whereas scholars come from hovels and mansions alike, more than half of them come from homes in the upper business or professional group.

Socioeconomic factors

It is possible that the above figures blur some of the actual facts regarding background, since in underprivileged groups the estimated waste of potentially high ability students alone is probably in the hundreds of thousands each year due to lack of adequate identification by the testing procedures in common use. Kenneth Clark (1956), in a follow-up study of students identified through the work of the Southern Project, which provided selection for attending college through guidance and scholarship aid, found that those who graduated in the top 10 per cent of their high school class were very successful in college in spite of the fact that they had received their training in segregated Negro high schools. Most of them came from higher socioeconomic backgrounds than was usual for their racial group, but had been racially isolated during their early years. Interestingly enough, an analysis within this racial group showed that those from lower socioeconomic status homes, although scoring lower on scholastic aptitude tests, tended generally to do even better in college than those from higher socioeconomic status families. When the quality of the various colleges admitting these students was held constant, 70 per cent of the lower socioeconomic group attained grades above C, while only 48 per cent of the higher socioeconomic level students managed to attain and maintain that standard. Among the highly selected Negro students, those with both high socioeconomic status and high scholastic aptitude test scores were relative underachievers in college, while those students of low socioeconomic status with high scholastic aptitude scores were overachievers, performing up to or beyond expectation in college. These findings suggest, therefore, that the students in an underprivileged population most likely to succeed in college are those with low socioeconomic family background and high scholastic aptitude.

Curry (1962) analyzed the effect of socioeconomic status on a younger group, 366 sixth graders in a large southwestern city. As did Svensson (1962), Curry found that socioeconomic status had no significant effect upon the scholastic achievement of the intellectually able pupils. However, socioeconomic factors did significantly affect the achievement of medium and low ability pupils, with the upper socioeconomic group favored. Frankel's (1960) data showed, in contrast, that achievers at the Bronx High School of Science came from home backgrounds with higher socioeconomic status and better educated fathers than did the underachievers.

Adult attitudes toward learning

The importance of attitudes toward schooling by parents, regardless of their social class origins was amply demonstrated in Kahl's (1953) large-scale study of adolescents' educational aspirations. He found that where the father was satisfied with "getting by" the son was less apt to consider going to college than in families where there was a striving to get ahead. Students from homes where there was apparent satisfaction with their present low status were generally bored with school, aspired to jobs like their fathers', and most preferred to "have fun" with their friends. Those students whose families believed in "getting ahead" took school much more seriously and aspired to better jobs than their fathers'. It would appear that within a given socioeconomic stratum a family's attitude toward its occupational status has a greater influence on the achievement expectations of the sons than does actual class membership. D'Heurle (1959) noted that achievers as young as eight years of age show an acceptance of adult values and a striving to live up to adult expectations, along with a strongly motivated need for approval, respect, and status from adults. Pierce and Bowman's (1960) study involving tenth and twelfth grade students concluded that the importance of parental attitudes toward education and toward diligence at school figured prominently in the success of able students. Parents of the achievers placed more emphasis on academic endeavors, personal responsibility, and independence training than did parents of the low achievers. Here again, the successful students showed a stronger identification with parents, whose values they were more likely to share.

A. Wilson (1959) adds another dimension to the socioeconomic factor by suggesting that the school climate may be a significant force in steering the motivation of high-ability students. He found differences in achievement and aspirations of gifted high school students to be related to the social class makeup of the school. Students of comparable IQ and very similar family background performed quite differently in schools which were predominantly middle class than they did in those which were predominantly lower class in their enrollment. In the lower-class school climate the bright youngster from a typical middle-class family tended to achieve less adequately and to show a lower level of educational aspiration than did comparably able students in the predominantly middle-class schools.

Family emotional climate

A generally favorable home climate understandably influences scholastic achievement positively. Kurtz and Swenson (1951) found home conditions of overachievers "more favorable" according to teacher ratings. Sutcliffe (1958), in a study of a large group of graduating high school seniors with IQ's above 110, of which half had average or below average marks and half had higher averages, found on the basis of a check list that the high achievers more frequently lived with both parents and had feelings of happiness toward home, parental attitudes toward friends, and occupation of the parents. Evidence presented by Powell (1963) suggests, on the basis of a measure of self-disclosure and security obtained from achieving and underachieving college students, that his underachievers showed a lack of emancipation from parents, a finding that might be indicative of certain inadequacies within the family milieu. Blackman's (1955) analysis of projective material on junior high under- and overachievers showed the environment of the underachievers to contain more elements of threat, frustration, hostility, and unhappiness. Shaw and Dulton (1962), using a parental attitude inventory for a comparison of high school academic achievers and underachievers, found that parents of the underachievers had significantly stronger negative attitudes toward their underachieving child. Disruption in family structure has also been found to be associated with underachievement by Ratchick (1953), Roe (1952), Granzow (1954), Ryan (1951), Terman (1947), Layton (1951), and Frankel (1960). Conklin's (1940) study of failures of highly intelligent high school pupils revealed that personality of the mother, home discipline, and parental disapproval of the child's chosen companions seemed to contribute to failure. Barrett (1956, 1957) found that the parents of the underachiever tended to show indifferent attitudes toward education and were more likely to be overanxious, oversolicitous, or inconsistent in their feelings toward the child. Homes of this investigator's subjects showed conflict, authoritarianism by parents, or domination by the child. In a six-year study of 34 underachieving boys at Loomis Academy, Holmes (1962) administered and interpreted four projective tests to each of the subjects. No distinct personality patterns were evident, but difficulties in relationships with one or both parents appeared in 30 of the 34 cases.

Burgess (1953) strikes a dissenting note in indicating that in her comparative study of over- and underachieving freshman engineering students the overachievers had greater limitations in their environment, were less satisfied with it, and were, accordingly, thought to view educational attainment as escape from restriction. Eckert (1935), on a personnel questionnaire, found that the superior college student in the upper quartile of grade-point distribution had a less favorable home environment than had the student in the lowest quartile. Musselman (1942) also inferred from his findings on the large high school group studied in Baltimore that whenever a pupil of superior intelligence has a handicap, such as coming from a broken family, being of foreign extraction, having parents in poor health, or having poor personality adjustment, such a student works harder in school to overcome the handicap and, consequently, his achievement ratio increases.

The majority of studies of home backgrounds fail to take into account the number of high achievers who have emerged from environments not regarded on the surface as conducive to high academic performance, nor do they shed light on the groups of young persons whose scholastic records are at variance with predictions of success based on the fact of their desirable home backgrounds. Such lack of definitive evidence suggests the importance of studying these factors of family education, occupation, socioeconomic status, and attitudes toward achievement, not as separate, independent entities, but as patterns of circumstances which tend to influence family relationships in particular ways, and might have a great deal of influence on the learner's school behavior. McGuire (1960), in studying the role of sex and community variability in test performance, proposed that there is a "life-style," independent of intelligence, which affects classroom learning. He also postulated that high family status promotes motivation for school performance.

Dynamics within family relationships

A concern with some of the more dynamic features of family relationships and values has yielded some provocative results in the area of father-son identification, early childhood training, and parental dominance.

Identification. The theory of identification derived from the work of Freud and developed and modified by contemporary writers (Bronfenbrenner, 1960) has provided models for several studies of underachievement. Westfall (1957), in his study of underachievement in the bright high school student, pointed to the finding that the nonachiever seemed to identify less with his parents, who themselves appeared to be less active and less supporting of him and his increased needs than parents of achieving students. Kimball's case studies (1952, 1953) of adolescent boys with a high level of intelligence in residence at a preparatory school who were failing in school work showed a poor father-son relationship in a high number of cases. The boys revealed in interviews and on projective material that there was never a warm, close attachment with the father. Either the fathers of this group had worked long and hard, which seemed to have brought about emotional distance between themselves and their sons, or they had been strict disciplinarians who attempted to dominate. The boys were uncertain about whether or not to follow their fathers' careers and showed resentment at pressures to do so. Of this underachieving group 41 per cent failed to give any response on a sentence completion test which could be classified as aggressive action directed toward removal of an irritant, while only 13 per cent of a control group of achievers failed to give such aggressive responses. Kimball saw the underlying aggression in the boys and their tendency to inhibit direct expression of aggression as resulting in so much guilt and anxiety that they were prevented from functioning well scholastically. She further observed that a high number of the boys showed primarily feminine identification, with strong feelings of inferiority and passivity, and prominent dependent needs. They were defensive about their ability and anxious to maintain a belief in their own superiority, which in their cases resulted in not working at school tasks for fear of failure. In other words, to try and to fail would be a confirmation of their feared inadequacy.

McClelland (1953) obtained boys' trait ratings of their parents and correlated them with certain measures of motivation for achievement. At the high school level, sons with high motivation for achievement scores perceived their fathers to be friendlier than did sons with low achievement motivation. The reverse, interestingly enough, was true at the college level where sons with high achievement motivation tended to perceive their fathers as unfriendly and unhelpful. A preliminary report by Gilmore (1952) involving a sentence-completion technique to separate 35 high achievers from 35 low achievers at the Massachusetts Institute of Technology found, conversely, that the achievers had happier relationships with their fathers and closer identification with their mothers than did the low achievers. Gowan's (1955) review of several studies of underachievement suggested, in general, that at the secondary school level underachievers perceive parental support and helpfulness in a negative manner. Kirk (1952), on the basis of case studies and the MMPI, discussed the basic symptomatology and dynamics of behavior to be found in college students whose academic performance is severely and chronically different from and inferior to their ability to perform well on tests. She noted that in a situation of counseling such a student usually has insight into his abilities, but gives unrealistic and superficial excuses for his inadequate achievement. His explanations often seem to reflect what he has heard; that is, he does not know why he is doing poorly, because he knows he has the ability. She concluded that academic failure may be an unconscious satisfying of hostility usually directed toward some family member who demands success.

Early training. The effects of experience and training in the first years of life on later scholastic performance represent a relatively new area of research endeavor. Winterbottom (1958) found a positive relationship between early independence training in the home and an individual's need to achieve as measured by projective tests. Siss (1963), in keeping with the findings of Winterbottom, found, in a study relating independence training to reading achievement, that third-grade boys whose mothers had favored early independence training were competent in reading and intellectual performance and showed more positive personality characteristics. The boys were not, however, easily differentiated from the boys whose mothers had favored moderately early independence training, but both groups performed more favorably than did the boys whose mothers had favored late independence training. Siss speculated that the high maternal demand implied in an early independence training attitude is relatively beneficial for the development of competent attributes. However, the mother favoring middle independence training may be more realistic in her demands since she obtains nearly equivalent results with her son despite making more moderate demands, according to Siss. Of interest also in Siss's study was his measurement of teacher values in regard to independence training and the interaction of these values with those of the mothers in his study on the reading achievement of third grade subjects. In brief, teachers' attitudes toward expectations were more variable than mothers' attitudes, but showed little relationship to the boys' performance levels in reading.

A study by Chance (1961) performed with first grade children tended to find the reverse of Siss's results to be true, namely, that when actual achievement was related to early independence training, children whose mothers favored earlier demands for independence made poorer school progress, relative to their intellectual level, than did children whose mothers favored later independence demands. Differences were greater for girls than for boys and greater in reading than in arithmetic. The author suggested that early independence training may in actuality be a form of greater pressure upon the child as well as a need for the mother to maintain a greater interpersonal distance between herself and the child. Along similar lines Rosen's (1956, 1959) studies suggested that there is probably a more important relationship between early achievement training and later achievement motivation than between independence training and achievement motivation. Rosen concluded from his findings that, for need-Achievement to develop, boys appear to require more autonomy from their fathers than from their mothers. While the dominant mother is more often perceived by the boys as imposing *her standards*, the dominant father is often perceived as imposing *himself*. Relatively rejecting, domineering fathers among Rosen's population, particularly those with less than average warmth, seemed to be a threat to their sons and a deterrent to the development of high achievement motivation.

Parental dominance. An association between parental dominance at home and a child's achievement at school has been an interesting theme followed by many investigators, with rationale forming two divergent points of view. On the one hand, authoritarianism has been seen as fostering submissiveness and/or conformity to parent and teacher achievement values such that school achievement is enhanced (Bishton, 1957; Drews and Teahan, 1957; Haggard, 1957; Holland, 1961). On the other hand, undue pressure and demands on the young person to achieve and to exert power through intellectual pursuits have been thought to have an adverse effect, contributing to rebellion, repressed hostility, and low achievement drive (Kimball, 1953; Pierce, 1961b; Strodtbeck, 1958). A corollary of this latter hypothesis would be that students who experience acceptance and affection from their parents, who feel valued more for themselves than for academic performance, and who share equalitarian values with their families would be more likely to achieve scholastically (Karnes, 1961; Morrow and Wilson, 1961a; Weigand, 1957).

Drews and Teahan (1957) adapted three subscales, the Dominating, Possessive, and Ignoring scales from Shoben's Parent Attitude Survey instrument, and administered them to mothers of high- and low-achieving gifted students and to a group of moderately able students, some successful, others unsuccessful, at the junior high level. Results showed that the mothers of the high achievers were more authoritarian in their treatment of their children. This was especially true in the cases of high achievers among the gifted students. It seemed evident to the researchers that the academically successful child could be characterized as one who has a rigidly designed place in the home, which he is expected to keep with docile acceptance. His parents convey the impression that they know what is best for him, and these adult standards are rarely questioned. Haggard (1957) noted that his third-grade, achieving subjects felt their parents were overprotective, pressuring for achievement, and lacking in emotional warmth. By seventh grade these students had antagonistic attitudes toward adults, although they got along better with adults and peers than did the low-achieving student, suggesting a developed ability to control hostility. Bishton's (1957) eighth-grade, high academic achievers tended to come from upper socioeconomic families. The behavior patterns of these eighth graders appeared to be submissive and conforming, accompanied by strongly motivated needs for approval and respect from adults. These studies seem to indicate that a home pattern of authoritarianism and constriction fosters achievement in school.

In contrast, Kimball's (1953) previously cited study of a small group of underachievers bears out the notion that domination on the part of the father interferes seriously with school performance. Strodtbeck (1958) studied the effects of the interpersonal relationships within families on the achievement-related attitudes of boys. He showed the importance of the power position of the father; i.e., boys with dominant fathers tended to be submissive, although the family interaction characteristics as he measured them did not account for achievement-related attitude differences. He also suggested that ethnic group values such as are evidenced in the southern Italian's greater loyalty to the family than to the community and belief in destiny outside one's self affect talented behavior adversely. In contrast, the Jewish acceptance of the necessity of leaving one's family to make one's own way in the world and belief in man's ability to control his future and perfect himself result in educational and occupational aspirations which affect academic achievement positively. Pierce's (1961b) study of the top 30 per cent in intellectual ability of tenth- and twelfth-grade students demonstrated that mothers of high-achieving boys received lower scores on the authoritarian-control factor, as well as on the strictness scale, although these mothers also provided evidence of holding stronger opinions regarding equality than did mothers of low-achieving girls. The investigators concluded that boys performed better academically under democratic attitudes, while girls performed better under authoritarian attitudes.

The positive influences on achievement of the more supportive and democratic families were borne out by Weigand's (1957) comparison of 17 successful and 17 unsuccessful college students comparable in ability. The successful group reported less stringent parental supervision of leisure time activities, greater encouragement by parents toward success in work and play, and a generally more permissive atmosphere in the home. There seemed also to be greater parental approval of vocational goals among the achieving students. Morrow and Wilson (1961a), using questionnaires and attitude scales, compared the reported family relations of 48 bright boys making high grades with those of a group making mediocre or poor grades. The two groups were equated for school grade, socioeconomic status, and intelligence. The results indicated that the parents of the group of high achievers reportedly engaged in more sharing of ideas, activities, and confidences; they were more affectionate, more trusting, more approving, and more encouraging with respect to achievement; they were less restrictive and severe. Evidently, the family of the bright achiever fosters positive values toward teachers and school and an interest in intellectual activities. No differences were found among families of underachievers and achievers in such characteristics as overprotectiveness, parental disharmony, irregularity of home routine, goals set for the children, or pressure for achievement. Karnes and associates (1961), in a study of elementary school children in the Champaign, Illinois school system, compared parental attitudes of academic underachievers and overachievers. Parents of overachievers on the Parent Attitude Research Inventory were less authoritarian-controlling, less hostile-rejecting, but also less democratic toward their children. On the Revised Parent Attitudes Scale of Ausubel, the overachievers saw themselves as more accepted and intrinsically valued by their parents than did the underachievers.

Vocational Aspirations, Interests, and Decisions

The largest number of investigations of the relationship of vocational aspirations and interests to the phenomenon of underachievement has utilized the familiar Kuder Preference Record and the Strong Vocational Interest Blank to tap characteristic occupational concerns. A smaller number of studies have looked to the possible connections between the time a career plan is

evolved, definitiveness of career purpose, and academic performance. The theme of realism of aspiration in conjunction with
day-by-day school performance has also led to some relevant
insights in regard to underachievement, as has one study on
the occupational motivation situation of high school students.

Vocational interests and goals

Pearlman's (1952) study of college freshmen, using the Kuder,
indicated that the male achievers expressed preferences for activities of an intellectual and research nature paralleled by
choices with a positive social service emphasis. The male underachievers were characterized by preferences for activities of a
manual type supplemented by activities associated with a strong
persuasive trend. Professional level objectives in the two groups
were similar and somewhat unrealistic for the underachiever,
whose present low performance would be likely to interfere with
attainment of aspirations. Diener's (1960) comparison of under-
and overachieving male college students revealed no significant
differences for any area of the Kuder except artistic interest,
which favored the underachievers. The Edwards Personal Preference Schedule favored the overachievers on most scales.

Morgan (1952) selected from 132 university sophomores, 40
achieving and 30 nonachieving students of high ability who obtained honor grades or whose grades fell below the mean average
of the freshman class. These two groups did not differ in variety
of interests as manifested on the Strong Vocational Interest Blank.
Types of interests indicated by patterns on the Strong blank
showed significantly more achievers with interests typical of
persons in social service or welfare occupations and significantly
more nonachievers with interests typical of persons in business
detail and business sale occupations. Also on the Strong blank,
the achievers scored significantly higher than nonachievers on
a scale of Interest Maturity. Ryan's (1951) study of under- and
overachievers in college showed the occupational scales of the
Strong Vocational Interest Blank did distinguish groups with
more than chance expectancy. Underachievers scored significantly lower on the Minister Scale and significantly higher on the

Masculinity-Femininity Scale. A later study by the same investigator, Ryan, in collaboration with Rust (1954), employed the Strong Vocational Interest Blank in an attempt to improve the best estimate of the grades of Yale Freshmen, an estimate based on the new student's adjusted high school record, scholastic aptitude score, and total of three College Entrance Examination Board scores. Agreement between stated occupational aims and inventoried interest was found to be unrelated to academic achievement.

Vocational decisions

The time, nature, and stability of career choices have been studied in order to determine their bearing on the achievement patterns of the academically able person. Williamson (1937) and Zorbaugh and Kuder (1937) were interested in the influence that having made a definite occupational choice had on college grades. Their findings showed no significant difference in GPA between students who had made an occupational choice and those who had not or were undecided. Weitz, Clarke, and Jones (1955) looked at the relationship between time of choice of a major field of study and performance and found that male students who reported selecting a major field of study before entering college performed better than those who reported having made no such choice.

Armstrong's (1955) secondary school underachievers, when tested on the Kuder Preference Record, appeared more likely than normal achievers to have stated vocational goals not in line with dominant interests, to have vocational interests set for them by others or to have none, and to have interests not satisfied by school. Carter and McGinnis (1952) found definiteness of vocational choice to be one factor which differentiated college freshmen having lowest and highest point-hour ratios, the difference favoring the high achievers. Nason's (1958) pattern of circumstances included presence of college plans and specific vocational choices as being among the factors related to high level achievement.

McQuary (1954) likewise determined that overachievers in college were more likely to have made vocational decisions prior to entering college. In contrast, college underachievers were uncertain about their vocational choice and indicated that they desired to go to college because their friends were going. Findings of Todd, Terrell, and Frank (1962), in a long-range investigation of the underachieving college student, highlighted sex differences in regard to ideal and actual vocational goals. A comparison was made of 177 normal achievers and 67 underachievers selected on the basis of being at or above the 80th percentile on an academic aptitude test, with a GPA either above 3 (normal achievers) or below 2 (underachievers), and showing willingness to participate in the study. The subjects were sophomores, juniors, or seniors enrolled at the University of Colorado in the spring of 1960. Findings were based on two personality inventories, the Goals Preference Inventory and the Inventory of Expectations, and a specially devised questionnaire, the Vocational Goal Questionnaire. Significantly more female normal achievers had identified ideal vocations or goals than female underachievers, whereas no significant difference existed between male achievers and underachievers. However, with respect to actual vocational goals, significantly more male normal achievers had made a decision than had underachieving males. For the female subjects, differences on actual vocational goals between the two groups did not reach significance. Male normal achievers also were more likely to relate their course work to future success in life than were the male underachievers. No difference was found between normal achievers and underachievers in expectancy for obtaining vocational goals, in spite of the fact that a significantly greater proportion of male achievers than underachievers expected success in their course work with their present effort. The authors concluded this phase of their study by underlining the greater need manifested by the normal achievers in contrast to the underachievers for academic achievement and recognition.

Super and Overstreet (1960), in their study of the vocational maturity of ninth-grade boys, demonstrated that grades and school achievement versus underachievement were related to most indices of their vocational maturity. Concern with choice and acceptance of responsibility were significantly correlated with the two school achievement measures. Specificity of planning was related to grades. Use of resources was related to achievement rather than underachievement. The correlation of their Vocational Maturity Index Total with grades was .38, or .29 with intelligence partialed out. The modest correlations of this study suggest that there are other variables to be taken into account in fully understanding the relationship of vocational maturity to grades.

The vast technological changes which are occurring so rapidly in our society are requiring increasingly specialized manpower. This means that the "early starter" and "long continuer" on a particular career path has certain advantages. Since some professional fields require that basic preparation be instituted early, the young person is often relatively immature and unfamiliar with any more than the rather obvious features of the world of work when he sets his occupational goals (Super and Overstreet, 1960).

Drews (1957) found that three-fourths of her gifted boys were planning their study for careers in science and engineering. And of 5,078 National Merit Scholarship and Certificate winners (1956), 60 per cent planned on similar courses of study and another 25 per cent on liberal arts study. The number headed for business careers was limited to 2 per cent. In this connection the findings of Thistlethwaite (1958) with reference to the National Merit Scholarship winners' major programs at colleges are interesting. It was revealed that at least three out of every ten scholars reported a shift in major field during or at the end of the first year. The most common shift was from the sciences to humanistic studies. History was the greatest recipient of scholars who changed their majors. Of consequence, also, was the shift reported from applied to nonapplied fields, with a very small proportion shifting the other way. The necessity for an early vocational decision and the influence on that decision of the present high status of the scientist in our society may operate to produce greater underachieving problems in a portion of our able students. In a study by Little (1959) of discontinuing and continuing college students at the University of Wisconsin, three-fourths of the dropouts had failed to meet minimum scholastic requirements, with courses in mathematics and science accounting for the greatest number of failing grades.

Realism in vocational choice

Westfall (1957–1958) makes this concluding observation regarding the vocational planning of his nonachieving high school students:

> In the area of vocational planning there is a need for careful guidance to prevent later disappointments arising from discrepancies between vocational ambitions and efficiency of achievement. Nonachievers seem more certain about vocational choices, but often these choices are not in harmony with their established pattern of behavior in terms of achievement. It is also well to recognize that the unrealistic job choices of the nonachiever often indicate a pattern of interest in music, art, and literary fields. More information and assistance are needed for these persons in the consideration of their vocational choices. (p. 392)

Jonietz's (1959) study of 57 liberal arts freshmen who had scored in the 90th percentile on the School and College Achievement Test produced some insights into the characteristics of underachievers. On the basis of their grades at the end of the first semester, she divided these students into three groups as follows: achievers, averaging 4.25 or higher on a 5-point scale; near-achievers with averages of 3.5 to 4.25; and nonachievers with averages below 3.5. The nonachieving group differed from the other two groups in that its members were more sure of their professional goals and expected to earn more money and greater fame, although they possessed less knowledge of the actual hurdles to overcome in reaching these objectives. The nonachievers also felt less responsibility toward society and regarded such values as "fame" and "fun" as exceptionally important. Jonietz concluded that these poor performers had false perceptions of themselves and society and would respond only to a radical attack upon their self-deceptions. Similar conclusions were reached by Iscoe (1959) in his study of probationary college students, 85 per cent of whom harbored the unrealistic belief that they would improve enough to be removed from probation, while actually only about 40 per cent succeeded in doing so.

Graff (1957) compared several occupational choice factors in normally achieving and underachieving intellectually superior twelfth-grade boys. The two groups differed on the Strong Vocational Interest Blank in adjustment to school work and in realism evidenced in occupational choice. The Portland Public School report (1959) described a comparison of 49 high-achieving boys with 49 underachieving boys who were equated on the basis of grade in school, socioeconomic status, and intelligence and compared for career outlook. Results showed the following: All the high achievers planned to enter college after finishing high school. Despite their mediocre or poor grades, 34 out of 49 underachievers indicated the same intent. Significantly more high achievers indicated that they would like to be and expected to be in professional, scientific, or engineering occupations. Significantly more underachievers than high achievers indicated that they would like to be in occupations involving adventure or excitement, for example, piloting planes, running night clubs, or playing professional sports. The two groups also differed in the amount of income they hoped for and expected to be receiving ten years hence. The high achievers hoped to be and expected to be earning more than the underachievers.

Krippner (1961) tested vocational preference of high-achieving and low-achieving junior high school students. More of the low achievers were undecided with respect to vocational goals. High-achieving girls most frequently ranked teacher as their first occupational choice, with secretary as second choice, and stewardess as third; low-achieving girls, on the other hand, ranked secretary as first choice, nurse as second, and teacher as third. High-achieving boys chose physician, scientist, and engineer in that order, while low-achieving boys chose physician, tradesman, and aviator. The investigator hypothesized that the low achievers based their choices more on social status than on real interest or ability.

Occupational motivation

Farquhar and Payne (1963) explored the nature of motivation within an occupational context, relating it specifically to grade-point average of under- and overachieving high school students selected from 4,200 eleventh grades in eight Michigan cities. Selection criteria for the two groups were carefully defined. Responses to a specially designed instrument, the Preferred Job Characteristic Scale, based on McClelland's need-Achievement theory, were factor analyzed. Although certain factors were identified, correlations with GPA were low. The authors concluded that the primary value of their study was to increase conceptual understanding of occupational-motivational complexes.

School and Study

School attitudes and study practices have been investigated less widely than other achievement-related factors. The direction appears to be consistent however, in that underachievers, by and large, hold negative views toward school-oriented activities, and their efforts to study are minimal and/or unorganized. To what extent these characteristics represent a cause of poor school performance or an outgrowth of it is difficult to determine.

Dowd (1952), studying underachieving college students of high capacity (those who exceeded 90 per cent of their classmates in scholastic aptitude but failed to exceed 50 per cent academically), reported that three-fourths of them studied fewer hours per week than the average achievers. The nonachievers also professed disliking their courses and professors, but it was not known whether personality factors caused feelings of dissatisfaction or whether these responses were solely an indication of projection after the fact of failure. Lum (1960) compared three small groups of college sophomores designated as over-achievers (.5 standard deviation above normal mean on GPA), underachievers (.5 standard deviation below normal mean on GPA), and normal achievers (within one half standard deviation of mean in either direction). Employment of the Brown-Holtzman Survey of Study Habits and Attitudes, an incomplete-sentence test to tap achievement motivation, and the Dole Vocational Sentence Completion Blank showed differences among the three groups to be primarily ones of attitude and motivation rather than recorded study habits. The underachieving subjects reported being more easily discouraged when confronted with long or difficult assignments, being accustomed to exerting only minimum effort in courses not liked, and procrastinating more on studying Darley (1937) noted the importance of considering clinically isolated problems such as failure resulting from poor choice of curriculum. In such instances, the usual attitude and adjective tests of maladjustment are not appropriate.

A relative decline in scholastic performance on standardized measures among underachievers was reported by Frankel (1960), who found that, whereas gifted achievers and underachievers were equally high in verbal and mathematical aptitude upon entering high school, the former group moved farther ahead on subsequent tests. The achievers expressed more positive feelings toward school and more interest in science and mathematics, devoted more time and used better techniques on study, and were more apt to plan college courses in pure sciences and in liberal arts. These findings are in general confirmed by a study of Wilson's (1962), who noted more negative attitudes toward school and teachers, lower grade-point aspirations, and less regular homework among high school boys making mediocre or poor grades than among boys making high grades. Westfall's (1957–1958) previously cited study found the Brown-Holtzman Survey of Study Habits and Attitudes to discriminate between those academically talented students who were doing well in academic activities from those who were not achieving satisfactorily. Major problems identified seem to reside in the motivational and attitudinal phases rather than in the mechanics of study. Applbaum (1961), analyzing a variety of factors characterizing 303 New York City high school students whose overall scholastic average for the first term of tenth grade was not commensurate with scores received on reading and computation tests, noted that the students themselves felt the primary reason for their underachievement was inadequate study. Phelps (1957), in a similar comparison of 100 achievers and 100 underachievers in an Atlanta, Georgia, high school, also found differences relating to school life. The achievers in his study were more frequent participants and spent more time in school-based activities, and their school attendance records were better. However, they revealed more problems in the social and recreational areas of the Mooney Problem Check List than did the under-achievers.

In the Portland, Oregon (1959), study referred to earlier, in which an extensive comparison was made between 49 high- and 49 low-achieving gifted boys who were equated in terms of in-telligence and socioeconomic status, results with reference to educational adjustment showed the high achievers to be more strongly motivated toward school work, less critical of school and teachers, and more likely to regard academic achievement as compatible with personal happiness. These high achievers also possessed superior work habits, broader cultural interests, and higher vocational aspirations, and expected to earn more money as adults.

Jackson and Getzels (1959), in their study of attitudes toward school among adolescents, concluded as follows: "Contrary to popular expectations the 'satisfied' and 'dissatisfied' students did not differ from each other in general intellectual ability or in scholastic achievement. Those differences which did appear were linked to psychological rather than scholastic variables" (p. 297). Miles (1954), in one analysis of attitudes toward school of the gifted children in Terman's study, reported that only 54 per cent of the boys and 70 per cent of the girls expressed a very strong liking for school. This finding suggests that too many of the academically able in their sample found school work unre-warding.

O'Leary (1955) developed a Work Habits Rating Scale which he applied to 55 junior high school students designated as over- and underachievers selected from a total population of 442 pu-pils. An obtained correlation of .63 between the scale and the survey achievement test suggests that study patterns are pre-dictive of a student's working up to his capacity. Malpass (1953), also studying junior high groups, analyzed scores from a battery designated as perceptual tests (Sentence Completion Test, School Pictures Test, and Personal Document Test) to discover the re-lationship between students' perceptions of school and their achievement (end-of-semester grades and standardized test scores). The obtained measures showed little or no correlation with the Stanford Achievement Test scores in reading or arithmetic, but there was a significant correlation between the perceptual tests and mean semester grades. Studies using the MMPI (Borow, 1945; Gough, 1946) show that curricular satisfaction, efficiency of planning and working, and motivation pertain to better achievement. Underachievers in Granzow's (1954) study were rated by teachers as poorly adjusted to school rules and procedures. Sutton (1961) analyzed individual school histories, self-reports, descriptive ratings by peers, teachers' observations of current behaviors, and personality inventories for children in three fifth grades. He concluded that a child's poor performance may reflect a lack of basic ability, motivation, or positive emotional involvement. A study is now in progress at the Horace Mann–Lincoln Institute (Goldberg, 1957) in which anterospective data gathered in fifth grade are re-examined after scholastic underachievement has become a more clearly identified problem in ninth grade. It shows that in fifth grade the potential underachievers were less often selected by their peers as being persons who would be helpful to them in doing their school work, although the teachers were rating them as equally successful academically as the future high achievers.

With the school as the main locus of the manifestations of and concern with scholastic underachievement in bright students, the bulk of research has tended to deal with nonschool-related dimensions. As is evident in this review, factors such as personality, adjustment, self-concept, peer attitudes, parental background, and socioeconomic aspects have received far more attention than have school and study. The very real possibility that underachievement may be, in part, a phenomenon of uneven, if not poor, teaching in the elementary grades, unchallenging material in the important transitional years of junior high, and rigid, traditional academic content in the high schools needs to be considered. Other factors which conceivably might account for the variance in performance may have to do with inadequately learned basic skills in subject matter areas, inefficient study skills, and differential abilities. Of greater import than self-reported attitudes toward school may be the deeper, and more difficult to obtain, genotypical picture of what accounts for such attitudes and how these factors influence performance. Gowan and Scheibel (1960) demonstrated a high correlation between reading ability and achievement in college, even when intelligence was held constant. They reported many gifted students as being seriously deficient in reading. Norman and associates (1962) studied 215 superior sixth grade children (California Test of Mental Maturity total IQ over 130) and compared achievers with nonachievers in terms of age, sex, IQ, and achievement patterns. They found a large disparity between the language and nonlanguage IQ's of the two groups. The mean nonlanguage IQ for achievers was 133.2 and for nonachievers 146.6, a highly significant difference. Norman and his associates speculated that the heavily verbal elementary school curriculum does not allow for the demonstration of the abilities tapped by the nonverbal function.

It is clear that the school's responsibility for its curriculum effectiveness and its methodology is enormous. Added to these demands is the critical one of the school's identifying high ability wherever it exists. Swanson (1954) interviewed men who, some twenty years earlier, had been superior high school seniors. In an effort to find out what factors had influenced some of these men to go on to college and the others to terminate their education after graduation, he found that one of the clearest differences was the simple fact that someone—a teacher, minister, relative, or friend—had encouraged the young, able student to continue his education. The men lacking any advanced study could not recall that anyone had ever suggested to them the advisability of further academic preparation. While today the recognition of the importance of a college education is much more widespread than it was in the 1930's, the means of obtaining it have increased in complexity and difficulty, and make even greater demands for wise direction and assistance from the school.

Motivation for Achievement

The bright underachiever is most frequently described as one who "could if he would" or one who "just doesn't seem to be motivated." Such a judgment is commonly followed by admonitions from teachers, guidance counselors, family, and friends to him that he "should buckle down and work," an exhortation which reveals a misinterpretation of the nature of the problem, a problem that is not so simple as to be overcome easily by the will to do better. All too often it is also an oversimplification to expect that an administrative provision, a new device, or a different set of materials alone will obtain different behavior on the part of the learner.

Need-Achievement theory

Investigations of human motivation have identified and studied both relevant voluntary acts and cognitively guided skills, as well as certain noncognitive and less consciously directed needs. McClelland (1953) has defined motivation as a condition of strong affective association, characterized by an anticipatory goal reaction and based on past associations of certain cues with pleasure or pain. He has theorized, as have others, that the basic motivational pattern for achievement is determined early in child-rearing practices. He has further stated that motivation for achievement is typified by competition with a standard of excellence, unique accomplishment, and long-term involvement. McClelland has taken the position that motivation for achievement can only be measured by a method which allows the individual to project his motivation in fantasy (Atkinson, 1958). By use of now standardized procedures, persons with high achievement drive (designated by McClelland as n-Achievement) can be differentiated from those of low achievement drive by presenting them with a series of pictures and certain directions for writing about the picture. Under test conditions set up to induce achievement tension, those persons with high need-Achievement drive tend to produce stories in which characters are described as wanting to get ahead, doing something useful about getting ahead, and thinking in advance about success and failure more frequently than are the characters portrayed in the stories produced by persons with low need-Achievement drive.

This theoretical development has furnished a framework for several studies dealing with the phenomenon of scholastic underachievement. Uhlinger and Stephens (1960) undertook to examine the relationship between achievement motivation and academic achievement in freshman students of superior ability and to assess the predictive validity of achievement motivation. The Edwards Personal Preference Schedule, the Goal Preference Inventory, an incomplete sentence blank, and three types of student grade-average estimates were administered to 72 honorary scholarship students. The hypothesis that high achievers evidence greater need for achievement than do low achievers was supported by only one of four measures. High achievers showed greater need for love and affection than did low achievers. Generally, high achievers had a greater expectancy for academic success and higher minimal grade goals than did low achievers. The investigators concluded that important inadequacies may exist in both the concept and/or the measurement of achievement need. Shaw (1961) used the Edwards Personal Preference Schedule, the McClelland Achievement Motivation Test, and the French Achievement Scale on a high school group of achievers and underachievers. Only French's instrument differentiated between male achievers and underachievers. Shaw likewise called for a critical re-examination of need-Achievement concepts and instruments, pointing to the possible fallacy in assuming that need to achieve would be constant in all areas of the individual's life space, or that it would necessarily result in observable production of a socially desirable sort, or that need to achieve and behavior would inevitably be congruent. He concluded by suggesting that intervening variables in the life situation of a given individual might prevent him from meeting any need to achieve. Herron (1962), through use of the Holtzman Inkblot Technique, the French Test of Insight, and a questionnaire administered to 180 subjects under either relaxed or achievement-oriented test conditions, called into question such negative findings concerning reported relationship of n-Achievement with academic performance. He concluded that intellectual achievement motivation is a unitary construct which can be largely defined by grade-point average corrected for scholastic aptitude and by questionnaire items whose content is related to attitudes toward education, intellectual activities other than school work, and study habits.

Pierce and Bowman (1960) looked carefully at achievement motivation and achievement values in their group of intellectually able tenth and twelfth grade students. On McClelland's TAT measure, tenth grade high-achieving boys scored higher on need-Achievement than their low-achieving peers. Twelfth grade high-achieving boys also scored higher on this than low-achieving boys, but the level was not significant. When the extremes in this latter comparison were reanalyzed using the 12 highest and the 12 lowest scores of the high and low achievers, the difference favoring the high achievers was significant. An internal analysis of certain categories pertaining to involvement, such as need, affect, anticipation of success, and instrumental activity relating to an achievement goal, showed such ability to become self-engaged in achievement tasks as a characteristic of the high-achieving boys. The same test did not differentiate between high- and low-achieving girls, a finding thought to reflect different cultural expectations; namely, that girls more often than boys aspire to marriage rather than to attending college and anticipating a career. Achievement values as measured by Strodtbeck's value scale and one by DeCharms confirmed the predicted difference in the tenth grade boys and girls, and in the twelfth grade girls. The investigators suggest that the reversal in achievement values in twelfth grade boys may reflect compensatory behavior on the part of the low achievers who had failed to live up to expectations held for them and might have become cognizant enough of the social values necessary for success to set out to say the "right" things on the testing instruments.

Bruner and Caron (1959) developed, through empirical analysis, a dynamic and cognitive picture of academic overachievement and underachievement in sixth grade boys and girls in a middle-class culture. The Wechsler Intelligence Scale for Children was administered to 64 subjects, school grades were converted into standard scores, and discrepancy scores between the two distributions were examined. The seven boys with the greatest discrepancy between IQ and school performance whose performance exceeded IQ were designated as overachievers; the seven in the opposite direction were designated as underachievers. On several measures including McClelland's TAT, Sarason's

Anxiety Tests, and some memory procedures intended to measure the efficiency of retention for achievement-related material in contrast to neutral material, the overachieving boys had a higher TAT achievement score than underachieving boys; tended to recall achievement-related words sooner; had less memory interference for achievement-related response words; and expended more effort to solve problems in competitive situations. Overachieving boys were characterized by more general anxiety and more anxiety with respect to academic testing.

McKeachie (1961), interested in this same problem of motivation, but at the level of predicting college success, took an adventurous leap by attempting to study the interactive factors of the individual's motives, the strategies he uses in attaining success or activating his particular constellation of motives, the ways in which different teaching methods affect such functioning, and the outcomes in terms of course grades. The results are too detailed to report here, but the direction of this type of research which recognizes the importance of the motivational variables, the variety of levels of interaction within the classroom, and the need for appropriate assessment points to a future direction, as yet relatively unexplored in its potential for understanding scholastic underachievement more fully.

Objective measures of motivation

Central to the position of McClelland and his research associates has been the notion that motivation for achievement can only be measured by a method which allows the individual to project his motivation in fantasy. However, Gough's success in assessing motivation using objective rather than projective measures has also made a contribution to the understanding of the role of motivation in academic achievement. Gough (1949; 1953; 1955) developed an instrument over the years now known as the California Psychological Inventory. Used most widely with high school students, the CPI results show that the more successful high school students tend to be less rebellious and more accepting of conventions and that their higher scores are suggestive of greater seriousness of purpose, more persistence in academic and scholastic pursuits, and more diligence and organization in their work habits. The same scales demonstrate, in contrast, that the underachiever is prone to impulsivity, dissimulation, and even delinquency.

Thorndike (1959), in a review of the CPI, described the development of the inventory through the assembling of a large pool of items thought to be related to something significant in personality, the identification of criterion groups that differed sharply in some attributes judged to be both socially significant and psychologically meaningful, and the development of scoring keys which included items found empirically to differentiate criterion groups. Thorndike grants efficiency in discrimination of the test with respect to the specific criterion dimension on the basis of which the items were selected. He suggests, however, that the criterion dimension may not have clear and distinctive psychological meaning, the dimensions used for describing individual personalities may not be efficient, and the separate scales may lack both independence and reliability. Although Gough's concern with the theory of socialization-asocialization as it pertains to the intellectual functioning of the bright person has furnished a substantial and fruitful framework for his investigations, Thorndike's critique suggests that the usefulness of the instrument has still to be substantiated.

Administrative and Counseling Provisions

Programs designed to overcome scholastic underachievement have included special recognition honors and broad attacks on the problem in city systems such as New York City and Champaign, Illinois, modifications of instructional and grouping procedures, and the development of individual and group counseling.

Special recognition

Thistlethwaite (1959) studied the effects of differing amounts of social recognition upon the educational motivation of talented youth. He compared two groups of Certificate of Merit winners in the 1957 National Merit Scholarship program. Results indicated positive effects of recognition, especially in the increases in favorable attitudes toward intellectualism, the number planning advanced degrees, and the number planning to become college teachers or scientific researchers. The latter effect was observed especially among students whose fathers were employed in non-professional occupations and among students who had only moderately high verbal aptitudes. In addition, increased rec-ognition was observed to increase the likelihood that the stu-dents would obtain scholarships. Stamatakos and Shaffer (1959) studied the influence of recognition and special attention on the achievement of superior college freshmen. Several groups of students were formed and given varying amounts of attention ranging from none to a combination of special lecture programs, a series of reprinted articles, banquets, letters of welcome from the dean of students, and monthly counseling interviews. No significant differences were observed in academic behavior. The results of this study cast doubt on earlier conclusions about meth-ods of stimulating superior achievement. The study is note-worthy, however, for its relatively clear design in which the four groups of intellectually superior freshmen were formed on the basis of random assignment in advance of any experimental treatment. Whitla (1962) studied the effects of "cram courses" on the College Entrance Examination Board scores and found that such intensive tutoring made no significant differences on performance. He concluded that proper methods of study, or-ganizational ability, and reasoning power result both from native abilities and several years of development.

Krugman (1960) reported on the Talent Preservation Project in New York City sponsored jointly by the Board of Education of the City of New York and the Columbia University School of Engineering. Students identified on the basis of IQ scores above 130, a composite score on the Iowa Tests of Educational Devel-opment at or above the 90th percentile, and any grade in the first three terms of high school below 85 were classified as un-derachievers. The project included 4,900 students in all five boroughs of the city, with a control group of 1,700 achievers. In addition to studying the characteristics of these groups, the project set up a variety of programs for working with the un-derachieving students ranging from group therapy and family casework services to tutoring, special help with work-study skills, cultural enrichment, and the like. According to Krugman, some outcomes became apparent almost immediately. Schools began to report at the outset that many students who had not considered themselves capable began to function better as soon as they learned the test results. In many cases families who had not been considering college for their boys and girls took a new look at their children and began thinking of college. In a substantial number of cases, counselors and teachers who had not considered particular students superior changed their approaches to these students and began to apply motivational and remedial techniques. Although the design of the project does not make possible a comparative evaluation of the various approaches, assessment is being made of the extent to which special efforts affected achievement patterns of gifted underachievers.

Instructional modifications

Hausdorff and Kowitz (1964) reported in a preliminary paper a study of interaction effects of various instructional programs on achievement of secondary students. Approaches in three school districts with a total of 800 tenth grade students included special instruction in reading and study skills within academic areas, special tutors in the same academic subjects, and no special treatment. Variance analyses of subclasses within schools indicated no differentiation among pupil populations in the study, that is, no significant gains in achievement. The investigator suggested the need for further differentiation of elements of instructional programs and study of the relationship of such elements to selected features of learning.

Warren and Iannaccone (1959), working only with poor achievers of average ability in a junior high school, organized two experimental and two control groups where various instructional procedures were carefully planned and carried through. It was found that the underachievers made significant gains scholastically in a so-called modified democratic atmosphere wherein they were encouraged to make suggestions on how the class should be conducted and allowed to make decisions in much of the planning of timing of work, seating arrangements, choice of certain parts of curriculum and even whether or not they worked at times.

Grouping modifications

In the Champaign, Illinois, schools, Karnes (1963) described the results of organizing an experimental class of elementary school underachievers. In contrast to 23 heterogeneously grouped underachievers, the 25 homogeneously grouped children showed a significant gain on measures of academic achievement, creativity, and perceived parent attitudes. No significant difference was shown in perceived peer acceptance; in fact, both groups decreased in peer group approval. However, the initially "higher average learning capacity" rather than the membership in a special class may have accounted for the observed improvement in the homogeneous experimental group. Miller (1962) summarized a study undertaken to determine whether counseling, tutoring, or regular class treatment was more effective in helping underachievers in the third grade. With 103 children identified by various measures, she formed three groups matched according to sex, age, and IQ. The first group was counseled individually twice a week, the second was individually tutored in reading twice weekly, and the third received no treatment. On two reading measures no significant differences were found among the three groups. McCracken (1960) studied the effects of a three-week training program in reading on gifted sixth graders and obtained favorable results in increasing reading rate and comprehension.

Counseling provisions

Counseling would seem to offer a more direct and personal approach than administrative procedures to the personality difficulties thought to be related to lowered scholastic performance. However, the process is not easily amenable to objective evaluation. To be sure, a counselor who sees bright underachievers individually, or in a group, will undoubtedly gain considerable insight into the dynamics of this problem, and will probably see evidence that the young persons themselves view their situation with less distortion as a result of the interaction. But how to show the extent to which such contacts directly affect school performance is quite another matter, and whether, in fact, counseling can directly affect learning performance is still largely an open question.

Winborn and Schmidt (1962) set out to determine the effectiveness of short-term group counseling upon academic achievement of potentially superior but underachieving freshman college students. Their results after six sessions over a two-month period showed significant grade-point average differences between the experimental and control groups, the mean GPA of the controls being higher. There were no differences on the California Psychological Inventory scores for both groups. The researchers concluded on a rather discouraging note that counseling actually produced negative effects on academic achievement.

Dragow (1957) postulated, on the basis of clinical studies over a five-year period, that among college underachievers a client's feeling of failure, or acceptance of the fact of failure, suggests a favorable prognosis and seems to expedite counseling. Motto (1959) takes exception to Dragow's conclusion that acceptance of failure is a necessary prerequisite for counseling readiness. Using as subjects 20 underachievers who were in the upper 10 per cent on the ACE or Ohio State Psychological Test and had college GPA's of less than C for at least three semesters, he noted that regardless of whether they had accepted the idea of failure or felt a need to change the curriculum, they responded positively to counseling. He saw the function of counseling to be helping the clients gain some insight into the feelings within themselves which had resulted in suppressed intellectualism.

Marx (1959) compared the effectiveness of two methods of counseling, individual and group counseling, with a group of 181 freshman academic underachievers. Of the 104 who reported for counseling, 46 were assigned randomly to groups; 58 were seen individually; and the 53 students who did not respond to the opportunity for counseling were used as controls. The counselees seen individually made significantly greater grade-point improvement than did the counselees seen in groups or the control group. Also, more of the students in the counseled groups completed the second semester than did those in the control group. However, the GPA for the total group counseled did not differ significantly from the control group. The results were cited as inconclusive by the investigator.

Kirk's (1952) observation is pertinent to the two preceding studies. She worked with clients seen at a university counseling center, whose scholastic grade records were much lower than their test performances. She postulated that these students did better on tests because the situation was largely impersonal, while the classroom situation, with an instructor in charge, aggravated the students' problems of hostility against authority. It is possible that most of the systematic studies of counseling results have not considered the lack of awareness in counselors of their own dynamics at the outset of treatment of underachievers. A second factor neglected by the researcher all too often is the slow and uneven rate of change inherent in any personality modification, particularly change in school functioning.

Ohlsen and associates (1960) reported on nine substudies primarily concerned with the extent to which group counseling improves the mental health and academic performance of gifted, underachieving ninth graders. The classroom in which the ninth graders were counseled was equipped with remote-controlled television equipment. Closed-circuit television was used to pipe the radio-video record to another room in which a four-man team of observers sat. Tape recorders also operated by remote control to make a complete sound recording of every session. Distinctive features of this study were as follows: it was conducted in an outstanding high school in which reasonably good counseling services were already provided; it was conducted in a school setting; analysis of the counseling process and gains achieved were studied by independent observers; the complete audio-video record made possible certain types of analyses not otherwise possible; the permanent record of the counseling process made possible reliability checks and further analysis at a later date.

In one of the early reports of these several studies positive changes in relations with peers, siblings, and parents were shown to have occurred among the counselees. Increased acceptance of self and others was apparent for the groups which had undergone therapy as opposed to the control group. However, changes in actual attainment as measured by teacher grades were not noted. In fact what changes there were at the end of the first semester tended to show a significant drop in teacher grades for the experimental group as compared to the control group. The authors concluded that group counseling per se did not result in improved performance for the gifted underachiever. When underachievement is not identified until grade nine, the problems associated with poor academic performance apparently are not easily remedied. Subsequent studies by Ohlsen and associates pertaining to counseling of underachievers dealt with methodological problems of data analysis rather than with outcomes relevant to the problem of underachievement.

Caldwell (1962), Harris (1962), and Keppers (1962) in independent studies each attempted to assess the effect of intensive vocational counseling, group therapy, and group counseling respectively on high school adolescents with scholastic underachievement records. While there were some positive changes in the counseled individuals, similar favorable outcomes were in evidence for individuals in the control groups as well. The changes were not of sufficient magnitude to furnish strong support for this approach to remediation of underachievement problems.

Calhoun (1956) approached the problem of academic underachievement in eighth graders on a much less intensive basis than Ohlsen by holding a minimum of three individual conferences with an experimental group during the school year. In these interviews test results were interpreted by the counselor, and the pupils were encouraged to develop plans to alleviate their underachievement based on the student's own analyses of the reasons for his problem. Pre- and post-standard achievement test results showed no significant difference between the experimental and control group. School marks of the experimental group, in contrast, were better by a statistically significant margin based on five report periods during the year. Ratings of pupil interest in school work also favored the experimental group. The author concluded that scholastic underachievement appears to be associated with a complex of factors and has to be dealt with on an individualized basis. The results reported by Calhoun add a more optimistic note concerning the effects of counseling as they indicate that as few as three individual interviews make a difference in GPA. Whether or not such gains are sustained would need to be established by further study.

McCarthy (1957) studied the effectiveness of a modified counseling procedure in promoting learning among bright under-achieving ninth-grade boys from 17 high schools in the greater Boston area. The 24 boys who showed the most marked discrepancy between ability and achievement at the end of the first marking period were identified and divided into a control and experimental group. According to the report, no group had more than one member from the same school; all had IQ scores of 125 or better; all were stable personalities; every participant had a school average below 75 per cent. Based on data procured from the subjects on the Biographical Inventory, the Kuder Preference Record, and the California Test of Personality, twelve "disguised" case studies delineated the more outstanding traits of the experimental members. These studies became the pivotal point of discussion for the experimental groups during the six one-hour counseling sessions which were scheduled for successive weeks in the spring of that academic year. No differences occurred between first quarter and final marks of the experimental group members as compared with the controls. Shifts in attitudes toward school did not differ, nor did the counselees' own attitudinal expressions as measured by the number of positive and negative statements occurring at the beginning and at the end of the counseling sessions change. Questions raised by the investigator include appropriateness of the nondirective orientation, the effect of the time variable since the sessions immediately preceded the end of the school year, and the effectiveness of the use of the disguised case studies. The project leader noted that while the introduction of a case study enabled the subjects to identify with the case being studied, discussions directed toward solution resulted in ego-defensiveness and resistance to any suggestions made by peers. Recommendations were made for a follow-up interview between counselor and each counselee and for a more active role on the part of the counselor in providing specific information to each subject regarding his ability, aptitude, interest, and goals.

Cohn (1962) reported a study on the values of group counseling for underachieving pupils who possess varying levels of learning potential and who show acting-out behavior. The project supports certain recommendations pertaining to needed dimensions in teacher attitudes, school administrative procedures, and classification systems applied to underachievers.

Roache (1963) described a project then in its fourth year in a small suburban New Jersey community to motivate bright underachievers identified on the basis of high inteligence test scores or rating in the 99th percentile on Verbal and Numerical sections of the Differential Aptitude Test and having three grades of C or lower in major subjects. Following comprehensive individual psychological tests, the subjects were scheduled for weekly individual counseling sessions. Detailed statistical analysis has not yet been published, but a preliminary evaluation shows that 71 per cent of the students who had been exposed to the program were no longer underachieving. At the high school level, also, Caldwell (1962) reported a controlled experiment to assess the effects of intensive vocational counseling on school achievement. He formed one control and two experimental groups, each with 25 high school students matched according to grade and sex. Two full-time counselors worked with the two experimental groups. At the end of the year, the counseled groups showed a significantly greater gain in marks than did the control group. Caldwell concluded, however, that all three groups continued to show marked underachievement, and that the counseling efforts had not accomplished their purpose if a shift from the underachieving to the achieving category is the criterion for success.

Another attempt to raise the performance level focused on underachieving junior high school students. Wilson (1956) worked with a group of 16 eighth graders whose IQ's were near or above 130 but who had earned few A's in the seventh grade. The investigator set aside for the students special periods of arithmetic instruction and a series of group therapy sessions. In English, science, and social studies, these students were absorbed as a group in a larger class of 35, the rest of the class being made up of bright youngsters who were not specially selected as gifted achievers. Teachers working with the underachieving students held meetings on the problems of the gifted and planned special projects for these students. Results showed marked short-term success, with the GPA's increasing from 2.76 (on a 4-point scale) in grade seven to 3.9 in grade eight. However, at midterm in grade nine, when all students had new teachers and more than half were in new schools, the underachievers regressed to a GPA of 2.97. The methods used in upgrading the students' achievement during the eighth grade were, nonetheless, deemed promising.

A description of programs of various types for underachievers in public schools and colleges and suggestions for organizing guidance and counseling services is found in a monograph published by the Department of Health, Education, and Welfare, titled *Guidance for the Underachiever With Superior Ability*, edited by Leonard Miller (1961).

Edelston (1950), a British author, who some years ago emphasized the relationship between the nature of underachievement and selection of appropriate remedial measures, described 18 case studies where educational failure in bright children had occurred. He categorized emotional conditions represented in the group as follows: disturbance of external origins such as poor home environment or an unsympathetic teacher; reaction formation to or rebellion against unwise handling at home or at school; infantile neuroses; defects of character of constitutional origin; and more severely abnormal psychotic disturbances. He recommended careful diagnosis, accordingly, and treatment which is appropriate to the diagnosis, such as increased educational pressure for some, psychiatric treatment for others, and remedial teaching for yet a third group.

A good deal of additional research is needed to discover ways in which the school can help young persons. A prior step to either administrative planning or counseling would involve much more careful academic, psychological, and possibly even psychiatric study. It is probably important to differentiate between the underachieving youngster who will rise to the occasion in the secondary school given some help and understanding and the young-ster whose problems are too deep-seated to be amenable to any help at that late date. Fliegler (1957) attempted to establish a typological distinction within the underachievement category. He differentiated between long-term and situational underachiev-ers—the long-term underachiever having problems predominantly stemming from the home since childhood, whereas the situational underachiever's problems spring primarily from the school envi-ronment. Extensive research is still needed on identification of potential underachievers in the elementary and early junior high school grades, in order that educational and psychotherapeutic efforts on their behalf can be initiated before these young persons become well adapted to their own poor work and study patterns and before their anxieties can channel their defenses into under-achievement.

CHAPTER THREE

Studying underachievers at Evanston Township High School

INTEREST IN INTELLECTUALLY SUPERIOR UNDERACHIEVERS and the school's provisions for them had for some time been a concern of the Evanston Township High School, Evanston, Illinois. This school is a large, suburban one located in a generally middle- and upper-middle-class university community. Enrollment at the time of the underachievement studies was around 2,700. Members of the guidance department of that school had made, a year before the study was initiated, exploratory efforts at finding out more about the underachievers in the school (Fox, 1953). However, the school was made even more aware of the problem as their project got underway to identify all students with outstanding ability. In checking the teacher nominations of all those who showed talent in one area or another, it was found that 120 students with IQ scores of 130 and better on at least one intelligence test had not been named by a single teacher. Here, then, were students who had potential for outstanding work in school but whose performance did not warrant their recognition as outstanding by any of the teachers with whom they came in contact. It was at this point that the Talented Youth Project, with Dr. Miriam Goldberg as chief investigator, and the Evanston Township High School joined forces to study underachievers at Evanston.

Two studies evolved subsequently. The first, to be referred to here as the Interview Study, will be described briefly in the first section of this chapter. The Interview Study reports on data obtained by school personnel on three groups of students. Two of them were similar with respect to IQ scores (125 or better), but differed in school grade average; and the third group was composed of students whose IQ scores were at or below the school median of 115, but whose school grades had gained them honor roll status. Findings were derived from interview summaries, school records, and teacher ratings. In general, this study was largely planned and executed by school personnel of Evanston with limited assistance from the Talented Youth Project staff during the preliminary stages. However, the project took full responsibility for analysis and interpretation of the data.

The Self- and School-Attitudes Study is presented in the second section. This investigation followed the Interview Study. It analyzed the results obtained from the use of two attitude inventories developed by the project staff and administered to four carefully selected groups of high-ability and/or high-achieving Evanston High School students, and to a fifth group, randomly selected to serve as a control group, heterogeneous as to ability and marks. A low-ability group was also added at the request of the school.

The Interview Study

Purposes

The Interview Study was designed to assemble such objective and subjective data as would be practicable and feasible for a large high school to collect on its own, and then to analyze this material for common trends, factors, or descriptive characteristics which would discriminate among three groups of students, namely, a group of students who could be identified as underachievers, a group of high achievers of comparable IQ, and a group of overachievers.

Subjects

An underachiever (U) was defined as a student whose lower IQ score on either of two intelligence tests was at least 125 and whose school grade average placed him at or below the average for the general population at Evanston. Thus, the average school grades for an underachiever could not exceed a mark of 3, the average grade which was achieved or exceeded by approximately 70 per cent of the total population. A high achiever (H) was defined as a student of comparably high IQ with a school average of 2 or above, which placed him in the upper 30 per cent of the population. An overachiever (O) was defined as a student whose IQ was at or below the school median of 115, but whose school grades gave him honor roll status—an average of approximately 2. It was the intent of the study to help the school identify 50 pupils in grades nine to eleven in each of the three categories and to explore similarities and differences among the students.

Data collection

Teacher interviews of students constituted the primary source of information. Interviews were designed to gather reactions of the kind not available from the students' present or past school records. Material dealt largely with students' feelings and attitudes toward school. For the interview schedule and instructions see Appendix A, Form I. Other information about the students was compiled from achievement, ability, and aptitude test scores, personal data records in the school files, grade records, and teacher ratings (Appendix A, Forms II, III, IV, and V).

Problems in data analysis

The use of the teacher interviews as the basis for obtaining data from the students defined as high, over-, and underachievers had certain advantages for the school's purposes. It served to involve the teachers actively in a search for a better understanding of the problem of underachievement and brought them face to face with the complexities and baffling uniquenesses which characterized the several groups. However, there was a wide variation in the quality of the interviews. The written reports differed markedly in length, depth, and objectivity of information. In most cases the material reflected a tendency on the part of the teachers to evaluate rather than to describe the situation of each interviewee. This imposed severe limitations on the use which could be made of the data.

A second limitation grew out of problems encountered in selecting students to meet the criteria set as the basis for categorizing the three groups. The teacher variation in grade distributions was so great that it became necessary to calculate a student's percentile standing in any given subject on the basis of the particular teacher's grade distribution. This process reduced the number of students available for comparison in each of the groups. Only 61 of the original group of 116 interviewees were eligible—24 high achievers (H) with IQ's above 125 and grades at or above the 75th percentile; 24 underachievers (U) with similar IQ's but grades at or below the 60th percentile; and 13 overachievers (O) with IQ's below 115 but grades at or above the 75th percentile.

Due to the unevenness of the interviews and the reporting, and to the small number of students in the groups, the identification of differentiating trends had to be curtailed and confined to a descriptive summary of comparisons. Since, however, this preliminary overview did lead to a more systematic and objective study the following year, a general discussion of the patterns of similarities and differences found among the groups through content analysis will be presented briefly below.

Results

Summary of interview data. Inspection of frequencies with which categories derived from the interview material occurred in the three groups showed the per cent of responses in any given category to be consistently similar for the O's and H's. Both groups tended to differ from the U's in direction, with positive differences favoring the O's and H's.

In general, the U's reported that they saw themselves less able or willing to compete for high grades, and they were less active in school governing affairs and seemed less dependent on the socialization function of the school. In answer to the question "How do you feel about school?" there were no differences between the U's and the H's. In both groups 80 per cent were rated as either very positive or positive in their attitudes. Both groups reported, in general, about equal satisfaction with their teachers and with the school program. The majority of the students reported no dislikes regarding school, and when there were dislikes expressed, these dislikes were toward a particular teacher or subject rather than toward school as a whole. Both groups planned to continue their education into college although the U's were somewhat less specific as to vocational goals. Only six H's and three U's mentioned specific career objectives.

The U's tended to see school authority and power vested in the adults rather than in the students, and at the same time turned to their friends rather than to teachers and counselors for advice and guidance. The majority of both the U's and H's reported making friends with ease and that most friendships (about 70 per cent) were with schoolmates.

Nor were there any differences in reports of out-of-school work activities. Only two U's and two H's reported holding regular after-school jobs. Both groups reported extensive participation in clubs and sports and spent free time on hobbies, listening to records or the radio, watching TV, and reading (the last two were mentioned more frequently by the H's than by the U's).

Perhaps most interesting was the difference in feelings about parental attitudes and pressures which characterized the two groups. The U's felt more pressure to live up to the high standards their parents had set and which they themselves had failed to meet; yet they saw their parents as less restrictive than did the H's about going out in the evenings, dating, and attending other nonschool functions.

From the interviews the U's and H's appeared to be far more alike than different. However, the incidence of responses in the various categories was, in many instances, too small to make comparisons possible. Few comparisons were made with the O group because of the small number of subjects.

Summary of record data. Categorization of information from the homeroom folders included socioeconomic status, parental education, leadership positions held by students, religious preferences, ethnic differences, and the like (Appendix A, Form IV). The only two categories which showed marked differences between the H and U groups were parental education level and leadership positions held in extracurricular activities. Differences in parental education level were observed only in attainment beyond the college attendance level. Parents of the U's were less often college graduates, or if graduates, they were less apt to have gone on to postgraduate work. The U's held fewer positions of leadership in the school than did the H's. A further trend was demonstrated in the analysis of the fathers' occupations: 94 per cent of the fathers of the H's were in managerial or professional jobs in contrast to 66 per cent of the U's fathers.

Summary of teacher rating forms. The teacher rating forms (Appendix A, Form V) provided information on the teachers' perceptions of the students' strengths and weaknesses, personality patterns, and behavior characteristics. Inspection of the ratings revealed that the U's had the greatest number of teacher mentions of weaknesses. Also, the U's received about as many negative as positive ratings from teachers. In contrast, the H's and O's received many more positive than negative ratings, a finding that suggests the extent to which teacher estimates tend to be associated with academic performance.

Conclusions

The results of the Interview Study, although inconclusive, uncovered enough trends to suggest the need for more systematic study of the three groups. From the interviews, the cumulative records, and the teacher reports, it became clear that the underachievers studied could be distinguished in some ways from the two groups of high achievers with whom they were compared on general attitudes toward school and on attitudes toward themselves as learners, but the available data did not allow for more specific conclusions.

Nonetheless, the categories derived from the content analyses of the interviews, the school records, and the teacher reports provided a wealth of material which, incorporated into more highly structured instruments, held promise for providing information on the students' attitudes toward themselves and toward their life at school. To be most effective such instruments would have to be appropriate for large-group administration within one or two school periods and sufficiently structured to insure comparability of response and ease of scoring.

As the next step in the studies of underachievement the material derived from the Interview Study was used as a basis for developing two instruments: one to assess the self-attitudes of the students and a second to gather more precise data on their attitudes toward their school. These instruments were administered to a new sample of students at Evanston Township High School in the spring of 1956. The development of the instruments, their administration and scoring, the sampling procedures used, and the findings will be discussed in the following sections of this chapter.

Self- and School-Attitudes Study

Purposes of the attitudes inventories

This study was designed for two purposes, each of which comprises a discrete portion of the total survey. The Self-Attitudes Inventory was used to discover more about the self-appraisals and aspirations of various groups of students in order to understand what relation such self-attitudes have to school learning as indicated by academic performance in the classroom. The decision to pursue the study of the role of self-attitudes in academic performance was stimulated, in part, by the dearth of information available on that topic at the time the study was undertaken. Although there can be no doubt that the image a person has of himself, as he now is and as he would like to be, colors his behavior in any task that confronts him, there had been little systematic research on how feelings about one's own abilities and personality characteristics interact with school performance. In addition, findings from the Evanston Interview Study suggested that self-assessments and aspirations as related to scholastic achievement merited further inquiry.

The School-Attitudes Inventory was employed to explore attitudes toward school and school-related activities of students of varying achievement status to determine what relationship, if any, existed between their level of satisfaction-dissatisfaction with school and their academic performance. Here, too, the Interview Study had yielded some trends which seemed to warrant more systematic pursuit.

Subjects

After consultation with the staff of the Evanston Township High School it was decided to identify five groups of students within the school population. Criteria for selection were as follows:

1. Underachievers (U) were students with IQ's of 125 or higher as the lower of two intelligence test scores (Kuhlman-Anderson Intelligence Test or Henmon-Nelson Test of Mental Abilities) and teacher grades below the 60th percentile.
2. High achievers (H) were students with IQ's of 125 or higher as the lower of two intelligence test scores but with teacher grades above the 75th percentile.
3. Overachievers (O) were students for whom the higher of the two IQ scores fell at or below the school median (115) and who had teacher grade averages comparable to those of the H group.
4. Low-ability students (L) were students with IQ's of 90 or below who were members of the Opportunity Classes. (Not all students below IQ 90 were in such classes.)
5. A random sample (R) of students was stratified by grade

Table III-1. Grade Level, Sex, IQ, and Average Grade Status of the Five Groups: High Achievers (H), Underachievers (U), Overachievers (O), Low Achievers (L), and Random Sample (R)

	Sex		Grade Levels				IQ (Mean of two tests)			Grade Average		
Group	Male	Female	9	10	11	12	M	SD	Range	M	SD	Range
H	34	16	16	12	12	10	132.9	5.7	126–149	1.6	.35	1.0–2.0
U	34	16	16	12	12	10	132.5	6.0	127–151	3.5	.56	2.7–5.0
O	24	26	16	12	12	10	109.2	4.5	89–114	1.8	.29	1.0–2.0
L	22	28	16	12	12	10	81.6	5.0	69–90	5.0	.78	2.7–6.0
R	22	28	16	12	12	10	112.3	14.8	70–157	3.4	1.38	1.0–6.0

level and sex as representative of the total school population. Characteristics of the five groups are contained in Table III-1.

Administration of the inventories

The inventories were administered to approximately five hundred students in the eight homerooms from which the random sample was to be drawn. In addition, all those identified as high, over- and underachievers who were not in the selected homerooms, were also tested. The Opportunity Classes of low ability students were also included. The instruments were administered by the guidance staff. Both the Self-Attitudes Inventory and the School-Attitudes Inventory were administered to the same groups of students, and both were completed at one sitting.

The Self-Attitudes Study

The Self-Attitudes Inventory. This inventory (Appendix B, Form I) was patterned on the work done by Bills *et al.* (1951). The inventory included two of the scales used by Bills: "How I am" and "I wish I were," thus allowing for three measures: an assessment of one's present status; an indication of wished-for or ideal status; and a measure of the discrepancy between the two. Two additional scales were included, one asking for the individual's perception of how others view him, titled "Most people think I am" (Sweet, 1929), and a second asking for an assessment of how "Most high school students are." These scales provided two additional measures of status-assessment as well as five additional discrepancy measures. Thus, ten global scores could be derived from the four scales.

The Self-Attitudes Inventory consisted of two portions, referred to here as *Abilities* and *Characteristics*. The Abilities section contained 25 items which enabled the student to rate himself on four types of abilities: (1) general personal abilities, such as *imagination* and *disposition;* (2) self-reliance abilities, such as *carry out responsibility* and *self-confidence;* (3) intellective abilities, such as *solve problems* and *think clearly;* and (4) special talents, such as *musical* and *artistic.*

The Characteristics section included 54 adjectives which called for ratings by the student on three types of traits: (1) social characteristics, such as *friendly* and *competitive;* (2) task-related characteristics, such as *studious* and *well-organized;* and (3) personal characteristics, such as *cautious* and *energetic.*

Reliability. A previous version of the Self-Attitudes Inventory (using all of the items referring to abilities but with some substitutions in the items pertaining to characteristics) was administered on a test-retest basis to 44 eleventh grade students in a New York City high school. The following reliabilities were reported: perceived abilities ("I am"), .69; wished-for abilities ("I wish"), .84; and discrepancy score, .78. The scales dealing with the perception by and of others were not included. A test-retest analysis of total scores on the abilities scale of 100 students in the latter part of the ninth grade in the Cheltenham Public Schools produced reliability coefficients of .78 for the perceived abilities ("I am") score, .87 for the wished-for abilities ("I wish") score, and .81 for the discrepancy score.

Scoring and analysis. For each of the 250 students in the sample, responses on each item on the Self-Attitudes Inventory were assigned a numerical rating from 1 to 5. On the Abilities section, 1 was "very great" and 5 was "somewhat small." Thus total scores on Abilities went from low to high, the lower score representing the higher assessment.

On the Characteristics section, 1 represented the lowest score, "seldom," and 5 the highest score, "most of the time." Thus, the higher the score on Characteristics the higher the assessment.

Separate total scores were derived for the Abilities section and the Characteristics section on the several scales, as were discrepancy scores. Other details of rating procedures and scoring are contained in Appendix B.

The scores of the five groups on each of the scales were studied by means of one-way analysis of variance. Where a significant F ratio was yielded in the analysis, individual group-to-group contrasts were made using the Scheffé method.

Results of Abilities scores. Six separate total score analyses were made on the Abilities section of the Self-Attitudes Inventory.

These will be included in the following order: (1) perceived abilities, (2) wished-for abilities, (3) discrepancy between perceived and wished-for abilities, (4) summary of perceived abilities.

1. *Perceived abilities:* In the global appraisal of their ability the groups differed considerably. The range of possible total scores, based on the 1 to 5 ratings on each item on the inventory, was from a high of 125 to a low of 25; the observed range was from 103 to 39. Thus no individual considered his ability on every item "very great," nor did anyone score himself on all the abilities as "somewhat small." The mean score for the total sample (all five groups combined) was 70.0—a mark just slightly above a consistent average position.

From Table III-2 it is apparent that perceived abilities ("I

Table III-2. Means and Standard Deviations of Scores on the Three Perceived Abilities Scales for Each of the Five Groups[a]

| Group | Perceived Abilities ("My ability is") | | Perceived Estimates by Others of Own Abilities ("Other people think my abilities are") | | Perceived Abilities of Others ("Most other people's abilities are") | |
	M	SD	M	SD	M	SD
H	64.6	10.0	63.6	10.8	72.9	7.1
U	68.9	9.9	69.3	10.6	72.5	7.5
O	66.4	9.7	65.3	10.0	70.1	6.9
L	77.1	11.4	74.2	12.8	66.5	12.1
R	78.3	11.3	71.7	12.3	71.1	9.5

[a] The higher scores reflect *lower* perceptions.

am"), except for the reversal of the R's and L's, went in the expected direction, namely the H's perceived their abilities most favorably, O's next most favorably, U's third, and L's and R's fourth and fifth respectively.

A one-way analysis of variance found that the five groups differed significantly from each other (Appendix B, Table B-I). The Scheffé test of the differences between the various group means showed that the H's and O's, both high-achieving groups in school, appraised themselves significantly more positively than did the L's and R's (Table III-3). The U's, whose intellectual

Table III-3. Significant Differences between Groups on the Three Perceived Abilities Scales

Perceived Abilities ("My ability is")	Perceived Estimates by Others of Own Abilities ("Other people think my abilities are")	Perceived Abilities of Others ("Most other people's abilities are")
H > L	H > L	L > H
H > R	H > R	L > U
U > L	O > L	
U > R		
O > L		
O > R		

ability was commensurate with the H's and better than that of the O's, appraised themselves somewhat lower than both groups, and rated themselves significantly superior only to L's and R's. Noteworthy here, also, is the failure of the O's to rate themselves significantly superior to the two high-ability groups, in spite of their school attainment record.

In summary, the analysis of group differences on perceived abilities led to the conclusion that the O's and H's differed little from each other in their appraisal of their abilities and viewed themselves significantly more favorably than did the L's and the R's. (The H's and O's also exceeded the U's, but the difference did not reach significance.) It appears that school achievement and its accompanying recognition and status were more effective than was measured intelligence in shaping self-appraisal of abilities.

The rank order of the five groups with respect to perceived estimates by others of own abilities ("Other people think my abilities are") showed that the H's rated themselves as viewed most favorably by others, followed in order by the O's, U's, and R's, with the L's seeing their abilities as least favorably viewed by others (Table III-2). A one-way analysis of variance applied to the mean scores yielded a significant F ratio (Appendix B, Table B-2). The Scheffé test applied to the several group means showed that the scores of the L's on perceived estimates by others of own abilities were significantly lower than those of the H's and O's, and that the R's scores were significantly lower than those of the H's (Table III-3).

With regard to how the five groups viewed the abilities of others ("Most other people's abilities are"), the L's evaluated the abilities of others more favorably than any of the other groups, differing significantly from the high ability groups, H's and U's (Tables III-2 and III-3 and Appendix B, Table B-3).

2. *Wished-for abilities:* It was anticipated that for a population as homogeneous as the Evanston student body in regard to socioeconomic factors, home backgrounds, and consistently high parental expectations for the children to succeed in school and go on to college, the "I wish" scores would be expected to reflect these social and familial values in two ways: First, the wished-for-abilities scores should distinguish between groups *less* than perceived-abilities scores. Concomitantly, the wished-for abilities could be expected to exceed perceived abilities for all groups. Second, since difference in achievement level between the U's and O's was related inversely to the intellectual status of the two groups, it was postulated that the higher achievement levels of the O's might be related to their higher level of aspirations as indicated by their "I wish" scores.

From Table III-4 it is apparent that wished-for-abilities scores only partly confirmed the first expectation of no difference be-

Table III-4. Ranges, Means, and Standard Deviations of Wished-for-Abilities ("I wish my ability were") Scores for Each of the Five Groups[a]

Group	Range	M	SD
H	25–66	41.8	10.0
U	26–65	42.1	9.2
O	25–61	39.4	9.4
L	33–79	54.7	13.4
R	25–68	47.2	12.2

[a] The *lower* scores represent the *higher* aspirations.

tween groups on ideal ratings of abilities. The three high ability and/or achievement groups did not differ significantly from each other. However, the R's and especially the L's exhibited higher scores and, thus, lower aspirations than did the other three groups.

A one-way analysis of variance of wished-for-abilities scores across the five groups produced a significant F ratio (Appendix B, Table B-4). The Scheffé test of the differences between group means showed that the L's were significantly lower in their ideal ratings than were any of the other groups (Table III-5).

Table III-5. Significant Differences between Group Means on Wished-for Abilities ("I wish my ability were") Scales

H > L	O > L	R > L
U > L	O > R	

The second expectation, that the O's would reflect a higher wished-for-abilities score than the U's, was not confirmed. The ideal scores of the O's did not differ significantly from those of the U's. The O's exceeded only the L's and R's to any significant extent. However, the mean scores for three of the groups went in the predicted direction—O's highest (39.4), H's second (41.8), and U's third (42.1) (Table III-4).

In summary, the analysis of group differences on wished-for abilities led to the conclusion that the high-ability and/or high-achievement groups were similar in their aspirations, all three groups scoring higher on ideal ratings than the slow learners or the average population. The slow learners were markedly lower in aspirations than were the other four groups.

3. *Discrepancy between perceived and wished-for abilities and between abilities as perceived by self and by others:* Perceived-abilities ("My ability is") scores gave some indication of how the students viewed, or at least reported, their present status with reference to a variety of skills, aptitudes, and characteristics. The wished-for-abilities ("I wish my ability were") scores indicated what the students considered to be ideally desirable for them. There was, therefore, some justification for considering the dis-

crepancy between the two ratings as a measure of self-satisfaction. The assumption underlying this concept suggests that the more nearly an individual's view of himself approximates his ideal image, or how he would like to be, the more satisfied he will be with himself as a person, no matter how high or how low his self-perception may be. And conversely, if the individual's view of himself is considerably different from his ideal-image, his self-satisfaction will be low. Thus, the discrepancy between the self-image and the ideal image adds another dimension to the analysis of self-attitudes, and offers the possibility of bearing some relationship to achievement differential.

It was expected with regard to discrepancy scores between perceived ability and wished-for ability that the satisfaction would be greatest for the H's and least for the U's; that the O's would be more satisfied than the U's and the R's, but less than the H's; and that the L's would be less self-satisfied than all the other groups except the U's.

The order of the mean total discrepancy scores of the five groups was in the predicted direction. The H's had the lowest discrepancy score and the U's the highest, indicating greatest satisfaction for the H's, least for the U's. The O's were more satisfied than the U's, but less than the H's (Table III-6). However,

Table III-6. Means and Standard Deviations of Discrepancy Scores between Perceived Abilities, Wished-for Abilities, and Perceived Estimates by Others of Own Abilities for Each of the Five Groups[a]

Group	Discrepancy between Perceived Abilities and Wished-for Abilities		Discrepancy between Perceived Abilities and Perceived Estimates by Others of Own Abilities	
	M	SD	M	SD
H	23.5	7.63	9.9	4.5
U	28.1	8.17	9.7	5.2
O	27.8	10.15	7.9	5.0
L	26.2	10.18	13.2	6.4
R	27.1	11.23	10.2	6.3

[a] The *lower* the score the *greater* the satisfaction.

the mean discrepancy per item tended to be small, approximately one point, ranging from an average item discrepancy of .94 for the H's to 1.12 for the U's. When subjected to a one-way analysis of variance the F ratio was nonsignificant (Appendix B, Table B-5). Therefore, the hypotheses pertaining to the effects of ability and/or school achievement on self-satisfaction were not confirmed.

One other discrepancy relationship was considered relevant for an understanding of the self-perceptions of abilities. In a comparison of the discrepancy between how the five groups viewed their abilities ("My ability is") and what they expected others' estimates of their abilities to be ("Other people think my abilities are"), the three high ability and/or achievement groups were significantly less discrepant than were the slow learners. That is to say, the H's, O's and U's perceived others' views of their abilities to be significantly more in concordance with their own estimates of themselves than did the L's (Tables III-6 and III-7 and Appendix B, Table B-6).

Table III-7. Significant Differences between Group Means in Perceived Abilities and Perceived Estimates by Others of Own Abilities

H > L
U > L
O > L

In summary, although the five groups did not differ significantly in self-satisfaction, that is, in the discrepancy between perceived and wished-for abilities, the direction of the differences was as predicted. The H's tended to show the greatest amount of self-satisfaction, the U's the least. Also, the H's, O's, and U's saw other persons' estimates of their abilities to be in concordance with their own to a significantly greater extent than did the L's.

4. *Summary of perceived abilities:* On the basis of total Abilities scores for the five groups studied, there appeared to be a high degree of realism within each group. By and large, their appraisals of their own abilities coincided more with their school achievement records than with measured intelligence.

On perceived abilities, the H's and O's rated their abilities most favorably, and differed significantly from the L's and R's but not from the U's. The U's also appraised themselves as superior to the L's and R's.

On wished-for abilities, the levels of aspiration of the H's, O's, and U's did not differ significantly from each other, but did differ significantly, in a positive direction, from that of the L's. The O's also exceeded the R's to a significant degree.

On self-satisfaction, as measured by the discrepancy scores between perceived and wished-for abilities, the means for all three high ability and/or achievement groups fell within a narrow range. The H's emerged as showing the greatest satisfaction with their abilities (lowest discrepancy between perceived and wished-for abilities), while the U's showed the least satisfaction, a difference, however, that was not statistically significant.

Results of Characteristics scores. Six separate total score analyses were made on the Characteristics section of the Self-Attitudes Inventory. These will be presented in this discussion as follows: (1) perceived characteristics of self and others, (2) wished-for characteristics, (3) discrepancy between perceived and wished-for characteristics, (4) summary of characteristics.

1. *Perceived characteristics:* In the global appraisal of their characteristics some differences among the five groups were apparent. The range of possible scores was from a low of 54 to a high of 270; the observed range was from 128 to 245. Thus, no individual characterized himself on every item as being that way "most of the time," nor did anyone score himself consistently as "seldom" possessing the given characteristics. The mean score for the total sample (all five groups combined) was 210.1. This score was relatively higher than the abilities score and well beyond what would be represented by a consistent average position (around 137).

From Table III-8, it is apparent that the total mean scores of each of the five groups are consonant, in general, with the expected direction, namely, the O's rated themselves highest on perceived characteristics ("I am"), and the H's next most favorably. (Note that the total scores are based on a 1 to 5 scale with 1 representing the lowest score, "seldom," and 5 the highest score,

Table III-8. Means and Standard Deviations of Scores on the Three Perceived
Characteristics Scales for Each of the Five Groups

	Perceived Characteristics ("I am")		Perceived Estimates by Others of Own Characteristics ("Most people think I am")		Perceived Characteristics of Others ("Most high school students are")	
Group	M	SD	M	SD	M	SD
H	203.2	22.4	204.5	21.3	190.08	17.9
U	193.4	20.3	191.3	25.0	188.50	20.5
O	206.2	19.6	207.2	21.7	192.27	20.1
L	200.6	21.4	202.5	21.8	196.44	22.0
R	202.1	19.9	202.8	19.4	192.58	21.1

"most of the time"; thus the *higher* score represents the more desirable status.)

A one-way analysis of variance applied to the mean scores, yielded a nonsignificant F ratio, approaching, but not reaching the .05 level of significance (Appendix B, Table B-7). Thus, differences in perceived characteristics did not distinguish among the five groups.

With respect to perceived estimates of own characteristics by others ("Most people think I am") the rank order of the five groups showed trends in the expected direction. The O's saw themselves as viewed most favorably by others, followed by the H's, with the L's and then the U's seeing their characteristics as less favorably viewed by others. The R's occupied the central position (Table III-8). A one-way analysis of variance applied to the mean scores yielded a significant F ratio (Appendix B, Table B-8). The Scheffé test applied to the individual group means showed that the H's and O's had scores significantly higher than did the U's. In spite of their high ability, then, the U's apparently believed that they were viewed by others less favorably than did the equally bright H's or the less bright but higher-achieving O's (Table III-9).

With regard to how the five groups viewed the characteristics

Table III-9. Significant Differences between Group Means on Perceived
Estimates by Others of Own Characteristics ("Most people think I am")

| H > U |
| O > U |

of others ("Most high school students are"), the direction of the
mean scores suggested that the L's and R's perceived others most
favorably and the H's and U's least favorably (Table III-8). A
one-way analysis of variance of the mean scores across the five
groups yielded a significant F ratio (Appendix B, Table B-9).
Differences of ratings of characteristics of others distinguished
between the H's and U's combined and the L's.

In summary, the analysis of group differences on perceived
characteristics of self and others led to the conclusion that on the
self-appraisal items the groups did not rate themselves significantly differently from one another, although the mean scores
were in the predicted direction. The O's rated their characteristics most favorably, and the U's rated theirs least favorably. In
general, on the Characteristics items, the U's self-ratings suggested a relatively negative picture. On the appraisals of how
other people viewed them and of how most students appeared
to them, the five groups differed significantly. The U's were significantly lower than the H's and O's in rating estimates of how
others viewed their characteristics, and the U's and H's combined
rated the characteristics of others less favorably than did the L's
(Tables III-8 and III-9).

2. *Wished-for characteristics:* In brief, the analysis of group
means on wished-for characteristics found few differences among
the high-achieving and/or high-ability and random groups. The
L's, however, were exceeded in their self-aspirations by each of
the other four groups, (Tables III-10 and III-11, and Appendix
B, Table B-10).

3. *Discrepancy between perceived and wished-for characteristics:* It was anticipated that the discrepancy between these two
assessments would yield a measure of self-satisfaction similar to
that discussed with regard to Abilities, namely, that satisfaction
would be greatest for the H's and least for the U's; the O's would

Table III-10. Means and Standard Deviations of Wished-for-Characteristics ("I wish I were") Scores for Each of the Five Groups

Group	M	SD
H	246.1	18.1
U	244.2	16.8
O	245.0	16.9
L	221.2	25.9
R	244.3	22.4

Table III-11. Significant Differences between Group Means on Wished-for-Characteristics ("I wish I were") Scales

H > L	R > L
O > L	U > L

be more satisfied than the U's and the R's, but less satisfied than the H's; and the L's would be less satisfied than all the other groups except the U's.

From Table III-12 the rank order of the five groups shows one unexpected reversal, namely, that the L's had the smallest discrepancy score on wished-for characteristics, thereby expressing

Table III-12. Means and Standard Deviations of Discrepancy Scores between Perceived Characteristics, Wished-for Characteristics, and Perceived Estimates by Others of Own Characteristics for Each of the Five Groups

Group	Discrepancy between Perceived Characteristics and Wished-for Characteristics		Discrepancy between Perceived Characteristics and Perceived Estimates by Others of Own Characteristics	
	M	SD	M	SD
H	49.26	20.3	23.46	9.6
U	58.52	17.6	30.36	17.0
O	52.44	29.4	23.70	9.4
L	47.34	23.0	35.96	15.1
R	53.48	17.4	27.42	10.2

the greatest satisfaction. The H's and O's, while not the *most* satisfied as predicted, were next in satisfaction; while of all five groups, the U's expressed the least amount of satisfaction. However, a one-way analysis of variance applied to the mean scores yielded a nonsignificant F ratio (Appendix B, Table B-11). Therefore, the expectation that ability and/or achievement would have significant effects on self-satisfaction with one's characteristics was not confirmed.

One other discrepancy relationship was meaningful with respect to the self-perceptions of characteristics. In a comparison of discrepancy scores between how the five groups viewed their own characteristics and how they perceived others' estimates of their characteristics, the two high-achieving groups (H's and O's) and the random group (R's) were significantly less discrepant than was the group of slow learners (L's). The H's, O's, and R's perceived others' views of their characteristics to be more in accord with their own estimates than did the L's (Tables III-12 and III-13 and Appendix B, Table B-12).

Table III-13. Significant Differences between Group Means in
Perceived Characteristics and Perceived Estimates
by Others of Own Characteristics

H > L
O > L
R > L

In summary, neither achievement nor ability was found to have significant effects on satisfactions with one's characteristics. The order of the mean satisfaction scores was from greatest for the L's to least for the U's with the H's and O's falling in between. The H's, O's, and R's also perceived others' views of their characteristics to be significantly more in accord with their own perceptions than did the L's, who showed the greatest discrepancy between their views of themselves and how they believed others perceived them.

4. *Summary of perceived characteristics:* On the basis of total scores for the five groups studied, the Characteristics did not differentiate as clearly as did the Abilities. The direction of the

self-assessments tended to coincide more with school achievement than with intelligence. The O's evaluated themselves the
highest; the U's evaluated themselves the lowest.

On wished-for characteristics the L's showed significantly lower
aspirations than did the other groups, pointing to the possibility
that the L's had placed a relatively realistic ceiling on their aspirations. The other groups did not differ significantly from each
other in their level of aspiration.

On self-satisfaction as measured by discrepancy scores among
the four scales, the five groups did not differ on the "I am"–"I
wish I were" differences. The H's, O's, and R's saw others' estimates of their own characteristics as significantly more in accord
with their perceptions of themselves than did the L's.

The School-Attitudes Study

The purpose of the school-attitudes portion of the study was
to explore attitudes toward school and school-related activities of
the five groups in order to determine what relationship, if any,
existed between their level of satisfaction-dissatisfaction with
school and their academic performance. The subjects were the
same as those used in the Self-Attitudes Study.

The School-Attitudes Inventory. This inventory (Appendix
C, Form 1) was constructed by examining the interview material
for recurring trends which seemed to reflect differences among
the high-ability and/or high-achieving groups in reactions and
opinions regarding school. Some related topics, not contained
specifically in the interview material, but which held promise
for a better understanding of certain nonintellectual aspects of
differential achievement levels, were added.

Thirteen separate sections in the inventory were developed,
each with its own format and set of items (Appendix C, Form 1).
The sections were as follows:

1. Student Preferences for School Subjects and Reasons for
   Preferences
2. Student Evaluation of the Importance of Academic versus
   Personal-Social Development as a Function of the School

3. Student Satisfaction with Academic and Personal-Social Learnings in School
4. Student Satisfaction with School Provisions
5. Student Participation in and Satisfaction with School Experiences
6. Student Perceptions of Determinants of School Leadership Positions
7. Student-Held Membership and Leadership in School Organizations
8. Student-Held Membership and Leadership in Out-of-School Organizations
9. Frequency and Amount of Time Spent in Out-of-School Activities
10. Student Selection of Confidants in Educational and Personal Problems
11. Student Ratings of Certain Parental Attitudes toward the Student's School Life
12. Student Selection of Optimum Working Conditions in School
13. Student Overall Evaluation of Total High School Experience

Scoring and analysis. The content of the inventory yielded information which was largely specific to Evanston High School, and descriptive in nature. Where appropriate, some tests of statistical significance were applied. Details of scoring are contained in Appendix C.

Results. The results will be summarized here under five main headings: (1) student reactions to school functions and provisions; (2) student participation in and satisfaction with school and out-of-school activities; (3) student selection of confidants in educational and personal problems; (4) student ratings of parental attitudes toward student's school life; (5) student over-all evaluation of high school experiences.

1. *Student reactions to school functions and provisions (Sections 1–4 and 12 of inventory)*: Student preferences for school subjects tended to reflect the emphasis of the school on academic areas for all groups (humanities, foreign languages, mathematics, and science) and did not differ significantly among the H's, U's,

O's, and R's. The L's, however, did differ in preference for business and vocational subjects (Appendix C, Tables C-1 and C-2). *Interest* was reported as the main reason for liking a subject in all groups. *Challenge* was seen as an important ingredient for the H's and O's, but much less so for the U's, L's, and R's. *Class atmosphere* was seen as a salient feature in liking a subject by the H's only (Appendix C, Table C-3). Disliking a subject was influenced more by *lack of interest* among the H's and O's than among the other three groups, more by *difficulty* among the U's, L's, and R's than the achieving groups, more by *lack of challenge* among the H's than the other groups (Appendix C, Table C-4). *Poor class atmosphere* was given more often as reason for disliking a subject by the high-potential groups (H's and U's) than by the less able.

The school's function was regarded by the H's, U's, O's, and R's as being mainly academic rather than personal-social (Appendix C, Table C-5). The L's, however, considered the school's function to be more related to the student's personal and social growth than to academic achievement. As a corollary, all groups except the L's saw the school as doing a better job in the academic area than in the area of student personal-social growth. With respect to the academic functions performed by the school, adequacy of college preparation was ranked first by all groups, and imparting knowledge was ranked second by all groups except the L's. The L's rated the school much higher on the nonacademic function of participation in school activities and organizations, and lower on the school's adequacy in imparting knowledge than did the other groups.

In a comparison of school provisions in 26 areas, the underachievers were the least satisfied with provisions and desired more opportunities in a larger number of areas than did the others (Appendix C, Table C-6). They not only sought more social opportunities, but expressed a desire for counseling, for more teacher interest in them, both personally and academically, and for some chance for independent work. All groups seemed satisfied with the organizational features of the school such as time spent in official class, classroom order, and the like. Apprehensions about the future were revealed in the desire of all groups for more counseling about college. Both groups of high achievers sought more opportunities of a special nature for learning, and the L's and R's, like the U's, reflected the need to have more teacher assistance and interest shown them.

In Section 12 pertaining to evaluation of school working conditions the three groups reported that they learned better under direction, structure, and regular evaluations. The U's favored more direction by students than did the H's, and the L's favored more than did the two achieving groups and the R's. It was considered possible that the U's responses here may have reflected more individual interests in hobbies and reading (Section 9) which they would have liked to share with others.

2. *Student participation in and satisfaction with school and out-of-school activities (Sections 5–9 of inventory)*: The picture of opportunities for students to engage in a variety of school experiences and their satisfaction with such experiences shows the high-ability, high-achieving group reporting the greatest involvement and the greatest satisfaction here. An exactly inverse relationship existed between the amount of participation reported and the amount desired, with the U's having had the least participation and wanting the most and, conversely, the H's having been engaged in the greatest amount of participation in school activities and desiring the least (Appendix C, Figure C-1).

The high-ability and achieving groups (H's and O's) reported belonging to more in-school organizations at the time of the study, and in the past than did the slow learners or the random group (Appendix C, Table C-7). The O's reported more leadership positions in these organizations than did the H's or U's, but, when the types of leadership positions were considered, the H's actually tended to occupy positions of greater responsibility more frequently than did the O's. The U's organizational affiliations were reported to be fewer than those of the H's and O's with respect both to membership and leadership (Appendix C, Tables C-7 and C-8).

With regard to out-of-school activities, the two high-achieving groups (H's and O's) participated about equally, although the O's reported spending three hours more per week on school assignments than did the H's. The U's were not engaged, according to their reports, in heavy out-of-school organizational activities, but they did emerge as more frequently engaged in social pursuits than the H's and O's, and in group pursuits more than the L's, who tended more than did members of other groups to "go out" alone (Appendix C, Table C-9).

3. *Student selection of confidants in educational and personal problems* (*Section 10 of inventory*): The five groups resembled each other in perceiving the frequency with which they discussed their problems—educational or personal—with adults to be between "occasionally" and "seldom." Educational problems tended more frequently to be discussed with parents and friends than with school personnel. The relative infrequency with which educational problems were discussed with school personnel may be a reflection of the amount of time available for such discussion rather than an unwillingness on the part of the students to turn to teachers and counselors for help. Yet this section, together with other findings pertaining to desired changes in the school, indicates that students felt that the school's guidance function was less adequate than it might be and strengthens the notion that students did not find school guidance as available or as satisfactory as they would like it to have been.

Students appeared, according to their ratings in this section, to discuss personal problems less frequently than they did educational ones. When they did choose to talk over their concerns, they confided mainly in their parents, especially mothers, and in friends of the same sex. In this regard, the O's stood out as being more dependent on their mothers as confidants, the U's on friends.

4. *Student ratings of certain parental attitudes toward student's school life* (*Section 11 of inventory*): High achievement, as represented by the H's and O's seems, at least in the student's perception, to color parental satisfaction with school life. It is especially interesting to note that the average students (R's) did not consider their parents as satisfied with his school work as did the O's and H's.

In general, the two high-achieving groups (H's and O's) did not differ from each other in the favorableness with which they perceived the attitudes of their parents toward Evanston High School. The U's understandably saw their parents as having a lower opinion of their achievement than did any of the other groups, while the O's perceived their parents as having higher interest and approval than the other groups, most noticeably in comparison to the U's and R's. Parents of the high ability and/or achieving groups manifested higher interest in college attendance than did parents of the slow learners (L's) while the slow learners reported more interest on the part of their parents in this matter than did the random group (R's).

5. *Student overall evaluation of total Evanston High School experiences (Section 13 of inventory)*: The groups ranked in satisfaction with school experiences as follows: O's, H's, R's, U's, and L's. The O's seemed to enjoy school the most, the L's, the least. On the five-point scale from 1, "almost entirely happy and enjoyable," to 5, "almost never happy and enjoyable," the general population (R's) reported a positive evaluation of its school experience—almost a 4, "generally happy and enjoyable"—whereas the U's and L's rated their school experience between "generally happy and enjoyable" and "just all right." The H's and O's saw theirs as more nearly entirely satisfactory.

Summary

Analyses of student records, teacher rating forms and interviews by Evanston Township High School staff suggested that the underachievers could be distinguished from the high achievers both in their attitudes toward school and in their appraisals of themselves. The material derived from the interview and record analyses was incorporated into structured instruments and administered to five groups of students: high achievers (high IQ, high teacher grades), underachievers (high IQ, low teacher grades), overachievers (IQ below the mean, high teacher grades), low ability students (IQ below 90 and in special classes), and a random sample of the total Evanston high school enrollment.

The findings from the self-appraisal study showed the same trends as found in the interview study. In general, achievement status appeared to be a more commonly used yardstick for self-appraisal than did measured ability. However, on ideal status, community and family expectations appeared to set common goals for all three high-ability groups and for the random sample.

Some dimensions of attitudes toward school did discriminate between the high and underachievers. The former were more satisfied with school, participated in more extracurricular activities and wanted less changes in the school situation than did the latter.

Although few specific items discriminated significantly between the high and underachievers, in aggregate, the low achievers appraised themselves and their school less favorably than did the equally bright or even the less bright high achievers.

CHAPTER FOUR

Studying underachievers at DeWitt Clinton High School

THE EVANSTON STUDIES were followed by three investigations of underachieving entering tenth graders of high ability in the De-Witt Clinton High School, the Bronx, New York. DeWitt Clinton is a boys' high school which draws from an ethnically and socio-economically diverse population. Moreover, since it enrolls students from the same geographic areas as does one of the special academic high schools, the proportion of bright underachievers relative to the school's total high intelligence group tends to be especially great. Those gifted students who functioned at an academic level commensurate with their intellectual endowment often found their way into the special school; those who were equally bright, but poor school performers, either did not apply to the special school or, if they did, were rejected. Thus, of the entering high-ability tenth grade students at DeWitt Clinton High School during a three-year period, about one-half fitted the description of underachiever.

Background of the DeWitt Clinton Studies

Purposes

The investigations undertaken at DeWitt Clinton had a dual purpose: (1) to gain further understanding of the characteristics

115

and attitudes associated with underachievement by comparing underachievers from a very different setting with the underachievers at Evanston and (2) to experiment with and assess the effectiveness of planned administrative and guidance intervention in raising the achievement level of tenth grade underachievers.

Plan

The investigation covered a period of five years from 1956 to 1961. It consisted of three separate studies, initiated in sequence in the fall semesters of 1956, 1957, and 1958 respectively: (1) The Homeroom-Social Studies Class (1956–1959) provided special grouping for four semesters. (2) The Geometry Special Class (1957) was studied for one year. (3) The Group Guidance and Study Skills Special classes (1958–1961) encompassed the full three-year period of high school for one group of underachievers and two years for a second group. The studies were developmental in nature in that the second undertaking was based on some observations and hunches formulated in the first study, while the third study drew some of the features of its design from conclusions reached in the two previous studies. Each study used a different group of entering tenth graders.

The main focus of these studies was on the effects of certain school provisions on scholastic performance. However, attention was directed throughout this work to the underachievers themselves—their backgrounds, family attitudes, classroom behavior, personal insights, friendships, educational and vocational aspirations, and their own attitudes about themselves, other persons, and the school.

Subjects

During the three-year period in which the three different administrative plans were initiated, 227 underachieving boys and 100 high-achieving boys were identified and assigned to experimental and control groups according to the designs of the separate studies. Each group of underachievers was selected on the basis of IQ scores on at least two group tests and on junior high school scholastic records. Detailed descriptions of grades, standardized achievement test scores, and sociometric ratings are contained in the reports of the separate studies.

Personality and Attitudinal Characteristics of the Underachievers

Certain characteristics of several of the groups of underachievers studied at Clinton will be discussed first on the basis of information obtained from recorded interviews. Secondly, general observations of the several groups based on the Self-Attitudes Inventory, conferences with parents, and evaluations by the several staff members involved throughout the Clinton project will be summarized.

Interview data

During the first year of the Clinton study, 26 boys, selected at random from the matched pairs of underachievers involved in the Homeroom-Social Studies Class, along with four high achievers, were seen individually for a fifty-minute interview. The purpose of the interview was to investigate some of the more personal components of achievement, such as the boy's perception of his own ability and achievement, his reactions to the new school, his plans for the future, his recollections of his academic performance in elementary and junior high school, his view of his parents' reactions to his school record, and the like.

The interviews were conducted by a psychologist on the project staff, and were electrically recorded, transcribed, and analyzed. Although there were insufficient data to quantify and treat statistically, certain trends emerged which might be considered representative of the situation of ninth and tenth graders whose school marks made it apparent that, even though they were intellectually able, they were encountering school difficulties. Statements from the interviews are grouped according to broad topics, and each one is identified as to whether it was made by an achiever (H) or an underachiever (U).

Self-appraisal of ability. In the interviews the underachieving boys tended to refer to themselves and their ability as "all right," "average," or "fair." They might see their performance in one subject as "pretty good," but by and large the picture they gave was one of minimal aspiration and an apparent tendency to see themselves as doing satisfactorily so long as they did not fail:

> I was just about average. (U)

> My ability, I guess, is fair, average. If I am with smart boys, I'm about average. I was at the top only in elementary school. I never thought of myself as a genius. (U)

> I don't know my IQ, but it's supposed to be around 130. In other words I am pretty average. (U)

> I just passed my subjects, and that's all I care about. (U)

> I just want to be an average kid, nothing special. Why should I be the smartest kid in the world? I wouldn't get anything out of that. I just want to be one of the crowd. (U)

> About halfway—wasn't at the bottom, wasn't at the top. (U)

In contrast the high achievers saw themselves as possessing good ability:

> I have a 130 IQ, and I'm told that's supposed to be pretty good. (H)

> I think I'm pretty smart, not a brain, maybe, but pretty accurate, and pretty good in my studies. (H)

> I had a 90 average in my junior high subjects. I think the opinion of the teachers was that I was an intelligent boy. (H)

Teacher appraisal of students. The responses of the underachieving boys to the question of how their teachers evaluated them were usually characterized by a "could if I would" attitude:

> My Spanish teacher thought I wasn't trying enough. (U)

> One teacher thought I was a smart boy, but pretty lazy. (U)

> My teachers tell me, too, I'll get along in high school and I'll pass everything, but if I work a little harder I could be an honor student. (U)

These boys also responded to this question in terms of the extent to which they felt a teacher liked them or was on their side, and how much they themselves liked individual teachers:

> They all liked me. I was a fairly nice boy—never caused any trouble. (U)

I know my teachers liked me a lot, and I liked most of my teachers. (U)

Well, I got to like a couple of teachers, got friendly with them, and for them I did outstanding work and they gave me special things to do. (U)

Somehow I didn't hit it off very good with teachers. I used to dread going to some of the teachers. (U)

These comments are not essentially different from those made by the high achievers:

I think most teachers like me. (H)

When a teacher does not favor a boy and not only not favor, but doesn't like him at all, and the boy can tell it, I think he will get discouraged and won't do any work. (H)

Parental attitudes. 1. *Expectations:* From the population studied there was general evidence of high aspiration on the part of parents for the boys to get good marks in school, attend college, and enter a professional field. The parents themselves had evidently been denied higher education due to the economic depression of the early 1930's and were very anxious that their children have the best educational opportunity:

My father (dairy store owner) started working during high school. He says what he missed, I should have. (U)

My father (printer) wants me to get the education that he missed. In blunt words he says that if I don't finish high school he's going to break every bone in my body. He says he'll work the rest of his life so I'll have an education. (U)

My father (florist) says, "You have to have a college diploma to get anywhere in the world." He could have had one, but he stopped because of financial difficulties. He wants me to have the advantages he didn't have. He wants me to be up in the world, to work hard, and earn money, but not work as hard as he does. (U)

In my case my parents want me to work, but they also want me to go to college and make something of myself. My father didn't have that. (U)

Parents of the high achievers held similar expectations:

My parents, who were born on the other side and had little education, want to see me go through college; they want the best for me. (H)

2. *Assistance with studies:* Boys differed in reports of amount of assistance they received from their parents. The impression

one receives is that this factor has little direct relationship to achievement level. High achievers stated:

> My father helps me, always helps me. (H)

> I do all my own homework. My parents recall people who have lived longer, and like that, but about school work, they've probably forgotten what they had. (H)

> My parents are very interested in my school work and they want me to get good marks, and they always help me every night—both of them always help me. (H)

Comments of underachievers were similar:

> My father wants to teach me more advanced Spanish than we are having in class. My mother, whenever I make a report, wants to see it, correct it, tell me I should have stuck to the point. She always checks my homework. (U)

> When I bring home a poor report card my father says, "It's OK. It's just one of the first." Then he puts me down, and he sits down, and we work together. (U)

> My parents leave homework pretty much up to me. They feel if I don't want to do it, I don't have to. It's just up to yourself to learn. (U)

3. *Pressures:* There was a clearly recurring theme from a number of the underachieving boys relative to parental exhortation and pressures on them to study:

> Last year when I wasn't doing too well in Spanish, they started hounding me. (U)

> When I got a low grade in math . . . he didn't say I had to study; he just said, "You can't go fishing, you can't do this, you can't do that. If you don't want to have some fun again, don't study." (U)

> My mother keeps saying, "You know you can do better. You know you have better ability than that." (U)

> My mother just feels that I ought to stay in the house and continually study and study. And that'd be the only way I'd get good marks. (U)

> My mother always told me I could do better, and my father usually agreed with her and said that I should spend more time on my homework. (U)

> When I bring home a failure or a not-too-good report card they really start arguing at me, and they say that I have the ability which is right

and that I should be doing better and they get after me to do my homework. (U)

Parental pressures, however, were also reported by the high-achieving boys:

I know that if I came home with marks that were terrible my parents would object. My parents are always pushing me to get good marks. They keep saying, "Did you do this and did you do that?" (H)

My parents make sure I get my work done. (H)

An apparently satisfactory solution had been arrived at by two boys and their parents. One said:

My parents don't press me to do my studies. They used to. They stopped sort of abruptly when they found out I knew I had to do it and I'd do it. They always used to keep saying, "Keep studying, do this, do that," and I never minded it except that they kept telling me to do it, and I already knew I had to do it. Even as far as practicing goes, my mother may drop a hint here and there, but I usually pick it up by myself. (U)

Similarly another boy stated:

My mother used to talk to me every night, so finally I got straightened out. She used to help me along, too, until finally I caught on and now I'm doing all right. She's very proud of me. (U)

4. *Approval:* As indicated in the previous section most of the comments regarding parental attitudes dealt with directives to improve and dissatisfaction with present achievement. Few of the boys mentioned anything approaching wholehearted approval and support from parents. Even when a high mark was received, parents tended to focus on the possibility of doing even better or warn the boy against not maintaining his level:

If I got 85 on a math test my father would say, "That's not good enough. You should have gotten a 95." If I came home with 95, he thinks I should get 100. He keeps shoving it into my head about studying and getting my homework. (U)

They feel that my general record in school is satisfactory, pretty good. (U)

When I bring home good marks they say, "Keep studying"—they don't say, "Stop," or "That's good enough," but they say, "You have to maintain that average—that's good, keep going." (U)

This same attitude is expressed by parents of the high achievers as well as the underachievers, although there were a few exceptions:

> If I bring home a good report card, he doesn't praise me or give me things, he just says, "You still have to study even though you got a good report." (H)

> The marks that I get—my mother tells me I could do better. She tries to get me to get the highest marks. (H)

Vocational choice. The majority of the boys expressed a definite vocational choice. Engineering, medicine, and dentistry were mentioned most frequently. Sports writing, law, commercial art, and the ministry were also selected as areas of specialization.

Attitudes toward teachers. Many of the questions in the interviews directed toward self-perceptions, ability, school success, difficulties, etc., were answered by the boys in terms of the teachers they had had. Nearly every boy described a helpful teacher in conjunction with a subject in which he had done well and an unsympathetic or unfair teacher in the instances of school failure:

> I had the same teacher for the seventh and ninth grades. And she was awfully interesting. Whenever I'd write a story, she'd take it home and read it, and she would tell me what she thought of it. She helped me very much. (U)

> There was one good teacher, a real good teacher. She was the best teacher I ever had. She taught English. First I thought she was a little hard, and then I got the knack of it, rules and so on. She's a great teacher, always cracking jokes. (U)

> Well, in high school here I like my teachers, and I find some of the work interesting, and I have the urge to do good work. Like in _____ and _____. Last year I tried to make my compositions so short, and now I think I have some of the longest work. (U)

> If I had had a teacher who could understand me and work with me, I'd try hard to do very well. (U)

> Especially in English, I didn't feel that some of the subjects we had to write on in compositions had anything to do with English at all. Some

of the teachers just didn't teach. They thought just because they were so big and we were so small we'd catch on in a jiffy. (U)

Oh, the algebra teacher was terrific. She was very good. I got a big jump on algebra. I mean everything in geometry now is relying on that algebra, and it helps a lot. She was very good. (H)

I know a lot of boys who are very low in their grades, and they had this one teacher in junior high school, and they gave all these boys to him—he started them working and they worked for once in their life, and they liked him—he was a good teacher, and they liked to work for him. (U)

The boys often described what they considered desirable in a teacher. A high achiever said:

Well, I like a teacher who knows boys—like some teachers, they just teach—they're strict, they don't do this and don't do that. I think the best teacher would be the one that is really interested in boys, really wants them to learn . . . and not just to teach. In science last year I got 99 on all my report cards. In my last report card I got 100. Now I would rather have gotten a 75 and learned something that year than get a 99 and didn't learn anything. (H)

The underachievers referred to other qualities in a teacher:

A lot of teachers I didn't respect in the least. I mean they had no control over the class or anything. Some didn't give you any interest in a subject. They're just there, and they say a couple of words, and they teach like a record. (U)

I think if the teacher has a somewhat cheerful attitude that it would sort of reflect on the kids. But if a teacher just walks around as if it's the end of the world, nothing's going good, and last year they were continually complaining about not getting paid enough. This makes the kid feel, "Gee, he's not doing anything. He's getting paid nothing. Why should we bother with him?" And as a result of that you had fights and so forth in the back of the room. (U)

In Spanish class, we wouldn't talk out because we respected the teacher and knew she wouldn't stand for such a thing. (U)

This teacher when she gave us *Ivanhoe* . . . and I liked *Ivanhoe* and it was very interesting, but instead of letting us read it and at the end making a summary, every night we'd have to go home and answer three or four chapters of questions, and you just can't grasp it, and you lose interest. (U)

I think the teacher should understand the student. You know what I mean? The course should be made so that it's interesting. It shouldn't be third grade stuff, like you had stories and everything. When you're explaining the parts of speech you have a story. That's not diverting you, that's interesting. Like when you do book reports, at the beginning of the term you tell the child when the book reports are due, you give a lot of time, you know. Sometimes the kid just doesn't want to pick up a book. And lots of times, say you forget your homework. A zero for this. A zero for that. You talk out of turn. A zero for that. (U)

Attitudes toward Special Progress classes. The junior high Special Progress (SP) classes, which permit boys who have IQ's of 130 and above and are accelerated two years in reading and one-and-a-half years in arithmetic to complete the regular three years of junior high in two years, were regarded as a mixed blessing by the underachievers interviewed. By chance, none of the high achievers interviewed had been in the SP program.

Also, I believe that teachers are continually degrading the kids in the SP's. I had an official teacher in the ninth grade, and all the time she was telling us what a lousy group of kids we were and that we think we're so smart and cocky all the time . . . but that really stands out in my mind . . . the fact that they kept degrading us. (U)

Well, I made the SP's and I'm sorry to say that I ever took it because I think it's very bad because a child is pressured so much, giving him three years' work in two years, and every time the teacher asks him, "Oh, you're in SP, you have a brain, you ought to be able to do it." (U)

Well, I was quite shocked that I made the SP's. I didn't realize I had the brain power for it. I enjoyed it very much. If you learned the work and could get ahead, you could skip. I really learned quite a bit from it. (U)

I didn't like the SP program at all. When I first entered it my sixth grade teacher said they'd look up to you and everything, but I found that none of the teachers liked us. None of them. I don't think some of the teachers liked the fact that our credit was more advanced than their credit. And I know when we were in the hall, they didn't turn around to see who was talking in the hall, and without turning their heads they'd say, "SP's, be quiet." . . . Some of the teachers say, "You're not so slow, you're supposed to be SP." They didn't realize the fact that the eighth graders had already started the eighth grade work. And, see, we were only working on the seventh grade work. So they said, "Well, you're supposed to be SP's, you're supposed to be smart, why don't you know this, why don't you know that?" And they kept that up for five whole terms. [*Interviewer:* They really resented this evidently . . .] They did, they did! I know my ninth grade teacher kept saying, "Fine. If I had this class in the seventh grade, I'd put them back and take them out of SP." (U)

Well, I'd say that junior high, because of the SP's, bolstered me a bit. Because in elementary school, well they just divided the class. And well, if you had just a little bit of brains, they'd throw you up in the top of the class, and this was all good, but you didn't learn anything more. As a result I just sat back and said, "Oh, I'm something special, I'm a freak." So while everyone else was working I'd take out a comic book or newspaper and read it, which I didn't think was right because I wanted to get something out of school. In junior high I was rather reluctant to go into SP's because I felt maybe it'd be just a little bit too much for me, but everything showed that I should get into it, and I found that the work was more interesting because it was on a higher level. (U)

I like the SP's very much. (U)

Explanations for difficulties. In addition to reference to individual subjects such as mathematics, language, English, social studies, etc. and to individual teachers as causes of school difficulties, the boys offered the following kinds of explanations for their inadequate school performance:

I don't know. I keep on telling myself, "I'm going to try my best. I'm going to try my best." But when the time comes, I always meet some fellow at school and we kid around, and I get in trouble, and there it goes right out the window. I can't help it. But I just don't know. (U)

In our junior high school if you had a good record, they looked at the record and you were expected to do more work. And if you got an 80, that was like another kid's 70. A 100 should be like a 90. I was told that I had a very high IQ, and every teacher said I could do much better work. If I got a 90, I should do more, and I didn't think that was right. You had to be better than everybody else, and higher. (U)

I'm lazy. I'd get better grades if I studied for tests. (U)

Well, every time we had a spelling test, we used to get terrifically long words to spell, and I always had butterflies in my stomach. And we used to get a lot of words, about fifty words on a test, and it was fairly rough, and the butterflies didn't help any. (U)

Well, I know I do all my work at home and everything. I don't know, but when it comes to tests, I guess I just goof on tests . . . all of a sudden my mind goes blank, and I don't know anything. (U)

Well, I guess this conduct and things sort of worried me. (U)

The thing I didn't like about that class was that I would write a composition and my handwriting wasn't good; but it was an essay, see, and I'd get a 75 because the handwriting by itself wouldn't be too good. (U)

I had to be absent, and when I came back I was completely lost. (U)

Well, I just feel out of place in a big group with others. I'm not like a . . . like a show in school. It takes me a good time to do that. Everybody staring at me. Expecting a big thing. (U)

A not unusual explanation of school difficulty was told graphically as follows:

I failed two subjects, Spanish and geometry. And I know the reason. I needed eyeglasses. I couldn't see the board, and for some reason, I don't know what it is—I don't think my parents have taught this to me because they go to the doctor, not for every little thing, but if it's an emergency . . . and I have a fear of all doctors. I don't know what it is or who I inherited it from. I inherited my eyes from my mother, though. And I was just deathly afraid to tell them because I didn't know what he was going to do—the eye doctor. And actually it was a fear of the unknown. Because of this my marks have been slipping. I couldn't see the board during tests. I'd get half the test done, but I still wouldn't go up to my mother and father and tell them. And everything else I'd tell them. I mean I went up for smoking—that was nothing. But something important like this . . . I just don't go to them. Well, finally my father came up with the brilliant idea and took me to the eye doctor, and he made an appointment. I read the first letter on the chart, and after that, nothing else. He slipped glasses on me, and I said "Wow" and I read every letter. (U)

Attitudes of and toward friends. The interview material did not give many leads on the extent to which a boy was liked and accepted by his peer group. Each one mentioned having friends, taking part in group pursuits of various kinds, and sometimes relying on friends for assistance. Some interesting material did come out, however, regarding attitudes toward the high achiever as listed below:

My friends all want to get good marks. They're all worried about failure in a subject. Nobody wants to fail, and they all try for an 85 or better.

[*Interviewer:* So that it's all right if they make good marks . . . they're not considered sissies for this? Does such an attitude exist at all, do you think?] Yes, definitely, because there are some boys who are classified as bookworms, and they're never downstairs or anything like that. They're upstairs all the time. They get good marks, but, I don't know, I don't feel it's worth that much. I'd rather get five points lower and be downstairs once in a while. (U)

Most of my friends are pretty smart, also. (H)

I'm average, a little above average. I think the ones who were geniuses . . . they were bookworms too much. They don't do anything after school. They don't participate in activities or anything. They just study, and I don't want to be like them. (U)

Being in SP's didn't make any difference. It was how you could play baseball or something—it didn't matter how smart you were. The kids who were not good in sports usually made it up on social activities . . . like there was one boy, he wasn't especially good in sports, but he was always around at all the dances, and he was the life of the party, and he was a pretty nice person to get along with, and we considered him like the rest of us . . . The kids outside the SP's sometimes called us names . . . like SP means "stupid people." (U)

Well, some kids study all the time, and maybe they don't know, but the class usually doesn't like them, and the class starts getting noisy and these kids sit down. Teachers, some teachers I know just go for those kind of kids . . . Well, there's one kid who was in our school last year —he was a brain in mathematics, and he knew what the Einstein theory was. He couldn't play baseball or anything like that, but when he got to school, he studied and got 100 in every subject. When he got home, he got right to his homework and started studying and went to bed about eleven. He doesn't have any physical life—you have to have physical and mental to keep well. That guy didn't have many friends . . . other kids practically made fun of him . . . If I really wanted to, I could get one of the highest marks in the class, but if I did that, I wouldn't have very many friends, and I think friends are important, too. (U)

People reacting to me as different really doesn't bother me. It sort of bolsters my ego a little bit. I ran around with a chip on my shoulder, but I knocked that off a long time ago, but you find out . . . "Well, gee, this fellow doesn't like this, and I like it." And I find out that everyone else, they sort of go toward this goal, and I've got it already. I'm just going to walk around with a chip on my shoulder. Then you meet other people who have the same interests. So you don't have a chip on your shoulder any more; you're just one of the group. I think that through different activities you meet kids like this. Once I thought that this was impossible, that I was like a freak . . . because everyone else just had a nonchalant attitude about the whole thing, about getting into high school; but I'm finding that kids have the same ideas I have, which is good, because then we can work cooperatively more or less. (U)

Out-of-school activities and interests. Boys from all groups mentioned sports more frequently than any other activity. Hobbies such as electronics, model building, collections, and scientific interests were second in frequency. Reading was third. In many instances boys indicated either extensive interest in one area or a wide variety of interests:

> I like to make models. I like to build things with my hands. I'm very good at that. I like to paint with oils. I do very well in that. I feel I always have to do something with my hands. I build something. Always attempting. They don't always come out. I do it. Even if it's not so good, I get a certain feeling out of it that it was mine, that I did it. (U)

> I have interests in radio and television. The time was when I wanted to become an amateur radio operator. But this is in the past. Right now I concentrate mainly on making money, which is a terrible thing, but I have a little servicing business going, more or less, and I pick up a little bit of money now and then, most of which goes either to the church organizations or different other expenses. I belong to the _____ Church. I've gone to conferences. I'm a member of the young people's society; I'm secretary there. I'm the organist for the Sunday School and the young people's society. I have played for church services and have taken part in worship services, etc. It's really my second life. (U)

> In the ninth grade I also took algebra, and we got into some geometry, and after we finished I just happened to go on beyond the basic in geometry. I got very interested in that, and I liked it. Different things fascinate me. I put more effort on them . . . I think if I get settled or if I know what I want to be when I grow up, I'll be interested in just one certain subject and concentrate on that. (U)

> I have a tropical fish tank, and I usually spend my time with my fish . . . or playing baseball, . . . but most of my time with fish. I got interested in them—well, they seemed fascinating, how they could live and multiply, and it seemed like a different world; so I started reading books on tropical fish, and then one day my uncle got me a ten-gallon tank with a cover on it and the different attachments, and gradually I got the accessories, and I have everything for the tanks now, and they're all bustling activities. (U)

Well, I didn't go out for the newspaper or anything, but the season now is hockey and basketball, and I get to go to the games. When I get home from the game, I write it up, you know, as if I were a reporter and compare it with how the actual reports are. During Saturdays and Sundays and during the summer I'm at Rockaway. That's where I work. We go there to the games and catch baseballs because that's what business we're in. We sell them. We get there early before most of the crowd is in. We practice to get as many balls as we can hold. And then we start selling them. (U)

I have a job at a photography shop, and I'm learning the trade there— it's very interesting. (U)

I like to play basketball. I collect stamps. And I build model planes and things. I like to swim indoors during the winter. I play a little football and baseball. I do a lot of reading. I have my own library in my home. I have around one hundred books—and I go to the library an awful lot. (H)

Oh, I read the complete Sherlock Holmes, Hemingway, Steinbeck— and I like science fiction. (U)

Whenever I'm bored or something I'll write a story or something. I find that interesting. It amuses me. (H)

Attitudes toward high school. By and large the boys felt the change from junior high to high school had been for the better. They mentioned a number of features which they viewed positively, and only a few which they viewed negatively:

In junior high I felt I could fool around and it wouldn't mean much, not even the low grades. But here I want to get as high marks as possible in the last two or three years so I will have a much better chance of getting into college. (U)

I don't think the teachers care to have enough time for you. Like in _____, my _____ teacher—all the kids in class were beginning to think she was very strict, you know, but none of the kids were learning their work, so one lesson she didn't teach any work, she simply stopped the lesson, and she was very good about it. She just took any question they wanted to ask her—about how to do the work in _____. And made it so much easier. The children were telling me after class, you know. And I think she's a very good teacher, one of the best I've known. (U)

I guess I grew up a little in high school. You get more freedom and you're on your own. They're not after you all the time and leave it up to you whether to study or not. You do certain things. The teachers leave it up to you. They figure you can make your own decisions. (U)

Like this year, I started off bad. I applied for a transfer. Teachers this year are giving me a fair chance. (U)

Well, now I'm with an older group. And I feel pretty much on my own. Not tied to my mother's apron strings. (U)

In high school most of the teachers are good—they know what they're talking about, and they know how to explain it to the children, I think. And it's a little harder in high school. You have to study. You can't kid around. Well, I think the main difference in high school and home-work is that it's not so much looking at a book—it's your ability and what you know—your mind and thinking things out. It's not really like opening up a book and saying now here's your answer—you have to think out answers for yourself. (H)

I think it's more interesting here than in the lower grades. I think it's the teachers—the atmosphere and things like that—so that maybe I have better teachers now. (U)

I think high school is quite a big step and I like it much better. You have more time to yourself. You have a period, if you're lucky, to study and maybe do your homework. (U)

I find high school now interesting, and I guess I realize now that I've got to work. I'm lazy when I can get away with it, and now I realize I can't. (U)

I think this is a very nice school—there's a variety of subjects and the periods aren't so long. And it doesn't get boring, and the teachers always have something interesting to teach, and I especially like _____ because you have to prove different things and I'm curious. (U)

Special comments

1. *Selection of friends:*

Well, SP wasn't that bad, but if I had to do it over again, I'd much rather take seventh, eighth, and ninth grades as whole years. And I also found that going into high school I'm at a young age. I'm only thirteen and a half and most of the children in my class are about to be fifteen. And I'm fit to play with them, but yet they're so much older and more mature . . . Well, I know I like to get along with older folks, and I don't like to hang around with children my age because like a lot of times in the eighth and ninth gardes they still haven't caught up to mature ability. I don't feel myself so mature, but the boys in my class have had an extra year and a half to develop, so that even though

I stay with them I'm sort of the young one of the group. And I get along with them, but feel sort of out of place when they look at me. They're all fifteen. (U)

Sometimes I feel a little younger or a little out of place with my class. It makes me feel like a mouse creeping up a big oak tree. The world is so big and you're so small. And you can't see at all. Or do at all. Well, sometimes it's as if everyone is watching me, to see how I'll do, to see if I'll fall back. And they think that just because I was in the rapid advance that I'm a genius. (U)

Most of my friends (the ones who have the same interest in hockey and baseball) are a year or two older than me. Most of my friends in this neighborhood are my own age. They all are, in fact. But there are two different sets of friends. The ones around here I'll play ball with, I'll go to the movies with, watch television with—things like that. Their parents don't let them do as many things. They're mentally not as old. They won't let them go downtown and things like that. These boys are older, and I've always hung out with older kids. (U)

2. *On being a younger brother:*

Well, the funny thing—see my brother went to this school and he really hit this school good because he pitched baseball for this school and got a scholarship to the college where he goes now. He really had recognition in this school, see. All the teachers respected him good, and at the end of the time—graduation—he got all sorts of citizenship awards and baseball awards and all that. And as soon as I come into this school— and I have a name that's unforgettable—as soon as I come in it's, "We expect this from you; we expect that from you," and that makes it tough, you know. I've got to watch my step. But I don't mind it. I'd rather have a brother like that than have one that I've got to be ashamed of.

Well, I feel more free in school than he did. He did everything to the tee. I feel that my brother . . . well, he has an excellent character. He gets along with everybody. He was very popular in school. Well, I seem to be the same way, but I don't know, I like to have fun in school. I don't like to do everything by the rules. But I always remember about him . . . and think . . . they're watching you, boy . . . and every time I do something wrong . . . there's nothing like it.

My parents, too. I mean, like anything I do . . . "Jerry (my brother) did this, and you should do the same. Jerry never had that when he was your age," and I get that thing.

In my junior high once—one teacher brought it up that I wasn't like my brother. In that way—I kept on hearing it, and I just blew up. My brother and I are two different people. It's not that I'm jealous of my brother—that's completely out of it—it's just like a phonograph record; they keep on doing the same thing, back and forth. There was one time —I did something—I can't remember what—and the teacher said "Your brother would never have done that," so I just blew up and I said that my brother and I are two different people. That's the way I feel—we shouldn't be compared. We are two different people. (H)

Summary of interview data. Pervading most of the interviews with the underachievers was a recognition that they were bright and potentially capable of outstanding academic achievement; but there was an equally strong resistance against making the necessary effort. "I could get the highest marks if I tried—but why should I?" was a commonly expressed sentiment, possibly masking discouragement, rebellion, or failure to face reality, but a strong determinant of behavior, nonetheless. They felt that they had been hounded to do better, and that this had been of no help to them. Even their own resolutions to "try harder" were short-lived. Some of them attributed their poor performances to bad teaching, unsympathetic teachers, and full classes. A few blamed their own laziness; still others rationalized their lack of study as the only way to make friends, to be part of the crowd—not different or too good.

General observations

Certain personality and attitudinal factors obtained on the Self-Attitudes Inventory and from informal contacts with parents of underachievers as well as from the impressions of the project staff will be summarized according to the underachievers' self-perceptions, educational and vocational aspirations, and family status.

Self-perceptions. The same Self-Attitudes Inventory which was given to the five Evanston groups was administered at Clinton to the various groups of high and underachievers.

A general view of the results suggests that the underachiever perceived himself as less able to fulfill the tasks required of him, less eager to learn, less confident of himself, and less ambitious than did the high achiever. But his level of aspiration in those areas was as high as that of the high achiever. Thus, the gap was great, perhaps too great for him to believe that any amount of effort would close it.

Educational and vocational aspirations. The wide gap between the underachiever's ratings of his present and ideal level was, in a sense, a reflection of the gap that actually existed between his present school performance and his educational and vocational aspirations. Although his grades were below average, he planned to go to college; although he was failing in mathematics or science, he planned to be an engineer or a scientist. For example, out of one group of 30 entering tenth grade underachievers, 19 listed engineering, science, or medicine as their vocational choice. The mean first year algebra grade for this group was 72.5; the mean geometry grade, 69.8 (a grade of 65 was passing). Similar patterns were observed in each of the groups studied.

The entering tenth grade underachiever at Clinton had aspirations much like those of the high achiever. This may perhaps be explained by the fact that throughout the elementary school years he, too, was an achiever. In very few instances were there indications of poor academic performance before the eighth grade. In fact, of the 227 underachievers studied at Clinton, about 40 per cent went through the Special Progress classes in junior high, which required, at the sixth-grade level, a minimum IQ score of 130 and acceleration of two years in reading and a-year-and-a-half in arithmetic, as measured by standardized achievement tests. In addition, a recommendation from their sixth-grade teacher was required, indicating that the student was mature enough, and his general academic performance good enough, to enable him to cover the three years of junior high school in two years.

For these bright youngsters, underachievement became observable in the eighth or ninth grade, rarely before. Thus, by tenth grade their aspirations continued to reflect their early successes, but their self-ratings of the abilities needed to achieve these aspirations tended to fall below those of high achievers. However, most characteristic of the underachiever was his failure to be moved to greater effort by the recognition of the gap. It was almost as if he expected some magic to take care of the situation.

As was noted in the interview material, the boys frequently externalized the blame by placing the responsibility for their present plight on a teacher or a poor school situation. They related their success in a subject to "a good teacher who made it interesting" and their failure to one who "didn't teach us anything." But other explanations were offered as well. Some youngsters justified their underachievement in terms of not wanting to be a "grind": "Why should I be the smartest kid in the world? I wouldn't get anything out of that; I just want to be one of the crowd." Some expressed strong negative feelings toward the boy who is "never downstairs or anything like that" (this statement obviously made by an apartment dweller); others felt that if "you got one of the highest marks in the class . . . you wouldn't have many friends."

A significant number blamed their own "laziness" for their poor behavior in class. There was a small group among the underachievers which was willing to settle for "just not failing." These boys were waiting to get out of school. Some of them were consistent truants; others did the minimum necessary to get by; still others did consistently failing work. But the majority of the students wanted to improve. They periodically "turned over a new leaf," promising themselves that they would try harder and do better. The good resolutions rarely lasted long enough to provide the necessary success for overcoming their inadequate work patterns.

Family status. Neither in Evanston nor in Clinton was any significant difference found between the socioeconomic status or the general educational level of the families of the high and underachievers. However, while more of the Evanston fathers of the high achievers than underachievers graduated from or went beyond college, this was not true at Clinton. Both groups were similar in number of children per family and in number of working mothers. Birth order made no difference.

But, despite similarity between high and underachievers in

most aspects of the family picture, disruption of the normal family was more frequently observed among the underachievers. For 118 underachievers at Clinton, there were 21 broken homes, through parental death or divorce, which in every case but one resulted in the absence of a father. In a group of 60 high achievers, there were only two fatherless families.

These findings suggested that the absence of a father from the family deprived the boy of an adequate male model and that the normal processes of identification might thus be more likely to be disturbed. However, since the majority of the underachieving boys did have fathers in the home, it became important to examine the role and status of the father in the family picture. From conferences with 20 sets of parents, it became apparent that in nearly every instance the mother was the dominant figure. She was more articulate, took the lead in the conversation, often answered questions directly addressed to her husband, and in some instances, belittled the husband's ability to be a positive force in the boy's life. Since there were no similar interviews with parents of the high achievers, it is difficult to determine to what extent the observed dominance of the mother rather than the father in situations relating to the son's education is a general cultural phenomenon and to what extent it was more common in the families of the underachiever.

Of some interest in regard to father-son relationships and the process of identification was the evidence that in a number of cases fathers who had high academic aspirations for their sons, particularly with regard to going to college, were not themselves college graduates, and apparently had not provided a model in regard to academic interests. The mother tended to take over this function in terms of exhorting the boy to study. One might speculate that many of the boys rebelled against the dominance of the mother and lacked a male supportive figure in their reaching out for their own male status. Both of these factors may have contributed to poor school performance.

The boys in the high-achieving and underachieving groups, in describing their families' attitudes toward their school work, reported high pressure in some instances and disinterest in other instances. In the two groups, the physical and psychological conditions for doing school work were rated by the boys all the way from excellent to poor.

Problem checklist

An analysis of parental ratings on a problem checklist found as many serious problems checked by the parents of the high achievers as by those of the underachievers. However, for the underachievers, the problems were more often related to school work. The underachievers themselves checked more serious problems than did the high achievers, and most of these problems were related to school work or to carrying out responsibilities.

Summary of informal observations

From the research studies at Clinton and Evanston, it would appear that comparisons of high and underachievers within a specific school situation do not reveal significant differences in the social factors usually associated with underachievement. However, the underachievers more often identified with the typical nonintellectual values prevalent in our culture. Regardless of their own socioeconomic status, the underachievers, unlike their achieving peers, viewed studiousness and high grades or interest in intellectual pursuits as making one a "grind." In reality, the high achiever was socially more active, participated in more extracurricular activities, had more hobbies, and more out-of-school interests, and was generally more concerned with social responsibility, which he considered himself better able to carry out, than the underachiever.

The Homeroom-Social Studies Class

The first study at Clinton, initiated in the spring of 1956 and terminating three years later, was designed to study the academic, personal, and social characteristics of underachievers and to assess the effects of grouping gifted underachievers in a homeroom section and retaining them as a group in one subject matter class taught by their homeroom section officer. It was hypothesized that if such students could share each other's problems, so to speak, and could at the same time become closely identified with and receive support from a teacher, their general school attitudes and performances would improve. In order to achieve the desired relationships, the teacher selected for the task had to be vitally interested in the problem, had to be warm and outgoing, and, above all, had to combine flexibility with maintenance of high standards.

Selection and grouping of subjects

Initially, 102 underachievers were identified at the time they were completing ninth grade. The selected students had IQ's of 120 or higher on either sixth- or eighth-grade intelligence tests and ninth-year grade averages below 80 per cent. To verify the intelligence ratings of the 102 identified underachievers, they were brought to Clinton in June of their ninth year and tested on the California Test of Mental Maturity. All students whose average score on the junior high intelligence test[1] *and* on the CTMM was 120 or higher and who did not fall below 120 on either measure were included for the study. Seventy students met the above criteria, and matched pairs were formed on the basis of IQ and ninth-year grade averages. One student from each pair was placed in the special class (designated as S), the other in the control group (designated as C). The control students were not identified to themselves or to their teachers and were randomly distributed throughout the homeroom sections and subject-matter classes of the grade.

In addition, a group of high-ability high achievers (designated as H) was identified—students with IQ's comparable to those of the underachievers, but with ninth-year grade averages above 85 per cent. No special provisions were made for this group beyond those normally made by the school for able students. This group was officially designated as an honors section.

Inspection of the junior high school records of the three groups

---

[1] The junior high test was either the Pintner General Ability Test or the Hennon-Nelson Test of Mental Abilities. In the case of those students who had been in the Special Progress classes during junior high, the sixth grade Pintner scores were used, since there had been no junior high retest.

and of the sociometric ratings[2] made in the junior high school classes from which the underachievers came showed that the S and the C groups did not differ from each other on any of the measures on which information was available at that time (spring, 1956). The H's differed from the other two groups not only in ninth-year grades—the basis upon which they were selected— but also on average IQ. However, the 5-point IQ difference, although significant, was actually not very large, and all three groups fell into the academically talented category. The only measure on which there were large differences between the H's and the S's and C's was in the relative number of positive and negative mentions received on a sociometric rating made by junior high school classmates. The underachievers (S's and C's) were nominated by their peers as potential failures in high school and in life, as most apt to get into trouble, and as least popular far more frequently than were the high achievers (H's), whereas the high achievers were more often rated positively.

It is noteworthy that even though the underachievers were characterized by low teacher grades, their performance in junior high school on standardized achievement measures of reading and arithmetic differed little from the performance of the bright high achievers. These findings (supported by similar findings from the junior high school records of subsequent groups) suggest that during the elementary and junior high school years most bright youngsters, regardless of classroom performance as reflected by school grades, acquire considerable mastery of basic skills and knowledge.

As a regular part of the school's testing program the subjects involved in the study were examined on the Iowa Tests of Educational Development (ITED) during the fall term of the tenth grade, after having been selected for the study. Results further supported the conclusion that achievement on objective measures

[2] Each of the junior high school homeroom sections in which one or more of the selected underachievers was located was asked to complete a sociometric survey which asked for nominations of best- and least-liked student, the one most or least apt to be successful in later life, etc. Returns were received for 49 of the students—24 S's and 25 C's. Since the H's were not identified until after they arrived at Clinton, sociometric ratings were available only on ten students who were in classes which filled out the surveys.

of academic mastery is more closely related to intelligence than to school grades. The combined group of underachievers (S and C) did not differ significantly from the H's on any part of the test. However, although the S's and C's were alike on all the junior high measures (Table IV-1), they differed significantly

Table IV-1. Status of Three Groups—Special Class Underachievers (S),
Control Group Underachievers (C), and High Achievers (H)—
at the End of Grade Nine

	S	C	H
Number	31	31	31
Average ninth-year grades	73.7	73.0	87.7
Range of ninth-year grades	56–79	61–79	84–94
Number from SP[a] classes	13	10	16
Average age	14.1	14.2	14.0
Average IQ[b]	131.8	131.6	136.0
IQ range	120–152	121–148	125–148
Average reading increment over grade[c]	2.24	2.56	2.51
Range of reading increments	1.0–4.0	.4–4.0	.5–4.6
Average arithmetic increment	1.4	1.5	2.0
Range of arithmetic increments	−1.3–4.0	−2.2–4.1	−1.3–4.5
Average positive sociometric rating	1.8	1.8	9.0
Average negative sociometric rating	17.0	19.8	4.9

[a] Special Progress.

[b] Where students were retested on the CTMM or had two IQ ratings listed on their record, an average score was used.

[c] Since the reading and arithmetic tests were given either in eighth or in ninth year, the means and ranges were calculated on the basis of increment over the grade in which the student was when he took the test. For example, if a student took either of the tests in eighth grade and received a grade equivalent of 10.2, his increment score would be 2.2. If he took the test in ninth grade and received a grade equivalent of 7.8, his increment score would be −1.2.

on the composite score of the ITED. This finding cast some doubt on the comparability of the two groups. By chance, the control students had started the tenth year with a significant edge over the special students.[3]

[3] As discussed on page 142, later comparisons of grades were based on analyses of covariance to account for differences on the ITED.

Organization of the special class, tenth grade

The plan to group one class of bright underachievers together for homeroom and one subject matter class with a highly competent and understanding teacher grew out of the belief that ideal teaching was a reasonable approach to ameliorating learning problems, particularly when the teacher combined pedagogical skills with active involvement in the school life of his students and awareness of their difficulties. Such a special class provision could be undertaken in any large high school, utilizing generally available personnel and facilities. It could lend itself to a combination of subjective and objective evaluation measures, as well as provide opportunity for direct observations of the subjects. These considerations made it an attractive experimental plan.

Since the plan of a combination Homeroom-Social Studies Class with the same teacher had to undergo two modifications during the second year of the study due to scheduling difficulties, the depth to which the effects of the first administrative plan could be studied were limited. However, changes in the original plan afforded some unexpected opportunities for observing the phenomenon of underachieving behavior in two additional settings. In brief, during the second year, the special class remained intact with its same homeroom teacher, but with a different social studies teacher each semester. Details of these arrangements will be described in a later section.

The experiment began in September 1956. The social studies class met the first period following the homeroom period, so that the group had the same teacher for the first two periods daily. The students were told that they were a specially selected group, placed in this class because of their high level of ability and their need for help in raising the level of their school performance. The teacher used many ways to communicate to them his interest in them and his availability for discussing any problems they cared to bring up. At the same time he indicated his high expectations for them in terms of study and work in social studies.

Evaluation of student performance
at the end of the first semester, tenth grade

Grade averages. At the end of their first semester at Clinton the students in the special class were compared to the controls and to the high achievers on school grades in each subject (see Table IV-2) and on participation in school activities. To what

Table IV-2. Teacher Marks, First Semester, Grade Ten, for the Three Groups (S, C, and H) in Five Subject Areas and Averages across All Subjects

Subject Area	S (N = 31) M	S (N = 31) SD	C (N = 30) M	C (N = 30) SD	H (N = 31) M	H (N = 31) SD	t test S vs. C	t test S vs. H	t test C vs. H
English	78	7.5	84	6.7	88	6.9	-3.52^a	-5.47^a	-2.32^a
Mathematics	71	11.8	76	19.1	87	10.2	-1.27	-5.73^a	-2.96^a
Social studies	82	11.4	82	7.8	86	6.7	0.00	-1.73	-2.17^a
Science	78	8.9	84	7.6	91	8.5	-2.81^a	-5.88^a	-3.42^a
Foreign language	70	10.8	74	11.4	85	8.7	-1.36	-6.03^a	-4.31^a
Average	76	7.3	80	7.4	87	6.4	-2.22^a	-6.32^a	-3.99^a

[a] Significant at or beyond the .05 level.

extent did a semester of the kinds of experiences to which the students in the special class had been exposed produce improvement in their school performance?

Improvement in grades over the junior high school was found for *both* groups of underachievers (S and C). Each group did, to some extent, turn over a new leaf and did benefit by the more adult atmosphere of the school. But, inspection of Table IV-3 shows that the S's did not improve more than the C's. On the contrary, as a group, the S's showed significantly less improvement. A part of this discrepancy was explained by the fact that only 25 of the C's, as opposed to all 31 of the S's, had taken five major academic subjects, and the lesser load may have made higher grades easier to attain. But this was only a partial explanation. A far more significant part of the difference in grades was related to the higher ITED scores that the C's had received.

Table IV-3. Increments in Grade Averages from the End of Grade Nine
to the End of First Semester of Grade Ten for Special Class (S)
and Control Group (C)

S		C		S-C Difference		
M	SD	M	SD	M	SD	t test
2.53	6.18	6.63	7.23	−4.10	8.97	−2.50[a]

[a] Significant at the .05 level.

When the student grades were treated by an analysis of covariance, controlling for initial status on the ITED composite
score, the differences between the special and control groups
disappeared. Thus, after one semester, membership in the special class had *no effect* on the scholastic attainment of the students
beyond the improvement related to the overall upgrading effect
of the school as a whole.

A tabulation of the school service activities of the S's and C's
did show that the S's evidenced a greater involvement with school
service activities than did the C's in all school functions except
publications and athletics.

Teacher and staff observations. The special class teacher, referred to in this discussion as Dr. K, and the HMLI project staff
members associated with this study observed the underachieving boys in the special class rather closely in a variety of situations. The teacher, especially, developed a close relationship with
the boys in his capacity as section officer during the homeroom
period, a time which touched on many aspects of the subjects'
school life. In his role as social studies teacher Dr. K also became well acquainted with the strengths and problems of each
boy. The project staff, through its interviews with the boys and
a leadership weekend[4] which they attended along with some

[4] Through the efforts of the DeWitt Clinton Alumni Association and a faculty
member of the school, the high school sponsored a series of leadership weekends.
Selected groups of boys were transported to a farm where they spent two days discussing personal, vocational, and social problems, and playing, eating, and rooming
together under the supervision of student counselors, school staff, and the leader.

of the school staff and the special teacher, became familiar with the life situations of many of the subjects. The staff also conducted a discussion meeting with parents of the boys in the special class. Some of the staff's impressions of the boys during this first semester of study will be discussed here.

Dr. K's first impression of the special group was that the boys were well behaved and attentive, but neither interested nor enthusiastic. While not overtly unhappy at returning to school after the summer vacation, the underachievers lacked the spark generally observed in honor students. Very few of them knew each other before coming to Clinton, but they were soon drawn into strong mutual friendships. In their special class they were extroverted, talkative, often boisterous; in other classes they tended to keep apart and were generally more subdued in their behavior. The boys' sharing two periods each day seemed to generate a feeling of belonging, security, and warmth. Later in the school year, when boys in other sections greeted each other happily after a holiday, these students were positively enthusiastic—almost to the point of hysteria. They continued chattering until they were called to order, and although they came to attention more slowly than other classes, they were never discipline problems; nor was the noise a sign of revolt or disobedience.

Their friendship ties strengthened as the semester progressed and gradually became inbred, in many cases precluding out-of-class associations. The boys met after school and during weekends, looking to each other for companionship outside of school as well as in it. Each boy found support in the recognition that problems which he had felt to be uniquely his own were shared by many of his classmates.

Upon entering high school, the underachievers seemed more afraid of school than hostile toward it. They had accepted a standard of mediocrity and needed strong incentives to increase their efforts. The teacher recognized the importance of giving these students sympathy, but not pity; guidance, but not overprotection; self-confidence and a sense of responsibility, but not

The boys in the special class were chosen for one of these weekends, giving the HMLI Project staff some excellent opportunities for informal observations of the subjects.

premature demands for independence. By creating a climate of acceptance and support, but at the same time holding up high standards of independent achievement, the teacher hoped to improve the students' attitudes toward school and eventually spur them to greater achievement.

Because of the fused homeroom and social studies period, the teacher did not necessarily have to terminate guidance activities at the bell. The 8:55 signal no longer meant, "Save your problem for tomorrow; now let us study the world's problems." Even though the social studies period was sometimes curtailed by a few minutes, once the lesson began the boys were attentive and worked with little waste of time or effort.

Since the social studies class was also the homeroom of the group, achievement in the class meant recognition and status among one's peers. The boys wanted to do well, not only for themselves but also for the teacher. Parents reported that the boys did much studying in all subject areas, but especially in social studies. The students became more willing to work toward better grades when they realized that any effort on their part would be commended and rewarded. Though standards were high, they were flexible and thus never unattainable. The teacher soon discovered that any procedure which could be perceived as rejection acted as a negative motivating force. For example, when several boys submitted poorly done homework which received low or unacceptable grades, they felt that their efforts were being rejected; consequently their homework became progressively worse. To remedy this situation, all homework offerings were accepted, but the inferior ones were put aside ungraded, and the students were invited to redo their assignments when time and inclination permitted. A few days before grades were to be entered on the report cards, the boys were apprised of the grades they could expect in the event that their assignments remained unimproved, and what they might receive if they reworked their assignments. Faced by the immediate goal of a higher grade, many of the boys did the work over.

Some students, who had seldom done homework in junior high school, questioned the necessity of doing written assignments. One student, for example, argued that he had little to gain from writing homework. The teacher gave him the option of doing his homework or taking a special short quiz on the assignment each time he did not do the written work. Faced with an unprejudiced choice, he generally preferred the written homework, but occasionally exercised his option to take the quiz.

The students were encouraged to participate in school activities. Almost every boy gave some service to the school in such activities as the lunchroom squad, the office squad, or some other special squad. They were novices at giving, but the pleasure of giving was infectious. In the section room, the pupils voluntarily helped each other or studied in groups. The area in which a boy was proficient became his badge of distinction. There was an awakening to the pleasure and prestige which accrue from helping others.

The class climate was such that the boys felt free to come to the teacher with personal as well as school problems. At all times they found an attentive listener, ready to help with support and suggestions geared to increase the youngster's self-confidence.

Through these personal contacts it soon became clear that, in many instances, there were serious misunderstandings and poor relationships between the boys and their parents which were related to school behavior. Y's fear of his father, for example, drove him to change four failing marks to passing ones on his first report card; G could visit his divorced father only when he had good grades. These were some of the burdens the boys brought with them to school. Parent conferences alerted some of the parents to their part in handling the boys' problems. For example, Y's father had never before realized the extent of his son's fears and was grateful for an opportunity to re-examine his relationship with his son. Direct contacts between the teacher and the parents resulted in greater understanding of the child at home and school.

In general, Dr. K reported that many of the boys in the special section seemed to have benefited greatly from their association with each other and their close identification with the teacher. He was confident that the semester's experience had had a positive effect on the boys.

Continuation of the special class. Despite the fact that an examination of the grades of special class members at the end of their first semester at Clinton did not support the teacher's subjective evaluation that the boys had benefited greatly from membership in the group, it was realized that one semester is a short time for significant changes to become apparent. The special class was accordingly maintained with the same teacher for a continuation of the homeroom-social studies combination for the second semester of tenth grade.

Evaluation of student performance at the end of the second semester, tenth grade

Grade averages. As noted in Table IV-2, the mean grades of the C's were higher than those of the S's in all subjects except history at the end of the first semester of grade ten. The differences reached statistical significance. In contrast, at the end of the second semester of grade ten, the S's had somewhat higher mean grades than the C's in all subjects except English, but none

Table IV-4. Teacher Marks, Second Semester, Grade Ten, for the Three Groups (S, C, and H) in Five Subject Areas and Averages across All Subjects

	S		C		H		t test		
							S vs.	S vs.	C vs.
Subject Area	M	SD	M	SD	M	SD	C	H	H
English	81	7.1	84	9.8	88	5.1	−1.50	−4.52[a]	−2.11[a]
Mathematics	75	13.9	73	14.1	83	9.1	0.56	−2.74[a]	−3.39[a]
Social studies	82	10.5	78	8.6	86	7.8	1.47	−1.72	−3.84[a]
Science	81	9.3	79	9.6	90	7.6	0.82	−4.19[a]	−5.04[a]
Foreign language	73	11.0	68	13.4	78	11.1	1.52	−1.78	−3.21[a]
Average	78	6.8	76	8.0	85	5.3	0.88	−4.56[a]	−5.33[a]

[a] Significant at or beyond the .05 level.

of the differences between the two groups of underachievers reached significance. Again, both underachieving groups were graded significantly lower than the H's in each subject and across all subjects (Table IV-4).

Table IV-5. Increments in Grade Averages from First to Second Semester
of Grade Ten for the Special and Control Groups

S		C		S-C Difference		
M	*SD*	*M*	*SD*	*M*	*SD*	*t* test
1.90	6.08	−3.90	7.13	5.80	7.88	4.03[a]

[a] Significant at or beyond the .05 level.

Comparison of increments. Inspection of Table IV-5 shows that
the S's improved in grade average for the second semester, while
the C's showed a drop in grade average. The S's improved in
all subjects except European history, where they remained the
same (Figure IV-1). This may have reflected the teacher's reluctance to be too lenient in grading his special class. C's received lower marks at the end of tenth grade than at midyear in
all subjects except English where they remained the same. The
differences were most striking in mathematics and science, and
total average. In fact, the S's made up their first semester def-
icit and, in all subjects but English, equaled or exceeded the
second semester marks of the C's (Table IV-4).

Figure IV-2 shows the changes in mean grade averages of
the three groups from the end of grade nine, through the first
semester of grade ten, to the end of grade ten. Examination of
Figure IV-2 shows graphically the patterns of achievement change
from the end of junior high school to the end of the first year in
senior high. The S's showed a consistent upward progression,
the H's a consistent but slight decrease, while the C's showed
a marked rise in the first semester at Clinton but a drop in the
second semester. These patterns suggest that despite a slower
start, the supportive atmosphere in the special class enabled
the students not only to sustain, but actually to exceed, the
gains they had made in the first semester. For the C's, the initially upgrading effects of the high school could not be sustained
in the absence of special help and support.

Teacher observations. After a year of close association with
the special class, Dr. K's belief that most of the students had

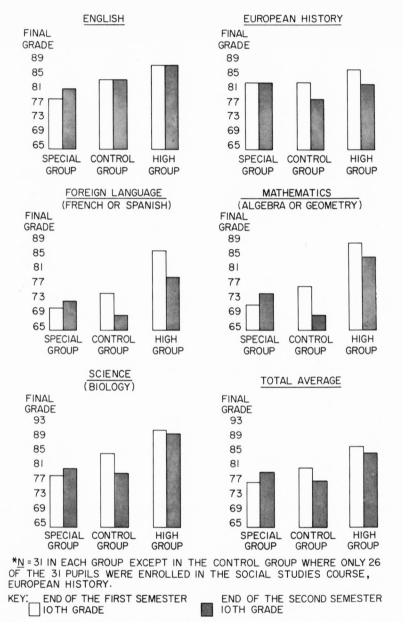

Figure IV-1. Changes in grade averages across five subject areaș for the three groups (S, C, and H)° from the end of the first semester to the end of the second semester of grade ten.

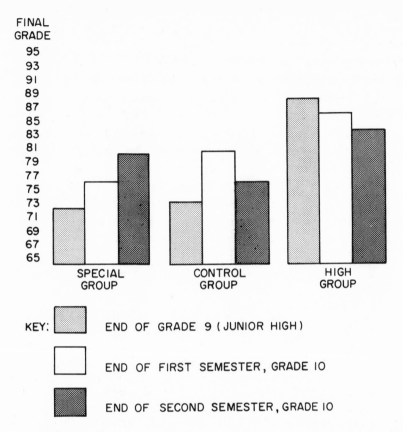

Figure IV-2. Changes in mean grade averages from end of grade nine to end of first and end of second semesters of grade ten for the three groups (S, C, and H).

benefited significantly from their year's experience was reinforced. The patterns of working with these students which were developed during the first semester were refined, and the warm, accepting climate of the class was retained, always balanced by holding up high standards as the ultimate goal.

No single incident, such as Dr. K's calling in a parent to praise her son's excellent work or giving a boy a twenty-five cent paperwork book to which he responded, "This is the first time anybody ever gave my anything in school," can be pinpointed as decisive in changing the achievement level of any one student. It was rather the entire range of experiences, interactions, and every-day relationships which the teacher saw as responsible for bringing about improvement in many of the boys. These included a carefully planned social studies program; expression of teacher interest; and the support that students in the special group seemed to give to one another. From these factors, some of the students managed to gain the maturity and confidence necessary for successful school work. For example, the boy who had changed his four failing marks on his first report card achieved an average of 86 per cent at the end of grade ten.

Along with assessing the factors which resulted in positive change for many of the students, the teacher recognized that these methods were unsuccessful in reaching some members of the group. At the end of the year, membership in the special group had had *no* observable effect on a number of boys. They presented a variety of negative attitudes, of which the descriptions below are but two examples:

> A had a record of thirty absences. His mother justified each and every one of them by telephone, in person, or by letter. The excuses ran the gamut from "It was very cold" to "His eyeglasses were broken." A December "chill" prevented A from attending the special camp weekend, where many friendships were cemented. A's continual absences made him almost a stranger. He formed no relationships with the other boys, and his attitude to the teacher was distant and impersonal. His work deteriorated, and by the end of the year he was in trouble with the police. His excessive absence was truancy, covered up by his mother's fear of letting the school know the true cause of his nonattendance.

> By unanimous consent, B was the class mime, and his stentorian bass voice did not increase his popularity with the teachers. His widowed mother reported that he had shown poor effort and had learned very little in junior high school. His high school grades were very poor. When questioned about his poor performance level, B stated, "It's too late to start learning now." Despite personal conferences and discussions, the teacher saw that he was not reaching this boy and could not find a way to help him change his negative attitudes.

However, Dr. K felt that many of the boys had begun to move in a positive direction both in their attitudes toward school and in their work patterns.

Summary comparison of improvers and nonimprovers in the special and control groups, tenth grade

Even though at the end of the tenth year the S's, as a group, showed greater improvement than did the C's, there were improvers and nonimprovers in both groups. In order to gain some insight into possible factors that were related to improvement, all the available material was reanalyzed, comparing students whose grade averages had increased by at least seven points from the end of the ninth year to the end of the tenth year with those who showed no improvement or a drop in grades. It was hoped that such an analysis might provide leads for selecting those junior high school underachievers who would probably become successful students in high school.

A total of 21 improvers were found, 12 from the special group and 9 from the control group; and 21 nonimprovers, 10 from the special group and 11 from the control group. The two groups differed significantly on the following items:

1. The scores of the improvers were significantly higher on the Iowa Correctness of Writing Subtest and on the Composite score.

2. On the Self-Attitudes Inventory, the nonimprovers showed a greater discrepancy between perception of their abilities and their wished-for ability status. This score is generally viewed as an index of adjustment and suggests that the nonimprovers saw their present ability to perform in various areas as too far from their desired ability to warrant making an effort to improve.

Other differences, although not significant statistically, showed certain trends: The incidence of divorces was greater among parents of the nonimprovers. Fewer of the nonimprovers had reached a decision on vocational goals. Fewer of the nonimprovers were the only or the oldest children, and fewer had older siblings in college who could act as achievement models for them.

Continuation of the Homeroom-Social
Studies Class into the eleventh grade

In view of Dr. K's conviction that the special class had been a valuable aid to the underachieving students, and in view of the objective evidence that membership in such a class resulted in greater improvement in academic achievement than would otherwise occur, it was decided to retain the group of underachievers as a unit, both in homeroom and in a social studies class for the eleventh grade of school.

Organization of the special class, eleventh grade

Certain school practices and scheduling problems at Clinton at the eleventh-grade level made it necessary to change three of the features which had existed in the Homeroom-Social Studies Class in tenth grade. These modifications altered the amount of time the special teacher could spend with the students, the membership of the group itself to a slight extent, and the nature of the expectations for high academic performance.

First of all, and perhaps most importantly, Dr. K was unable to continue as the group's social studies teacher, although he continued to function as their homeroom section officer. This resulted in the group's contact with Dr. K being limited to twenty detail-loaded minutes per day. Secondly, several students who had shown marked improvement in academic grades were permitted to transfer to squad sections in order to encourage their interest in special service activities. Thus, even in homeroom, the special class group of the tenth grade did not remain intact in eleventh grade.

Thirdly, it was decided that the S's, on the basis of an evaluation of their tenth grade work, appeared to be ready for regular honor work in social studies. It was thought that such a program would test the former underachievers in a situation where they could expect no special support or consideration, such as Dr. K had provided, other than what would normally be afforded honor students. The teacher selected to teach the special class was one who for many years had been eminently successful in working with honor classes. She was encouraged not to modify her usual procedures of expecting the students to perform at a consistently high level and of making no allowances for failure to meet high standards. Accordingly, the S's would be taught impartially as students who had superior academic ability and who would be expected to perform at a level commensurate with such ability.

Evaluation of student performance at the end of the first semester, eleventh grade

Grade averages. An analysis of grades showed clearly that the new arrangement for the S's had *not* proved satisfactory. The gains which they had made during the tenth grade were not sustained in the first semester of the eleventh grade. The S's final grades no longer exceeded those of the C's, and in social studies fell below, with an average drop of 16 points from the end of grade ten to the middle of grade eleven. This compared unfavorably with a zero drop for the C's (Table IV-6).

Table IV-6. Teacher Marks, Second Semester, Grade Ten, and First Semester, Grade Eleven, for the Special (S) and Control (C) Groups in Five Subject Areas and Averages across All Subjects

	S					C				
	Grade Ten Second Semester		Grade Eleven First Semester		Mean Differ- ence	Grade Ten Second Semester		Grade Eleven First Semester		Mean Differ- ence
Subject Area	M	SD	M	SD		M	SD	M	SD	
English	81	7.1	81	9.7	0	84	9.8	82	10.0	−2
Mathematics	75	13.9	68	14.2	−7	73	14.1	68	15.5	−5
Social studies	82	10.5	66	13.1	−16	78	8.6	78	13.0	0
Science	81	9.3	66	10.9	−15	79	9.6	68	13.8	−11
Foreign language	73	11.0	71	9.2	−2	68	13.4	71	11.4	+3
Average	78	6.8	70	8.0	−8	76	8.0	73	8.1	−3

A comparison of grades at the end of the first semester of the eleventh grade of the S's and C's showed no significant differences in English, mathematics, science, foreign language, or total average. The C's, however, received significantly better marks in history (Table IV-7).

Table IV-7. Teacher Marks, First Semester, Grade Eleven, for the Three Groups (S, C, and H) in Five Subject Areas and Averages across All Subjects

	S		C		H		t test		
							S vs. C	S vs. H	C vs. H
Subject Area	M	SD	M	SD	M	SD			
English	81	9.7	82	10.0	87	9.1	−0.48	−2.51[a]	−2.47[a]
Mathematics	68	14.2	68	15.5	80	10.6	0.00	−3.81[a]	−3.62[a]
Social studies	66	13.1	78	13.0	89	5.1	−3.25[a]	−9.95[a]	−4.78[a]
Science	66	10.9	68	13.8	83	10.5	−0.57	−6.26[a]	−4.86[a]
Foreign language	71	9.2	71	11.4	84	13.5	0.00	−4.53[a]	−4.11[a]
Average	70	8.0	73	8.1	84	10.0	−1.52	−6.12[a]	−4.78[a]

[a] Significant at or beyond the .05 level.

A comparison of the decrements of the two groups in grade averages from the end of grade ten and the middle of grade eleven found that the special class had lost significantly more than the control group (Table IV-8).

Table IV-8. Decrements in Average Marks from the End of Grade Ten to the End of the First Semester Grade Eleven for the Special (S) and Control (C) Groups

S		C		S-C Difference		
M	SD	M	SD	M	SD	t test
−7.27	6.02	−2.33	8.61	−4.93	9.58	−2.82[a]

[a] Significant at or beyond the .05 level.

Although the S's had been assigned to a highly skilled teacher for social studies, the fact that the group retained its identity appeared to have unfavorable consequences in this instance. The teacher was unable to handle the boys as a group, and the boys' marks reflected this.

Teacher and staff observation. The boys and the teacher had been in conflict throughout this semester, almost from the beginning. The teacher, expecting high quality performance, was unable to accept the erratic, tardy, and often slipshod work of the students. The techniques which she had found eminently successful with honor classes over the years were completely ineffectual in this situation. Insistence on the boys' toeing the line led to ever greater resistance, which was expressed in poor work, disturbing behavior in class, collaboration on assignments, and constant chatter and giggling.

By the end of the semester she was convinced that the group should not be kept together, contending that the close relationships among the boys resulted in mutual support for negative behavior, a condition which impeded learning and fostered poor character development.

The boys, however, continued to express satisfaction with being together, especially in their homeroom section. Even the students who had been encouraged to transfer to various special service sections at the beginning of the semester visited the special group regularly and repeatedly requested to be transferred back. They were not critical of their new sections, but rather wanted to return to old friends and to the mutually supportive atmosphere which characterized the special group.

In only one case was such a transfer effected. A boy who had been doing well in the tenth grade was now failing two subjects. His mother came to school to request the transfer, reporting that her son's work had suffered and that he had lost interest in school. When Dr. K pointed out that the boy would not have any more time for study in the special homeroom section than he now had, the mother stated that it was not the extra time, but rather the teacher, the boys, and the feeling of belonging to the original group which had made the difference in her son's school performance. The boy was reassigned to the special homeroom section and passed every subject. His mother reported a marked improvement in his attitude toward school.

But for most of the boys, remaining together in the brief homeroom period was not enough to counteract the growing conflict in their social studies class. Dr. K felt that his contact with the students was perforce too limited to allow for discussion of personal problems or for needed help with study skills.

Evaluation of the special class. The grade records of the S's and observations of their behavior in the first semester of the eleventh grade did not support the hypothesis that the underachievers who had shown improvement as a result of a year's involvement in a warm, accepting, and flexible situation would sustain their gains when held to uniformly high standards, both of conduct and of achievement. The short period that the boys continued to have with their effective homeroom teacher in eleventh grade apparently did not provide enough encouragement or help. These boys had grown to know each other well, and supported each other not only positively, but also in an adverse sense—in various infractions of the rules, uncontrolled behavior, and poor effort. It would seem that the fact of being together did not, by itself, produce improvement; on the contrary, it may have encouraged undesirable behavior. The important element was, in all likelihood, the performance of the teacher, Dr. K, in utilizing the group spirit constructively.

Perhaps the fact that the underachievers had a woman teacher for social studies may have failed to meet one of the basic needs of this group—identification with a father figure—a need that was recognized from the tests and interviews and was reported here in a previous section. The further experimentation at Clinton was planned with this factor in mind.

Continuation and evaluation of the special class, second semester, eleventh grade

During the concluding semester of this two year study, the S's were again retained as a unit for social studies and were programmed with a male teacher, Mr. M. (Three of the original 31 students had been failed at mid-eleventh grade in social studies. The second half of the eleventh year social studies class thus had 28 students of the original group.) Forewarned by the reports and experiences of the two teachers who had previously handled the S's, Mr. M did not expect the group to meet as high academic standards as an honor class.

Mr. M's experience with the group corroborated the impressions of the two previous teachers that the group lacked emotional stability and self-control. He found that any attempt at humor sent them into gales of laughter, and, therefore, he maintained a serious, work-oriented atmosphere throughout the term, even avoiding an occasional joke.

He was especially interested in the students' great desire to participate in group discussions and recitations. He sensed that this behavior represented a need to gain recognition rather than a desire to move the discussion forward. To solve this problem without injuring feelings required skill on the part of the teacher.

Mr. M found that homework of a factual nature was completed and handed in on time. Any assignment, however, which required independent thought and organization of material was subject to delay, stalling, and non-completion. Aware of the dangers of stern rebuke and unacceptance, on the one hand, and of allowing the students to get away with inadequate performance on the other, Mr. M followed a middle course. He proceeded to accept assignments that were handed in late and gave students a chance to rework assignments which had been poorly done, requiring that they incorporate suggestions for improvement. In addition, he devoted several class periods to practical demonstrations of how to do an assignment. Throughout the lessons he paid individual attention to each student and tried to understand him in terms of the particular problems and weaknesses which that student presented. While creating a warm and accepting climate in the class, allowing leeway in performance standards, and consistently showing an interest in the individual problems of the students, Mr. M also concentrated on teaching the group much-needed study skills. He felt that the group could use much more of this sort of help than time and subject-matter demands allowed.

At midsemester on the uniform social studies examination in economics, the S's performed at approximately the same level as the H's. Eighty per cent of the class received grades of 80 or above. Only two students received failing grades.

At the end of grade eleven, the grades of the S's did not differ significantly from those of the C's in any subject or on the aver-

Table IV-9. Teacher Marks, Second Semester, Grade Eleven, for the Three Groups (S, C, and H) in Five Subject Areas and Averages across All Subjects

								t test	
	S		C		H				
							S vs.	S vs.	C vs.
Subject Area	M	SD	M	SD	M	SD	C	H	H
English	77	10.9	77	13.4	87	5.2	0.00	−4.89[a]	−4.23[a]
Mathematics	69	20.3	64	18.4	81	10.2	0.96	−3.10[a]	−4.68[a]
Social studies	80	11.7	75	15.5	89	6.3	1.26	−3.94[a]	−5.06[a]
Science	71	11.8	70	10.9	80	10.4	0.34	−3.19[a]	−3.70[a]
Foreign language	70	11.8	70	14.7	85	8.8	0.00	−5.73[a]	−5.02[a]
Average	73	11.5	71	11.2	84	6.0	0.50	−5.40[a]	−5.95[a]

[a] Significant at or beyond the .05 level.

age across all subjects. Both underachieving groups, however, continued to be graded significantly below the H's (Table IV-9).

In comparing grades received at the end of the first half of grade eleven with those received at the end of the year, the S's showed a slight drop in English (4 points) and in foreign language (1 point); a slight rise in mathematics (1 point) and a somewhat larger rise in science (5 points). The greatest change was marked in social studies, with an average gain of 14 points. On the average, the S's gained 3 points, bringing their grade average back to where it was at the end of grade nine.

The C's showed a slight loss in total grade average (2 points), and losses between 1 and 5 points in all other subjects except science, in which they gained 2 points.

A comparison of the increments (or decrements) of the S's and C's from the end of the first to the end of the second semester of grade eleven (Table IV-10) showed that the two groups did not differ significantly from each other in degree of improvement.

Mr. M believed that the improvement in social studies over the previous semester was clearly related to a relaxation of tensions, an attempt to assess the characteristics and problems of the students, and deliberate experimentation with various procedures of helping them improve their learning. However, large class size and shortage of time prevented exploring the many possible tech-

Table IV-10. Increments in Grade Averages from First to Second Semester of Grade Eleven for the Special and Control Groups

S		C		S-C Difference		
M	SD	M	SD	M	SD	t test
3.0	10.8	−2.0	9.9	5.0	16.6	1.47

niques in sufficient depth to arrive at an optimum set of procedures.

Summary and conclusions of the two-year Homeroom-Social Studies Class

At the end of two years' study of the effects of the homeroom-social studies grouping plan for underachievers, it was found that there were no significant differences in marks between the S's and the C's for any subject. For both groups at the end of grade eleven, individual subject grades and average achievement fell significantly below the grades of equally bright high achievers (Table IV-9) and placed the underachievers at about the mean for the school as a whole. Nor did the picture change appreciably during the twelfth grade. Despite continued attention paid to the S's in the school, they finished their high school careers at a performance level only slightly above the one at which they entered; did not differ from the ignored C's and, except in social studies, remained significantly below the level of the equally bright high achievers to whom they were compared (H's) (Tables IV-11 and IV-12). On the New York State Regents Examinations the C's achieved higher mean scores than the S's in seven out of eight subjects (all but foreign languages). In mathematics and biology the differences were both educationally and statistically significant. Figure IV-3 shows the grade averages for the three groups from end of grade nine to end of grade twelve.

By graduation the majority of the S's were not accepted by the colleges of their choice; many had dropped out of the academic stream and made no educational plans beyond high school;

Table IV-11. Teacher Marks, First Semester, Grade Twelve, for the Three Groups (S, C, and H) in Two Subject Areas[a] and Averages across All Subjects

	S		C		H		t test		
							S vs. C	S vs. H	C vs. H
Subject Area	M	SD	M	SD	M	SD			
English	81	10.3	82	11.4	92	4.3	−0.16	−5.93[b]	−5.02[b]
Social studies	87	7.5	80	15.2	90	6.7	1.82	−1.66	−3.60[b]
Average	80	8.6	78	9.8	88	7.1	0.84	−4.01	−4.66[b]

[a] Comparisons could be made only in English and social studies since these were the only subjects which were taken by all or almost all of the students. The remaining subjects were largely elective.

[b] Significant at or beyond the .05 level.

some few dropped out before graduation. These patterns were no different for the C's. In each, about 10 per cent of the students improved greatly and achieved honor school status. None of the S's won a State Scholarship, while three C's and five H's were among the winners. The experimental effects, although apparently significant after the first year of the special class, showed no significant carry-over into the eleventh and twelfth years of school.

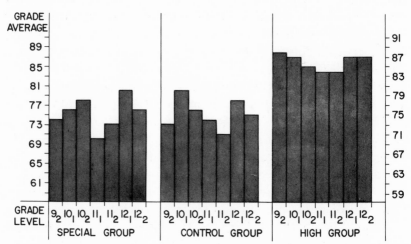

Figure IV-3. Mean grade averages of special (S), control (C), and high (H) groups from end of grade nine to end of grade twelve.

Table IV-12. Teacher Marks, Second Semester, Grade Twelve, for the Three Groups (S, C, and H) in English[a] and Averages across All Subjects

| Subject Area | S | | C | | H | | t test | | |
	M	SD	M	SD	M	SD	S vs. C	S vs. H	C vs. H
English	78	8.6	79	10.1	89	4.2	−0.14	−6.77[b]	−5.51[b]
Average	76	8.0	75	10.5	88	6.6	0.26	−6.47[b]	−5.99[b]

[a] In the last semester of grade twelve English was the only required subject. In all other areas, students took a variety of elective courses so that comparisons were not possible.

[b] Significant at or beyond the .05 level.

The Special Geometry Class

Purpose of the study

The preceding study led to an examination of other possibilities for working with underachieving groups. Although the number of low grades and failures had decreased during the first year at Clinton among the boys in the special class, those failures or near failures which remained were either in mathematics or in foreign language. Actually, these two subjects also accounted for the greatest number of ninth-grade failures. Very low passing grades in one or both of these subjects were marked even among otherwise high-achieving students. Therefore, it was decided to experiment with a special mathematics section which could be assigned to a teacher interested in the problem, flexible in his approach, and highly competent in the subject field. Plans to have similar special classes in French and Spanish had to be dropped because of scheduling difficulties.

Identification of students and organization of the class

There was little difficulty in finding students with IQ's above 125 and ninth grade elementary algebra grades below 75. In most instances, these students were two or more years accelerated in arithmetic according to eighth- and ninth-year standardized test scores. A few students were included who were at, or slightly below, grade level on the standardized junior high school arithmetic test if their IQ's and reading scores were especially high. Seventy students were selected, paired on IQ, ninth-year mathematics grades, and junior high arithmetic grade equivalents. Students who failed algebra were included, with the hope that in a different, less computational mathematics, such as geometry, they might succeed.

Because of the discrepancy in scores on the Iowa Tests of Educational Development between the S's and C's noted in the previous Homeroom-Social Studies Class experiment, the ITED were given to potential students for the special class in geometry prior to selection. Composite as well as quantitative scores were considered in matching students for this investigation. As in the previous experiment, one student from each pair was placed in a special section (Special Geometry Class) and the other scheduled into regular geometry sections (control group). Table IV-13 shows entering status of these two groups of students.

Table IV-13. Status of Special Geometry Class (S) and Control Students (C) at Entry into Grade Ten

	S (N = 31)		C (N = 31)	
	M	SD	M	SD
Ninth-year grade average	73.7	4.7	74.2	4.3
Ninth-year mathematics average	68.2	6.3	69.1	5.9
IQ	132.0	9.5	130.6	7.2
Arithmetic grade equivalent	9.2	1.4	9.8	1.5
Reading grade equivalent	10.8	.8	11.0	.8
ITED-composite score percentile	89.4	5.8	88.4	7.9
ITED-quantitative score percentile	73.2	17.1	71.0	16.4
ITED-reading-natural science score percentile	89.2	8.5	86.3	11.6

While the basic geometry content for the special class and the classes in which the control group functioned was essentially the same, the approach in the special class stressed concept formation and minimized drill and memorization. Considerable attention was given to the development of better work-study skills through homework assignments, frequent quizzes and tests, and discussions of ways of organizing one's self to attack a geometry task. The normal syllabus was enriched with many opportunities for individual problem-solving, represented by the challenge of geometry teasers on which the students could work.

Evaluation of student performance in geometry at the end of the first semester, tenth grade

Teacher grades. At the end of one semester there were no differences in teacher grades for the special group (S) and the control group (C) in any subject, not even in geometry. Here, as in the first semester of the Homeroom-Social Studies Class previously described, relatively low geometry grades in the special class may have reflected the reluctance of a conscientious teacher to overrate the students and thus unfairly contaminate the results of the study. A comparison of grades for the two groups (Table IV-14) showed no significant differences.

Table IV-14. Grade Averages of Special Geometry Class (S) and Control Group (C) in Five Subjects at the End of the First Semester of Geometry

Subject Area	S M	C M	S-C Differences M	SD	t test
English	78.7	81.0	−2.3	11.4	1.12
Social studies	76.6	77.9	−1.3	13.8	.53
Foreign language	68.0	69.7	−1.7	15.5	.58
Mathematics (Geometry I)	72.5	73.1	−0.6	15.8	.21
Science	75.0	78.4	−3.4	17.7	1.05
Average	72.0	74.5	−2.5	12.6	1.09

Test scores. On a more positive note, a standardized test of first-semester plane geometry[5] showed that the two groups were significantly different both in average scores and in distribution (Table IV-15).

The mean for the Special Geometry Class was at the 47th per-

[5] Harold E. Jeffery, *Seattle Plane Geometry Test for End of First Half-Year*, Form AM. Yonkers, N. Y.: World Book Company, 1951.

Table IV-15. Scores on the Seattle Plane Geometry Test (Form AM) for the Special Geometry Class (S) and the Control Students (C)

Group	N	Mean Standard Score	SD	Per-centile	Median Standard Score	Per-centile	t test
Special Geometry Class	31	111.7	10.7	47	113	52	6.76[a]
Control group	30	106.3	8.7	36	105	32	
Combined group	61	109.0	10.1	41	109	41	

[a] Significant beyond the .01 level.

centile (range from the 6th to the 95th). For the C's the mean was at the 36th percentile (range from the 2nd to the 74th). Comparison of the mean difference between the S's and C's using matched pairs was significant beyond the .01 level of confidence ($t = 6.76$). The medians were even more disparate, falling at the 52nd percentile for the S's and at the 32nd percentile for the C's. The distribution of scores in the control group was approximately normal, unimodal, and showed slight positive skewness. The frequency distribution for the special class tended to be bimodal and negatively skewed.

The work in the special class seemed effective in motivating almost half of the students to a high or fairly high level of performance. However, about one third of the students who were frequently absent, or who appeared too disinterested or too disorganized to respond to the enthusiastic atmosphere of the class, were not reached at all.

In addition, students who did show considerable improvement in mathematics over ninth grade did not necessarily improve comparably in other subjects. In fact, in one or two instances, mathematics became an all-absorbing interest, and these students tended to neglect their other studies. At any rate, after one semester it was clear that becoming successful in a subject area of former failure or near-failure would not be reflected in improvement in other fields of study.

Teacher appraisal. The teacher who worked with the Special Geometry Class found that most of the boys seemed responsive to the challenge of a conceptual approach to mathematics with a minimum of emphasis on drill and memorizing. The teacher also found that about half of the boys showed few problems other than those which could be attributed to poor work habits and under-stimulation in their earlier mathematics experience. However, the remaining students appeared to have deep-seated attitudinal and personal problems which continued to block their achievement despite the more individualized and intellectually challenging atmosphere of the class. Among these students was a group frequently truant from school.

Even in the relatively more disturbed group there were several boys who became intensely interested in the work and achieved at a high level. These boys showed particular interest in topics that were not a part of the syllabus but which could be pursued individually. One boy, for example spent much time attempting to solve the problem of angle-trisection. He would not accept the teacher's dictum that the problem was impossible—an attitude which would have caused him considerable trouble in his algebra classes—for he insisted upon reaching his own conclusions. As he investigated the problem, the boy gained an increasingly mature point of view about it and about the deduction process, a major aim of the course at this stage. Other problems that aroused wide interest and brought forth extra individual efforts included constructions by means of compasses alone, constructing models of rather complex solid figures, and difficult examples of proofs of original exercises.

The problem of work habits was approached through regular homework assignments, very detailed tests, and, later in the term, daily quizzes. Through frequent class discussions the students were made aware of the importance of regularly completing assignments. The need for correct form as well as correct content was emphasized, and any display of effort, even when not crowned by success, was praised. Many of the boys welcomed these procedures and very soon were performing well on homework, on recitation, and on the periodic tests.

Not all the boys improved in their work habits, and a great variety of individual responses was evidenced. Some handed in shoddy and sporadic work, accompanied by a plethora of excuses;

others failed entirely to comply with requirements; still others were absent whenever a test was given. At the first marking period (about the sixth week) the teacher announced that this grade would be based only on test results with no penalty for poor or missing homework. He warned that, beginning with the next marking period, there would be heavy penalties—even possible failure—for an incomplete homework record. Student reaction to this warning varied. One of the three most flagrant violators of the regular homework rule (the angle trisector) received a high rating, and from that point on, never missed another assignment, achieving a final rating of 97. Two others with equally bad homework records and comparable classroom and test achievement, continued to be remiss in turning in assignments and were failed at the next marking period. One of them changed after this and continued to perform successfully to the end of the term. The other (an overweight boy with apparently a great many problems) continued to do work of a very fluctuating quality to the end of the term.

Based on his estimate of the potential mathematical ability of the students, the teacher felt that more than half were performing near optimum at the end of the semester. In most instances, this meant an achievement grade of 80 or higher. Two failing students were included in this category, since, despite most conscientious efforts, they were still unable to do the work, and therefore considerable doubt was cast on their aptitude for mathematics. Individual tutoring in these two cases—and in some others—might have improved achievement.

Five of the 31 boys did outstanding work. Included in this group were the two who initially exhibited serious difficulty in accepting class routines. One student showed such a high level of achievement in all areas that he was included in the advanced scholarship class.

The most difficult boys to reach were the truants. Of five such boys, one showed marked improvement in attendance and classwork after a conference between the teacher, the boy, and his mother. Three others improved in attendance but not in performance, but one showed no improvement at all and was placed, as stated above, in a class for truants.

By the nature of the study, the basis of communication between pupils and teacher was related primarily to class work and only incidentally to personal problems. However, an unusual number of parents made a point of visiting the teacher and expressing concern about their boys' achievement. The boys frequently came to the teacher after school hours for help and talk, and such conferences seemed to have a positive effect on their performance.

Conclusions regarding the Special Geometry Class

The results of the Special Geometry Class were uneven, at best. The S's showed no more improvement as far as class grades in mathematics were concerned than did the C's who were scheduled in the usual way. Marks in courses other than geometry were not influenced by the help obtained or progress made in the special class. Some better effects were demonstrated on a standardized test in geometry, and a few students made remarkable gains during the semester as compared to their low level of attainment in junior high school mathematics.

At the end of the first semester, the special class was retained as a unit, except for four severe failures who had had excessive absence records; all others were permitted to go on to the second semester's work. Scheduling demands made a change of teachers necessary. A young teacher, interested in the problem of underachievement, who had been working under the former teacher's close supervision, was assigned to the class. The class atmosphere seemed to change, however, as many of the students lost their sense of enthusiasm derived from close identification with the first teacher. The group's achievement fell considerably below the first-semester level. A few of the outstanding improvers finished the year well, but the majority did no better than the C's either in class marks or in grades on the New York State Regents Examination (Table IV-16).

Like their predecessors in the Homeroom-Social Studies Class, the underachievers in the Special Geometry Class reached the end of high school showing little improvement over their entering status, and none beyond that of the C's. The amelioration apparent during the intensive phase of the program showed no carry over into the following years (Figure IV-4).

Table IV-16. Grade Ten Teacher Marks for the Special Geometry Class (S) and the Control Group (C) in Five Subjects, Averages across All Subjects, and New York State Geometry Regents Examination Scores

Subject Areas	N (Pairs of students)	S M	C M	S-C Differences M	SD	t tests
English	26	79	83	−4	8.8	−2.32[a]
Social studies	12	80	79	1	15.6	−.06
Foreign language	25	70	70	0	19.6	−.12
Mathematics	18	70	66	4	12.4	.28
Science	26	76	78	−2	10.1	.02
Average	26	74	75	−1	9.6	−.44
Regents scores	21	66	75	−9	27.7	−1.46

[a] Significant at or beyond the .05 level.

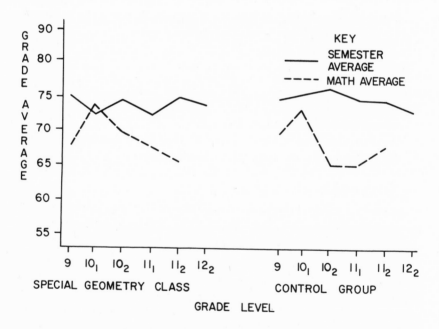

Figure IV-4. Average semester grades and average mathematics grades received by Special Geometry Class and control group from end of grade nine to end of grade twelve. (*Note:* Most of the students did not go on in mathematics beyond the end of grade eleven.)

The Group Guidance and Study Skills Classes

Assessment of the two previous intervention plans intended to ameliorate underachievement pointed to several conclusions: First, it became increasingly evident that academic underachievement is a symptom of a wide variety of differential achievement strengths and weaknesses, as well as basic personal and social problems, and that the seriousness and duration of the underlying problem should determine the extent and kind of help a student needs, academic or psychological, or both. Furthermore, there were probably some students who by high school age were beyond profiting from any help which could be given directly by the school. Unfortunately, it was not possible to arrive at criteria for making a prognosis on the basis of the kind of information which could be collected in the school.

For those students for whom it was possible to effect improvement, two factors appeared to be crucial: (1) assistance in mastering the skills of learning which many of the underachievers had failed to acquire in the earlier grades; and (2) identification with a teacher who was consistently interested and supportive, who viewed each student as an individual and accepted him as a bright and able person with a need for special help (for boys this probably means a male teacher).

Purposes and plan of the Group
Guidance and Study Skills classes

To meet the two needs discussed above, a program had to be devised which would place the underachievers in regular contact with a carefully selected teacher for long enough periods to allow for individual guidance and instruction in learning skills. It also seemed advisable to separate the teaching function from the guidance function for these adolescents, so that the person who was working closely and personally with them would not have to grade or evaluate them. It seemed wise not to group these students together in a subject class, since they tended to give each other negative support which often could not be adequately handled within the classroom context. Based on what had been learned about the needs of underachieving boys and what had emerged as the strengths and weaknesses of the first two approaches to the problem, a three-year plan was devised for another incoming group of tenth graders.

Identification of students and organization of Group Guidance and Study Skills classes

Eighty-five students with IQ scores over 125 and ninth-year grade averages below 80 per cent were identified, and three groups matched on intelligence, age, membership in Special

Table IV-17. Test Scores at the End of Grade Nine of Three Groups of Underachievers (A, B, and C) and Two Groups of Scholarship Students (S) Participating in the Group Guidance and Study Skills Program

Test	Group			
	A	B	C	S
IQ:				
N	29	29	26	63
M	133.1	133.9	135.2	131.2
SD	6.59	7.27	8.06	9.79
Ninth-year reading:				
N	29	29	26	63
M	11.9	11.8	11.9	12.0
SD	.70	.83	.60	.71
Ninth-year arithmetic:				
N	29	29	26	63
M	10.6	10.7	10.4	11.7
SD	1.56	1.37	1.53	1.01
Ninth-year grade average:				
N	29	29	26	63
M	73.5	74.5	74.1	87.3
SD	5.38	4.26	5.76	4.34
ITED composite:				
N	26	25	26	42
M	19.4	17.4	20.2	20.6
SD	2.08	3.88	3.02	2.17
ITED quantitative:				
N	26	25	26	42
M	17.8	19.5	17.5	21.6
SD	2.76	2.50	4.88	3.04

Progress classes during junior high school, and reading and arithmetic scores were organized. Data from the ITED were also considered in the selection (Table IV-17).

Two of the groups, designated A ($N = 29$) and B ($N = 29$), constituted special groups placed in homeroom sections with carefully selected teachers. The third group, designated as C ($N = 26$), was distributed among the remaining sections and acted as a control group. Each special section (Groups A and B) remained together for a daily study period immediately following the homeroom period supervised by their section officer. Thus a full hour was made available daily for the purposes discussed above. The teachers involved, together with the HMLI Project consultant, planned how the time should be divided among individual conferences, group discussions, and instruction in skills. Each of the two groups, A and B, was to have remained intact for the three years of high school, if at all possible, with the same teacher. However, any student who attained honor roll status (an average of 85 per cent or higher) after the first year was to be permitted to use some of the study period time for school service. A comparable group of two classes of high-achieving, high-ability scholarship students (designated as S) was also included for comparison purposes.

The teachers of the special classes were released for one period per week for planning together, sharing their successes and problems, and keeping a record of the work of their class. Group size was to be kept to 29 students to enable the teacher to pay maximum attention to the students' individual needs.

Evaluation of student performance at the end of two semesters, tenth grade

HMLI Project Staff appraisal of the teaching of the special classes. The Group Guidance and Study Skills classes again permitted the comparison of the effects of special and nonspecial treatment, as in the two previous studies; in addition, they allowed for a comparison of the effects of two highly dissimilar teachers. One of the teachers (with Group B) was exceptionally warm and outgoing, spent much time with individual students, made contacts with parents, and acted as a buffer for his boys with the rest of the school personnel. He provided remedial instruction in foreign language to some of the boys and used a portion of the daily hour to help individuals or the whole group with some of the problems they encountered in their homework. He was consistent in his approach to the boys and greatly beloved by them.

The second teacher (with Group A) was a blustering hail-fellow-well-met, who never attained a consistent approach to the group. At times he was totally permissive, allowing every kind of activity—reading comics, doing assignments, rough-housing, etc. At other times he would demand absolute quiet, forbidding the students even to do their homework during the hour. He took little personal interest in the boys or in their families, and some of the students developed an active dislike of him.

Grade averages, end of grade ten. At the end of grade ten comparisons among groups by analyses of variance revealed that the grades of the underachieving students in the special classes (Groups A and B) did not differ from those of the control group (Group C). Nor did the two special classes differ from each other (Table IV-18). However, when the three underachieving groups combined were compared to the two S groups, significant differences were obtained in every subject, favoring the scholarship students. At the end of tenth grade, the gap between the underachievers and the high achievers was greater than it had been at the beginning of the tenth grade or at midyear.[6]

Evaluation of student performance, eleventh and twelfth grades

Assessment at the end of grade eleven. The three classes of underachievers (Groups A, B, and C) had remained relatively intact through grade eleven. However, in each of the groups, but especially in Groups B and C there was considerable attrition due to school changes and dropouts. In addition, two students from Group C and one from Group A had been moved into one

[6] Analysis of teacher grades in the middle of grade ten found significant differences between the underachievers and the scholarship students only in foreign language, mathematics, and science. No significant differences were noted in English or social studies.

Table IV-18. Grade Ten Teacher Marks for Three Groups of Underachievers (A, B, and C) and the Scholarship Students (S) in Five Subject Areas and Averages across All Subjects

Subject Area	Group			
	A	B	C	S
English:				
N	28	27	24	63
M	78.8	82.6	81.7	88.1
SD	8.34	8.29	10.07	4.97
Foreign language:				
N	28	27	23	63
M	68.9	69.4	68.7	84.6
SD	12.7	16.5	9.32	8.24
Social studies:				
N	28	25	24	63
M	79.2	84.8	79.1	90.4
SD	10.43	9.31	13.85	4.76
Science:				
N	28	27	24	63
M	75.0	76.9	78.0	86.8
SD	9.81	12.88	10.96	5.54
Mathematics:				
N	28	27	24	63
M	71.3	72.8	72.3	85.3
SD	13.91	16.06	12.24	8.47
Semester average:				
N	28	27	24	63
M	74.3	77.1	75.8	86.8
SD	8.32	8.90	8.64	4.49

of the S groups. Of the original 29 pupils there were 26 left in Group A (one was added in tenth grade and brought the total up to 27), 23 in Group B, and 22 in Group C.

Because of the many problems encountered in Group A, some of the students were moved into Group B for the twelfth grade, while a few were moved into regular sections and no longer had a guidance period.

Grade averages at the end of grade eleven. A comparison by analysis of variance of teacher grades in each of the five academic subject areas and across all subjects found no significant differences among Groups A, B, and C (Table IV-19). However, in Groups A and B fewer pupils dropped foreign language or science

Table IV-19. Grade Eleven Teacher Marks for Three Groups of Underachievers (A, B, and C) and the Scholarship Students (S) in Five Subject Areas and Averages across All Subjects

Subject Area	Group			
	A	B	C	S
English:				
N	27	23	22	63
M	79.3	81.8	83.3	87.0
SD	8.73	7.74	6.39	4.33
Foreign language:				
N	23	20	17	63
M	66.70	69.3	74.4	82.0
SD	11.21	9.36	8.64	7.55
Social studies:				
N	26	23	20	63
M	78.8	82.6	79.4	88.0
SD	13.48	8.27	11.38	4.23
Science:				
N	23	23	18	63
M	69.6	70.7	70.0	82.4
SD	9.64	10.64	10.57	12.34
Mathematics:				
N	25	23	22	63
M	73.0	75.0	74.0	82.4
SD	9.46	13.73	11.05	7.01
Semester average:				
N	27	23	22	63
M	73.0	75.7	76.1	84.4
SD	6.89	7.49	10.74	4.16

than was true of Group C. This was largely due to the intensive efforts made in the special sections to have students continue in the academic stream and make up failures rather than drop out of subject areas.

Assessment at the end of grade twelve. At the end of the last year in high school, 66 of the original 94 underachievers were still at DeWitt Clinton. Analyses of cumulative grades and other performance records were made on the basis of the students' original tenth-grade placement, regardless of their homeroom sections in grade twelve. Only Group B remained relatively intact as a class, retaining 22 of its initial 29 students.

Cumulative grade averages. Comparisons by analyses of variance of the final averages of the students who participated in the Group Guidance and Study Skills classes found no significant differences among the three groups of underachievers. Groups A and B did not differ from each other nor did these groups, singly or combined, differ from Group C. However, each of the three underachieving groups, singly and combined, differed significantly from the S Group in each subject area and across all subjects (Table IV-20 and Figure IV-5).

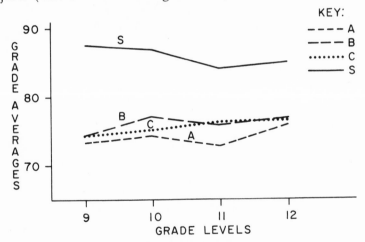

Figure IV-5. Grade averages of three underachieving groups (A, B, and C) and the scholarship students (S) in the Group Guidance and Study Skills classes from end of grade nine to end of grade twelve.

Comparisons of performance on New York State Regents Examinations and on the Scholastic Aptitude Tests (Verbal and Mathematical) showed no differences among the underachieving groups (Tables IV-21 and IV-22). Nor did the groups differ on number of discharges, dropouts, transfers, failures, repeaters, or scholarship winners (Table IV-23).

Table IV-20. Final Averages at End of Grade Twelve (Cumulative over Three Years) in Five Subject Areas and All Subjects Combined for Three Groups of Underachievers (A, B, and C) and the Scholarship Students (S)

	Group											
	A			B			C			D		
Subject Area	N	M	SD	N	M	SD	N	M	SD	N	M	SD
English	24	80.0	5.59	22	82.1	5.69	20	82.6	4.44	62	87.0	4.31
Foreign language	24	70.1	7.15	22	70.5	9.64	20	70.3	7.22	62	81.9	7.56
Social studies	24	80.9	6.73	22	82.6	7.30	20	82.0	6.04	62	88.0	4.25
Science	24	74.9	5.94	22	75.7	7.43	20	74.7	6.38	62	83.8	6.40
Mathematics	24	74.6	6.72	22	75.6	9.31	20	74.7	6.77	62	82.4	7.05
Average	24	76.1	4.70	22	77.3	6.66	20	76.9	4.66	62	84.6	5.10

Table IV-21. Number of Underachieving Students (Groups A, B, and C) Who Took and Number Who Failed New York State Regents Examinations in Each Subject

	Group					
	A		B		C	
Subject Area	Took	Failed	Took	Failed	Took	Failed
English	25	0	23	1	20	0
Social studies	25	1	22	1	21	2
Foreign language	18	2	16	1	15	5
Science:						
Biology	26	4	26	2	23	1
Chemistry	16	8	21	10	17	9
Physics	12	5	13	1	9	3
Other	5	2	2	1	2	0
Mathematics:						
Geometry	5	3	24	10	13	3
Math 10	23	9	1	0	10	1
Intermediate algebra	16	2	14	3	12	1
Math 11	8	2	8	0	6	0
Trigonometry	8	7	11	3	7	2
Advanced algebra	12	8	13	7	9	4
Other	7	2	3	0	2	0
Total	206	54	197	40	166	31

Table IV-22. Final Grade Averages, Regents Examinations Scores, and
Scholastic Aptitude Test Scores (Verbal and Mathematical) for
Three Groups of Underachievers (A, B, and C) and
Scholarship Student (S)

	Final Grade Average				Regents Examinations Average				SAT (Verbal)				SAT (Mathematical)			
Group	N	M	SD	Range	N	M	SD	Range	N	M	SD	Range	N	M	SD	Range
A	24	76.1	4.70	69–83	24	69.5	7.34	54–78	22	486.2	79.80	354–628	22	546.8	54.40	434–707
B	23	77.3	6.66	71–85	23	71.7	7.59	58–90	23	503.9	80.29	367–668	23	546.9	68.94	399–697
C	20	76.9	4.66	71–84	20	71.7	6.56	58–82	19	516.2	77.40	352–623	19	530.7	42.30	416–627
S	62	84.6	5.10	69–93	62	78.6	7.72	59–90	58	519.0	67.91	374–690	58	561.7	45.34	338–757

Table IV-23. Summary Data for the Three Groups of Underachievers (A, B,
and C) in the Group Guidance and Study Skills Classes at the End of
Three Years

	Groups		
Students Who:	A	B	C
Won State Scholarships	4	3	5
Carried five or more major academic subjects per term (30+)	0	0	3
Took College Board Examinations	22	23	19
Were held back	2	2	0
Were required to attend summer school in order to graduate by August, 1961	1	2	1
Graduated in January, 1961 (in three and one-half years)	2	0	2
Transferred to other high schools	2	2	4
Left school to go to work or were discharged (17+) before graduating	1	3	3
Failed one or more courses	16	11	15
Took one or more Regents Examinations	27	26	23
Failed one or more Regents Examinations	22	20	18

Concluding observations on the Group
Guidance and Study Skills classes

None of the comparisons between Groups A and B and Group
C proved statistically significant. Neither were the differences
between Group A and Group B significant. In each group about
one quarter became high achievers, and this number did not

differ significantly from one group to another. The majority of students retained their initial status, showing neither marked deterioration in school grades nor any noticeable upgrading of their work. The expectation that providing underachieving boys with a male teacher who could act as model, friend, guide, and helper would produce upgrading effects on achievement did not materialize.

Discussion of the DeWitt Clinton Provisions for Modifying Scholastic Underachievement

The outcome of the first two Clinton studies strongly pointed to the importance of the teacher who works with underachieving students. Underachievers appeared to do best when the teacher was able to accept their limitations and be sufficiently flexible to allow them the leeway they seemed to need. They also responded to high standards on the part of the teacher. In these cases, the teacher taught a subject and most of his contact with the group was in a teaching-learning situation. The third study, which placed the pupils in a guidance situation with a selected teacher, did not show equally positive effects.

One would like to believe that the initial improvement noted in the first experiment would have carried over into the remaining years had the teacher remained with the group. But the last experiment cast real doubt on this supposition. All underachieving groups, whether under special treatment or not, showed some improvement at the end of the first year—an improvement over their junior high school performance—but these gains seemed to drop off as the more demanding eleventh grade work was undertaken. Even the theory that identification with a warm, accepting, and consistent teacher would have positive effects, as was seen in the first two procedures, is open to question when the data of the last study are considered.

Although the special treatments undertaken at Clinton did not produce any significant or lasting results (of course, the effects may become apparent much later), about 20 to 30 per cent of all entering tenth grade underachievers improved significantly during the three years of high school, regardless of whether they received special attention or not. This phenomenon makes the use of control groups in this kind of research essential, since teachers and guidance counselors who work with such students are generally convinced that their efforts have produced positive changes, whereas an equal amount of positive change seems to take place even without special efforts.

The experiments described here, as well as the impressions of people who have worked with gifted underachievers in classes and in counseling relationships, suggest that efforts initiated at the senior high school level show little promise of success. For many of the students, underachievement seems to have become a deeply rooted way of life, unamenable to change through school efforts. The three-year high school may not provide enough time for the underachiever to build the needed helping relationship with an accepting and respecting adult and to free himself sufficiently from his dependence on the teacher to pursue his goals independently. Early identification of the potential underachiever, in terms of cognitive as well as sociopersonal factors, might enable schools to engage in preventative rather than curative programs for these gifted students.

CHAPTER FIVE

Review
and implications

A FINAL LOOK at the studies conducted in the Evanston Township and DeWitt Clinton high schools confirms the complexity of the underachiever's situation, provides some leads for practice, and indicates directions for further inquiry. Phenomenological factors related to the underachiever's self-concept, self-ideal, motivation, and adult models will be discussed, together with some of their implications. Results of the several experimental grouping plans to provide means for remedial approaches to underachievement in the high school will then be summarized.

Phenomenological Factors

Self-concept and school achievement

The finding that a positive self-concept appears to be more related to school mastery than it does to intelligence in high school students was borne out consistently for the groups studied. The high and low achievers did not differ significantly in self-estimates of their ability and characteristics when these were compared for personal and social dimensions. But, on school-related or task-oriented items the differences clearly distinguished between the two groups, suggesting that underachieving young persons appraised realistically the discrepancy between their

181

ability and their performance. This result held true regardless of geographic location (Illinois and New York) or socioeconomic level.

The dilemma of ascribing cause or effect to self-concept in scholastic attainment poses problems not readily amenable to present research methods. However, certain theoretical models, particularly those cast in a longitudinal framework, offer promise of determining the interactions of consistency and change in school performance with those of personality factors. White (1959; 1960) extends the model of psychoanalytic ego psychology to include the concept of competence—the whole realm of learned behavior whereby the child comes to deal effectively with his environment. White presumes the presence of what he terms "effectance motivation," which has its immediate satisfactions in a feeling of efficacy and has adaptive significance in the growth of competence. He then traces the acquisition of motor, linguistic, cognitive, and social behaviors at the various chronological stages of development. Activities which are ends in their own right in the earlier life of a child, such as his exploratory play, his acquisition of motor skills, and his first rewarded verbal responses, become gradually associated with good performance capability in himself and may serve later directly and indirectly as the means for the attainment of a variety of ends. Applied to school achievement, White's focus would postulate that later academic skill and satisfaction in mastery might well be related to earlier acquired competencies and to the pleasures derived from such competencies. Put more concisely, "I can do" becomes "I am," in that satisfaction in mastery becomes linked to the self-concept.

Support for such a position is seen in the findings of the Kagan and Moss (1962) study of psychological development, wherein their subjects were studied continuously from birth through adolescence, and then studied as adults. Those children with intense strivings for mastery during the early grades of school, six to ten years of age, were found likely to maintain this behavior predisposition in later years. Kagan and Moss consider that primary events in the first school years include the realization that mastery of intellective skills is both a cultural requirement and a source of satisfaction and that this orientation is critical for later learnings.

Significant differences in grade-point averages evident in high-ability secondary school students were found by Shaw and Mc-Cuen (1960) to be equally significant in the academic records of these same students when they were in the elementary grades, beginning in third grade for boys, and sixth grade for girls. Their findings suggest the prospect of earlier identification of school difficulties in bright pupils than has commonly been reported in the literature. Selection of such students at a young age, and study of such relevant variables as White's competency and Kagan's mastery strivings in relation to the course of under-achievement over time might yield a deeper understanding of school problems and better predictors than are now available.

A second finding regarding the self-concept of the under-achieving boys, one revealed more clearly in the DeWitt Clinton interviews than on the attitudes inventories, was their tendency to minimize their ability by ascribing to themselves such evalua-tions as "pretty average," "about like others," or, at best, "maybe a little above average." This tendency seemed to be an effort to avoid both social ostracism from peers and more stringent de-mands from adults. Unfavorable references to boys who were "too smart," "an Einstein," or, as one youth put it, "a bookworm, too much," appeared to be associated in their minds with all study, no friends, no fun, and even being actively disliked, par-ticularly if they did not have athletic ability, social talents, or a host of companions to compensate for obtaining high marks. Similarly, viewing one's self as having high ability seemed to portend longer and more difficult assignments from teachers, and greater dissatisfactions in parents with a boy's current achievement status. To this group of underachievers, "You have what it takes, if you just use it," promised only the dubious re-ward of higher expectations for them, the attainment of which, regardless of the effort they expended, would always fall short of adult standards for them.

Information pertaining to the actual requirements expected of bright students is not available, but according to numbers of the underachievers in these studies whose past school records were mediocre or poor and whose parental and teacher dissatisfactions with them were great, the added burden of considering themselves "bright" was not one they readily assumed. Attitudes toward excellence have been discussed extensively elsewhere (Barzun, 1959; Brameld, 1955; Mead, 1954). Inquiries by Coleman (1961) and Tannenbaum (1962) showed outstanding school attainment was not supported by the peer culture. Coleman's subjects ranked good grades, or "being smart in school," sixth out of eight criteria required for membership in the "leading crowd." When asked to rank hypothetical characters on acceptable traits and general popularity, Tannenbaum's students ranked *lowest* the one described as brilliant, highly studious, and nonathletic. To the subjects in Tannenbaum's study it was greatly preferable to be average, not overly studious, and athletic.

It is patently clear that the existing value systems regarding learning at all levels of education and the school's competition and reward practices influence the attainment attitudes of young persons. It would seem that schools need to examine the operation of these systems as they influence student performance and aspirations.

Ideals and school achievement

Evidence in the HMLI studies showed a much wider gap between the underachiever's estimate of his task-related abilities and characteristics and his ideal than was true for the achiever. Although as a group the underachievers recognized that their own performance was less than satisfactory and perceived their day-to-day attainments as minimal, their aspirations concerning "what they would most like" to be and to do resembled closely the aspirations of the achievers in almost every respect. Another example of the gap between achievement and aspiration was the consistent trend demonstrated by the underachieving groups at both schools to aspire to professional occupations even though their daily class performance was so poor as to make such choices almost wholly unrealistic.

The fact that the underachiever saw himself as having to travel a greater distance than the achiever to move from his present position to the one he viewed as desirable in the future in itself presented a number of problems for him. First of all, it meant that he was thereby exposed to more pressures from adults to achieve. For instance, if he were failing geometry or science and professing his intention to study engineering in college, he would probably be open to, and have to absorb in some fashion, more pointed questioning by a guidance counselor, more frequent discouragement from a teacher, and more intense exhortation and penalties from his parents than would the achieving student or the student who professed lower aspirations. Attention directed to the underachiever because of his manifest inconsistencies could be the cause of even greater stress and require him to call into play some type of defensive maneuver. Feelings of guilt for not achieving, combined with despair at the remoteness of satisfactory attainment, could result in several strategies for reducing conflict. He might be made so anxious by the disparity that he would mobilize his energies for work and actually begin making satisfactory progress in school. Or he might find his position so uncomfortable that, even though continuing to go through the motions of attending classes and voicing his high goals, he would actually just "give up" in terms of making any real effort. A third possibility is that he might withdraw entirely from school-oriented demands, become truant, and eventually drop out of school.

In reviewing the school history of a number of these bright underachievers, each of these three patterns was evident. This phenomenon of the existing discrepancy between present and wished-for status has a definite note of tragedy in it, calling for counsel in helping the young person to either mobilize his resources to move closer toward his goal or to face realistically the limitations within which he must live. At the same time the well-meaning friends, family, and school personnel who constitute an "onward and upward cheering section" need to give serious thought to the extent to which their efforts could accentuate rather than relieve serious problems of the underachiever.

Motivation and school achievement

One of the primary concerns of these studies was to tap the underachiever's view of his problem. How did he evaluate himself? How did he feel about his self-image? Did he want to change himself? How did he account for his school behavior? Whom did he hold responsible for his functioning?

As indicated previously, the underachieving groups did not differ markedly from their achieving peers in self-concept, except as this pertained directly to mastery of school-related tasks. On the School-Attitudes Inventory used in Evanston the level of satisfaction with school, participation in school and out-of-school activities, desirable and undesirable features of the school, and reactions regarding good and poor teaching were similar for both groups. However, in the interviews at DeWitt Clinton and the two informal weekend discussions another trend became evident: among this group of underachievers many repeatedly ascribed the initiative for success, or for failure, to a particular teacher. Teachers seemed to reap the major portion of the blame for the poor school record and, just about as frequently, the credit for a student's having performed well in a particular class. While no one would question the central position of the teacher in achievement patterns of young adolescents, these underachievers seemed to place an inordinate amount of responsibility in the hands of the teacher.

A theoretical model which combines Caron's (1965) study of the effects on learning of achievement-oriented and knowledge-oriented conditions and Miller and Swanson's (1960) study of inner conflicts and defense suggest some avenues for explaining the phenomenon of the underachievers making the teacher the culprit, so to speak. Caron calls attention to the "reading and studying behavior of our harassed students," which seems to be predominantly directed toward such extrinsic goals as good grades, parental and teacher approbation, and avoidance of failure. When this dependency on outside motivational factors occurs and, as in the case of the underachiever, is not rewarded, is it possible that he then shifts his behavior from seeking reward to projecting blame? Miller and Swanson empirically tested hypotheses about the social origins and child-rearing practices that predispose children to favor particular methods of resolving conflict. While school achievement was not a variable in their research, the finding that the seventh to ninth-grade boys in their

Detroit sample coming from working-class homes tended to use denial as the first line of defense when under stress, while boys from middle-class families used displacement, projection, reversal, and a turning against self, supplies confirmatory evidence for the tendencies exhibited by the underachievers in this study, who also represented a middle-class population. This notion certainly warrants practical studies in classrooms where Caron's distinction between extrinsic and intrinsic motivation could be examined for relevance to achievement level, and where the well-established diagnostic groupings of Miller and Swanson might be investigated so as to understand better both the antecedents of underachievement and the defenses engendered by it.

In addition to blaming the teachers, the underachievers also tended to blame themselves to some extent for their school performance, but in the rather superficial platitudes voiced by their parents and teachers, such as: "If I just studied more . . . if I weren't so lazy . . . if I applied myself, I could do it." This self-blame resembles, also, the behavior described by Miller and Swanson of turning criticism inward. When questioned further regarding their reasons for *not* so applying themselves, the boys seemed at a loss for any explanation. One answered, "I keep on telling myself, 'I'm going to try to do my best, I'm going to try to do my best,' but when the time comes, well I get in trouble, and I can't help it. I don't know." There is reason here to presume that irrational factors were operative, and that a good number of the students were simply quite unable to function better, even though they might attempt to do so.

Numerous attempts to explain the kind of irrational factors which prevent a young person from meeting one of society's first demands, that of satisfactory school work, draw on clinical insights regarding school phobias and evidence regarding emotional factors connected with reading problems. However, such attempts have usually failed to come up with generalizations which can explain the precise nature and functioning of dynamics that keep bright students from achieving to their full capacity. Whether such generalizations may ever be possible is doubtful since the phenomenon of underachievement itself appears to be so multi-faceted.

Nevertheless, certain theoretical and experimental work in progress promises more information regarding such unconscious factors as anxiety (Sarason, 1960; Spence, 1958; Taylor, 1956) and achievement motivation (Atkinson, 1957, 1960; McClelland, 1958). Taylor and Spence have been concerned with the formulation of a theory which could help explain why individuals who are hypothesized to have learned to respond with fear in achievement testing and other situations which threaten noxious consequences show an accompanying decrement in performance of some types of tasks but not others. Sarason's work has also focused on the response of the individual when differential anxiety is aroused and on an interpretation of the different kinds of task-relevant or task-irrelevant responses which are induced. He assumes that responses which in the past have been reinforced by reduction of fear—the so-called avoidant responses—are more strongly aroused in the highly anxious, and more debilitating for good performance. Anxiety, then, may contain some important clues to the disparity between ability and performance which seems on the surface to be so inexplicable.

Another research endeavor (summarized in the review of the literature in Chapter Two), that of need-Achievement (McClelland, 1953), has provocative implications for the understanding of the functioning of the underachiever. Atkinson (1960), for example, conceptualizes two dispositions activated in a performance situation: one, the "achievement motive," or the capacity to derive satisfaction from successful exercise of skill; the other, the "motive to avoid failure, an independent capacity to experience shame, humiliation, and embarrassment as a concomitant of failure." He postulates that these two opposing tendencies, to approach and to withdraw, are inherent in any activity when the behaving individual expects that his performance will be evaluated and that the outcome will be either a personal accomplishment or a sense of incompetence. He bases a number of predictions on this model, among them that individuals whose need for success is stronger than their fear of failure will try harder and perform better than individuals with the reverse pattern, i.e., those whose fear of failure is stronger than their need for success. Atkinson also theorizes that the greater the uncertainty of the outcome, the greater the effort that will be expended. The growing evidence from this evolving theory suggests that neither personality factors nor situational factors alone affect behavior, but rather that personality factors, including the unconscious ones, must be studied as they are engaged by known external factors. Studying such variables in the context of the school setting poses enormous, although not insurmountable, research problems.

Adult models and school achievement

In the DeWitt Clinton studies where the subjects were all males, two possible problems with regard to parental influences were identified. First, a larger proportion of underachievers came from disrupted families where there was no adult male in the home than was true of the comparable achieving group. Ramifications of this situation are well known, especially as they pertain to the growing adolescent boy. Secondly, the underachievers who came from homes where the father was present made frequent references to their father's college aspirations for them, but their mothers seemed to be more involved with the boy's school performance. In a series of interviews with both parents of one of the groups of underachievers, the mothers tended to dominate the interview. The fathers in this sample were largely from clerical, sales, and small business occupations. A number had been unable to attend college themselves because of the depression, and while they were serious about wanting their sons to attend college, the fathers did not themselves furnish learning models. Kimball (1952, 1953) who studied high-ability boys failing in their classes at a preparatory school found a poor father-son relationship in a high number of cases, apparently related either to emotional distance or to strict dominance on the part of the father. Kirk (1952) in working with a similar group of low-achievers at the college level presented evidence of a relationship between academic failure and hostility toward a family member who demands success. This dimension of the extent and nature of family involvement, while not studied systematically with the HMLI underachieving groups, suggests an area of needed exploration. Rosen's and D'Andrade's (1959) methodology for observing boys aged nine to eleven engaged in certain problem-solving tasks in the presence of both parents offers new ways of looking at family interactions. Their findings that, in order for high need-Achievement to develop, a boy required more autonomy from his father, "a beckon from ahead rather than a push from behind," and a high degree of involvement from the mother including both reward and punishment, for instance, are illustrative of variables which may be shown to have saliency for underachievement. As yet, however, the relationship between need-Achievement and academic achievement has to be demonstrated, a condition also requiring exploration if the theory of projection of motivation in fantasy is to have viability for application to problems of school attainment.

Effects of Grouping Plans on Underachievement

The grouping plans initiated at the DeWitt Clinton High School over a total period of five years, involving three different groups of incoming tenth graders who had been designated as underachievers in junior high school and comparable groups of high achievers, comprise a multi-faceted basis for the conclusions to be discussed here.

The overall result of the three main grouping studies, the Homeroom-Social Studies Class, the Special Geometry Class, and the Group Guidance and Study Skills classes, points to the general failure of such special administrative provisions to reverse the course of academic underachievement, at least to an extent greater than might have occurred by chance in the regular programming and instruction of the school. However, although the special classes did not make a significant difference in the grade-point averages of the underachievers as a whole, they did appear to benefit certain individuals. In addition, the process of selecting the underachievers for study, pooling observations by the teachers and researchers, and gaining intimate knowledge of the life situations of some of the individuals was illuminating.

The teacher-student relationship

The idea persists among educators as well as researchers that the teacher makes—or can make—the difference. What the ideal characteristics of such a teacher may be are not readily amenable to scientific scrutiny, since random descriptions of successful teachers will vary on almost every trait, ranging from strict to lenient, hard to easy, warm to detached, understanding to impersonal, young to old, and all degrees in between. The boys in these studies seemed agreed that a teacher should know his subject matter and be able to keep order. But what is more important here is that even when teachers for the special classes were selected on the basis of being highly competent (in the judgment of the school administration), experienced, well-regarded by their colleagues, and well-trained, the effect of such teachers appeared negligible in altering the pattern of underachievement.

Explanations for the teachers' shortcomings here might easily involve the whole panorama of educational philosophy and pedagogy. However, the important question to be raised has to do with the apparent inability of the underachieving students to profit from what could be assumed to be better-than-average teaching. One wonders if the boys found it difficult to trust authority, particularly a school authority. Could it be that, instead of being motivated by the encouragement they received from the teachers to do better in school, they leaned on this understanding and interest to enhance their position of poor achievement? Or, in instances where they actually did perform better for the teacher of the special class, as was true of some boys, was it impossible for them to respond in a similar manner to the more impersonal type of teaching? Did they need this type of teacher over a longer period of time or for more subjects during the day in order to show lasting improvement?

The fact that we have such meager findings on the effectiveness of different teachers and teaching methods can probably be attributed to the simple reason that teachers and teaching methods affect different students differently. In a study of teacher-pupil interaction at the college level, McKeachie (1961) suggests that the cues provided a student by his teachers may activate motives or skills which have previously been latent, may maintain the activation of motives or skills already active, may frustrate expectations previously elicited by the total environment, or may arouse uncertainty and anxiety about the likelihood of success or failure in reaching his goals. Three components of measurable student motives in a classroom situation were examined by McKeachie: affiliation, need for power, and achievement. Teacher behavior was then classified in terms of standards of achievement, personal interest in students, organization, and testing and feedback. Interactions between student motives and teacher characteristics were subsequently studied for effects on learning and attitudes regarding the learning experience. McKeachie implies a need in educational planning to discover a more specific approach to what constitutes effective teaching for an individual student. Thelen's (1961) approach to teachability grouping suggests one such method. For the underachieving student such an analysis may be even more crucial. This calls for learning how to categorize teaching situations in terms of their relevance for individual differences in abilities, in habits, and in characteristic approaches to learning.

While replication of McKeachie's type of study is not readily feasible for a school in selecting a teacher for its underachieving group, administrators could be continually aware of the need for special considerations in instruction for the underachiever. Competent teaching may have an especially important influence on learning in the earlier school years where the bright child is still achieving at grade level without any apparent difficulty, but is also forming attitudes in relation to the learning models with which he comes in contact. Perhaps the fact that boys rarely encounter a male model in these formative years may carry special meanings in regard to masculinity and academic learning. Or, as boys mature, the present inferior status of the teacher in our society may affect adversely the school functioning of students. Such subtle attitudes could have as great an influence on learning in high school as any teacher or teaching method.

The finding in these studies that the teacher's influence was not sufficient to make a difference in the achievement pattern of this small number of subjects strongly supports the need to investigate further what qualities in a teacher and what methods are most helpful, what the learner's attitudes regarding learning may be, and what school years are crucial if the teacher is to be an effective agent in preventing the onset and continuation of poor school performance.

Special class grouping of underachievers

It is generally agreed that special grouping of students for a particular purpose does not of itself guarantee attainment of that purpose, but may serve to facilitate instruction by narrowing the range of abilities, interests, or talents. Membership in two of the three special classes at Clinton was based on a combination of high ability and a record of a poor grade average in junior high school. The third class (the Special Geometry Class) was selected on the basis of high ability and low marks in one subject, junior high school mathematics. The Homeroom-Social Studies Class and the Group Guidance and Study Skills classes were based on the belief that bringing together such a group would enable the teacher to focus, in a helpful sense, on such common problems of the underachievers as poor study skills, irresponsibility about homework assignments, negative attitudes toward learning, and the like, to the benefit of all. It was also thought that any rewards by the teacher for improvement in effort or achievement might act as a spur, not only to the boy who had earned the recognition, but to the rest of the group as well.

It is possible that such positive effects actually did take place slowly within the first year of the Homeroom-Social Studies Class, since the grade-point average of the boys in this group did exceed the average of the boys in the control group to a significant degree. Consequently, at the end of the tenth grade, it seemed that the esprit de corps of the special class was high, its enthusiasm for school and for school activities was very positive, and the prospects for the group's next two years in high school were not only improved, but even very hopeful. This optimistic position was held in full cognizance of the fact that certain of the boys in the special class had not improved in their marks or in their general attitudes, and indeed seemed to have such serious problems that good school adjustment for them was extremely doubtful. Nevertheless, the outcome of the second year of the Homeroom-Social Studies Class dimmed the original hopes considerably. Despite the fact that the boys saw their former teacher daily for homeroom period, this brief contact was not sufficient for them to maintain the gains they had shown during the previous year or to overcome the negative attitudes engendered by the high, relatively inflexible standards of their new social studies teacher. Here the boys' tendencies toward impulsivity, defiance of authority, erratic work habits, and boisterousness seemed to be reinforced by each other's presence and to militate against any benefits to be gained by some of the excellent qualities of the teacher. Such tendencies, although they abated somewhat during the next semester when there was another change in instructor, still prevented optimal performance. This same phenomenon seemed to be at work in the other special classes: the Geometry Special Class and the Group Guidance and Study Skills classes. In fact, as indicated in a previous section, when one of the teachers was inconsistent in one of the latter groups, the effect on the group was so chaotic that the group had to be disbanded.

The HMLI project was based on a special grouping plan which applied to only two of eight periods during the day and involved too small a sample to make definitive conclusions; however, the findings raise serious questions about the practice of placing school failures together for remedial purposes, particularly if such failures consist of a group with good academic potential. Perhaps this is the time when a boy most needs association with peers who are meeting the demands of school successfully, particularly with reference to appropriate behaviors and positive attitudes toward learning. Since the underachieving boys often voiced apprehension about the negative effects of being thought a "grind," "an apple polisher," or "an honor roll student" by his peers, day-by-day exposure to some of the rewards of academic success may be more important, even if these have to be observed in others rather than experienced by one's self.

Special grouping apparently affects learners differently. What kind of underachiever is likely to modify his performance when in contact with high achievers? Do such contacts prove to be discouraging to other types of underachievers? Is there an essential difference between grouping boys together who show an underachieving pattern related to personality problems and grouping students together who have a particular weakness in a content area due to a lack of background information or skill? Such questions can only be answered through a series of studies similar to these, where attempts are made to isolate such variables and study the interactions.

The specificity of underachievement

One question that needs to be asked in relation to special grouping plans for modifying underachievement is whether the underachievement is a pervasive pattern contributing to lowered performance in all areas of endeavor or reflects special weaknesses in one or two areas so severe as to lower markedly the overall record. Determination of these differences may then dictate differing avenues of approach. General underachievement more likely may be related to personality difficulties, and assistance of a psychological nature may be the most necessary first step. Greater specification of the age at which school difficulty became apparent would also furnish some important clues as to the nature of underachievement.

If, on the other hand, the underachievement occurs in one content area (such as mathematics or foreign language), as tended to be true of a number of the subjects in these studies, the obvious first action should be in the determination of the processes or functions which may be responsible for the difficulty. Not unrelated here would be the strength of the teaching staff in the subject area in question, as well as the attitudes of the young student toward the subject in which he is doing poorly.

Those high ability students who have outstanding success in science and mathematics and who barely achieve average grades in the social studies or in English raise other questions. Since there is a greater variability in subject grades for gifted students in high school than at the elementary level, is this a reflection of the fact that general intelligence becomes increasingly specific with age? Or, is the nature of the subject matter in high school such that abilities other than those measured by general intelligence tests are called into play? Because the proportion of general ability as compared to specific ability differs for different subjects, mastery of a subject such as a foreign language may depend less on general intelligence than on some other ability not yet identified, while success in English or history, both of which require the kind of verbal behavior measured by intelligence tests, can be more readily predicted from a knowledge of general intelligence.

The evidence from studies of ability differentiation with age are not conclusive. Doppelt's (1950) findings suggest that up to age 16, at least, IQ scores explain only a third of the achievement variance. Multi-dimensional assessment of intellectual ability undoubtedly needs more systematic study. Guilford's (1959) three dimensional model of intellectual functioning, for example, suggests that there is considerable independence among the components which represent the interaction of various operations, products, and contents. Should it be demonstrated that specific school subjects depend more heavily on certain cognitive abilities than on others, then the IQ may prove to be no longer valid as a predictor of academic performance in these subjects. Consequently, students now considered underachievers because of their inadequate performance in such subjects might instead be working well within the limits of their capacity. This might be especially true of those high IQ students who do poorly in mathematics, an area hardly tapped by present measures of intelligence, or in foreign language, where very little is known about the cognitive abilities required for success. A more refined and differentiated approach to the measurement of intelligence would provide more valid predictive information. It could result in removing some of the pressure now being exerted on many high IQ students to excel equally in all subjects.

The work of Kagen, Moss, and Sigel (1963) on conceptual preferences in young children promises to contribute relevant information regarding the nature of the analytic attitude in response to stimuli. The authors propose, for instance, that conceptualization tends to be based on two fundamental orientations: egocentric and stimulus-centered. In the egocentric orientation concepts are derived from the individual's personalized, affective classification of a group of stimuli; that is, the individual uses his personal reactions to the stimuli or his personal characteristics to arrive at a basis for similarity among the stimuli. In the alternative orientation, stimulus-centered, the concepts are derived from aspects of the external stimulus; the individual's personal feelings are not part of the categorization. Work is in progress now to seek antecedents of the particular analytic style (such as constitutional, biological, and parent-child interactions). Undoubtedly, consideration will be given eventually to ways in which the particular analytic style functions in the various subject matter areas and to the advantage or disadvantage of the school learning tasks encountered by the student.

Witkin (1962) has been measuring field-dependence and independence, now called "global" versus "differentiated," "articulated," or "analytical" personality organization, and relating it to functioning of intelligence as well as to feelings, motives, and defensive systems. Of relevance to our concern with a more differentiated approach to cognition are the findings of Witkin that field-dependent or globally organized subjects do less well on block-design, picture-completion, and object-assembly parts of standard intelligence tests, and on insight problems. These same subjects, however, perform as well or even better on the vocabulary, information, and comprehension sections of intelligence tests than do the independent or more psychologically differentiated subjects. The ramifications of these findings for specific school performance have yet to be reported, but the possibilities again reinforce the differential nature of intelligence, which leads us to expect differential performance to a greater extent than may have been true in the past.

Perhaps one final research note might be introduced here, that of Hunt's (1961) proposition that intellectual capacities are based on central processes hierarchically arranged within the intrinsic portions of the cerebrum and that the encounters that children have with their environments, especially during the early years of their development, may be the key to both the rate of their intellectual development and the level of their adult intellectual functioning. He suggests moreover that the optimum rate of intellectual development would require self-directed interest and curiosity, and genuine pleasure in intellectual activity, fostered by early rich intellectual encounters in order to maximize a child's intellectual development. This conclusion points to the relevance of studying early childhood learning patterns, rather than adolescent ones, if the nature of underachievement is to be more clearly understood and modified.

The Interview Study–
Evanston Township High School

Form I
Interview Schedule and Instructions Form

I. Interview

(Prior to the interview each interviewer will have had an opportunity to look through the pupil's folder.)

It is agreed that at the outset we should make clear to the pupil why he is being interviewed. He should feel that we are concerned about him and the others and that any information that he might give us might help us in helping him and the others.

It should be made quite clear that any direct use of information from this interview will be made on a confidential basis. He should understand that the more frankly he speaks the more valuable the interview will be to him and to others.

Following the introductory remarks, we might begin the actual questioning in any manner and in any sequence which is most comfortable and effective for us. The questions that appear below merely indicate the kind of information sought. How we get at that information is up to us. It is well to note, however, that we should be prepared for rebuff or for student's trying to direct the interview his own way. We should be sure to get reactions and answers to all of the questions which follow and yet certainly be flexible enough to pursue promising leads.

We are after information suggested by these questions:

1. How do you feel about school?
2. How do you feel about the subjects you are taking?
3. How do you feel about your teachers?

4. How do your parents feel about ETHS?
5. How do your parents feel about the subjects you are taking?
6. What is your parents' reaction to the way you are getting along at school?
7. What are your parents' plans about your education?
8. What do you expect from high school?
9. What do you plan to do after high school?
10. What things do you like best about school?
11. What subjects do you like best in school?
12. What things do you like least?
13. What subjects do you like least?
14. What seem to be your strengths?
15. What seem to be your weaknesses?
16. When you have problems, with whom are you likely to discuss them?
17. When you have very personal problems, with whom do you share them?
18. How helpful is our regular counseling or guidance program to you?
19. Where do students usually make their best friends?
20. How easy is it to make and keep friends at ETHS?
21. Who are the most outstanding or the most important people in school?
22. Who do people in this school think are the "wheels"?
23. What do people think about the "brains"?
24. What do you think about competition around here?
25. What offices have you held in school? Outside of school?
26. What special interests and hobbies do you have within and outside of school?
27. How do you apportion your out-of-school hours? (Reading, TV, Movies, Study, etc.)
28. What activities do we have that you would enjoy participating in?
29. What are some of the activities which the school does not have that you would like to see included?

Summarize the salient features of the interview with the student, then have him evaluate to you what the interview meant. Indicate again our interest in him and hope that we will all profit from this and the other interviews. In these

202

steps we can uncover misunderstandings and misinterpretations. Above all we can leave the student with good feelings about the interview.

In dictating your notes on each interview indicate your overall impressions about each pupil and his situation. This will provide perspective to the many answers reported.

II. Information Obtainable from Room Directors and Counselors*

1. Kinds of friends pupil has.
2. Family situation
3. Interests and hobbies
4. Teachers, persons who know pupil best
5. Kinds of difficulties pupil has had
6. Socio-economic status of family
7. Pupil's attitudes and emotional status
8. Acceptance by his peers

III. Information Obtainable from Records*

1. Physical, health record
2. Socio-economic status (father's occupation, mother's employment), ethnic and religious groups (church attendance), neighborhood
3. Family situation
4. Pupil's stated interests
5. Out-of-school jobs held
6. Number of brothers and sisters

*Much of this data is to corroborate information gathered in the interview; much is to add to and fill out information obtained from the pupil himself. The interviewer may familiarize himself with this material in preparing for his interviews, but he will not be the one charged with collecting and recording it.

IV. Below are points to hit hard in your evaluation-summaries. Apparently some of these are easy to dodge. I think we need to pin ourselves down to answering these questions if

203

our material is going to be of greatest value for the study itself but more importantly to the kids involved and their counselors, departments, activities sponsors, parents, etc.

1. Why is the student achieving well or over-achieving? What points, brought out in your interview, seemed to point to the answer(s)?
2. How do adults fit into the picture of his achievement?
3. What is your overall impression of his full school (curricular and school-related extra-curricular) experiences? (job, etc., experiences as well)
4. How has the school been helpful? How has it failed to be helpful?
5. How accurate a picture can your report give of this pupil? (What was his reaction to the interview?)
6. WHAT RECOMMENDATIONS (TO WHOM) WOULD YOU MAKE CONCERNING THIS STUDENT THAT MIGHT HELP HIM AND OTHERS IN THEIR WORK WITH HIM? (WHAT SPECIFIC INFORMATION SHOULD BE PASSED ON TO WHOM?)

EVANSTON INTERVIEW STUDY

Form II

Achievement, Ability, and Aptitude Scores Form

| Name | Home Room | Class |

IQ Scores _____

Achievement Reading _____   Vocational Interest Natural _____

Achievement Math _____   Vocational Interest Mechanical _____

Achievement English _____   Vocational Interest Business _____

Achievement Total _____   Vocational Interest Arts _____

    PMA   Verbal _____   Vocational Interest Scientific _____

    PMA   Space _____   Vocational Interest Verbal _____

    PMA   Reason _____   Vocational Interest Manipulative _____

    PMA   Number _____   Vocational Interest Computative _____

    PMA   Word _____   Vocational Interest Levels _____

    PMA   Total _____

Teachers - English _____

      Foreign Lang. _____

      Math _____

      Nat. Science _____

      Social Studies _____

      Art _____

      Music _____

      Indust. Arts _____

      Home Econ. _____

      Bus. Educa. _____

      Speech _____

      Health & P. E. _____

205

EVANSTON INTERVIEW STUDY

Form III

Grade Record Form

Name		HR		Class

REVIEW OF PREVIOUS REPORTS (Part of Interview-Studies No. 2 and No. 3)

To gather data on the "high achiever" that is comparable to that already obtained on the "under-achiever", previous reports are revised and the data summarized below.

	English	For. Lang.	Math.	Science	Soc. Std.	Art	Music	Ind. Arts	Home Ec.	Bus. Ed.	Speech	H. E. = P. E.	Absence
Grade (Yr) 12 (1st S)													
Grade (Yr) 11 (1st S)													
Grade (Yr) 10 (1st S)													
Grade (Yr) 9 (1st S)													

	Eng.	Lit.	So. St.	Mth.	G. Sc.	Mus.	Arts	Man. Art	All Art	P. E.	Sch. Cit.	Absence (Half Days)
Grade 8												
Grade 7												

Grade 6	Kind of comment
	Areas of favorable comment
	Areas of unfavorable comment

Grade 5	Kind of comment
	Areas of favorable comment
	Areas of unfavorable comment

206

EVANSTON INTERVIEW STUDY

Form IV
Student Personal Data Form

Name	HR	Class

DATA FROM HOMEROOM FOLDER

The following is information gleaned from the records of the first 50 pupils studied in connection with our study of "under-achievers" (pupils with high IQs and average or below-average marks).

*1. Past serious illnesses   (including approximate dates)

*2. Present state of health

3. Date of "Student's Personal Data Blank"

4. Family situation   (Both parents living & together, etc.)

5. Father's occupation

6. Father's education

7. Mother's employment

8. Mother's education

9. Church preference (father's)

*Information will be provided by Health Services

10. Church preference (mother's)

---

11. Number of brothers and sisters

---

12. Hobbies and interests

---

13. Extra-curricular (In and outside of school activities)

---

14. Offices held honors received in activities (IN and outside of school)

---

15. Out of school jobs

---

16. Able to study at home

---

17. Subject liked best

---

18. Subject most difficult

---

19. College plans

---

20. Occupational-professional interests, aims

---

21. Names of several close friends, associates

Form V
Teacher Ratings of Students

Name_____ H. R. ____Class_____

Home Room Director_____

Counselor_____ Teacher _____

   This pupil, according to our records, achieves well in school subjects. He averages in marks at least ahead of 4 out of 5 pupils in our school. He may be achieving where he would be expected to achieve or he may be overachieving. Would you answer very briefly the questions which follow concerning this student? Answer only the questions where you can do so readily and without research. This information will supply us with data supplementary to an interview that we have had with this student. Incidentally, we are also combing the records and folders for supplementary data. We are eager to get from you your personal reactions and special information you may have that we might not find elsewhere.

1. With what kind of students does this student associate around school?

_____

2. How does he get along with other students? Is he well accepted?

_____

3. Is he well accepted by adults at school?

_____

4. What is the family situation? (Harmonious, both parents living and together, etc.)

_____

5. If you know the parents, do they allow the student too much freedom, etc?

6. What is the family able or unable to provide the student? (Encouragement, guidance, etc.)

7. What is the religious and nationality background of this pupil?

8. What is the family's socio-economic status? What kind of neighborhood do they live in? What kind of position does the father or mother hold?

9. What are the pupil's special interests in your class?

10. What hobbies and other interests do you know of?

11. What kind of difficulties has the pupil had?

12. What are this pupil's attitudes toward school?

13. What are this pupil's strengths?

14. What are this pupil's weaknesses?

15. How would you account for his high level of achievement?

210

The Self-Attitudes Inventory–
Evanston Township High School

EVANSTON INTERVIEW STUDY

SELF-ATTITUDES INVENTORY

Name _____ Home Room _____ Grade 9 10 11 12

last name   first name   middle name   (Circle appropriate number)

SCHOOL _____ Date _____

PART I

DIRECTIONS:

Below is a list of adjectives. At the left of each adjective is a blank. These blanks are headed I AM. Write in each blank in this column the number which best describes the kind of person you are. Do not spend too much time on any one adjective.

Write

5   if you are this sort of a person MOST of the time.

4   if you are this sort of a person a GOOD DEAL of the time.

3   if you are this sort of a person about HALF of the time.

2   if you are this sort of a person OCCASIONALLY.

1   if you are this sort of a person SELDOM.

At the right of each adjective is a blank. These blanks are headed I WISH I WERE. In each blank write the number which best describes how you wish you were.

Write

5   if you wish you were this sort of person MOST of the time.

4   if you wish you were this sort of person a GOOD DEAL of the time.

3   if you wish you were this sort of person about HALF of the time.

2   if you wish you were this sort of person OCCASIONALLY.

1   if you wish you were this sort of person SELDOM.

I AM	I WISH I WERE		I AM	I WISH I WERE
____ 1. accurate	____		____ 4. argumentative	____
____ 2. agreeable	____		____ 5. attractive	____
____ 3. ambitious	____		____ 6. bored	____

I AM		I WISH I WERE	I AM			I WISH I WERE
_____	7. bossy	_____	_____	23.	fearful	_____
_____	8. careless	_____	_____	24.	friendly	_____
_____	9. capable	_____	_____	25.	generous	_____
_____	10. cautious	_____	_____	26.	helpful	_____
_____	11. cheerful	_____	_____	27.	interesting	_____
_____	12. clear-thinking	_____	_____	28.	irritable	_____
_____	13. clever	_____	_____	29.	jealous	_____
_____	14. cliquish	_____	_____	30.	kind	_____
_____	15. competitive	_____	_____	31.	lazy	_____
_____	16. considerate	_____	_____	32.	likable	_____
_____	17. cooperative	_____	_____	33.	loyal	_____
_____	18. dependable	_____	_____	34.	modest	_____
_____	19. easy-going	_____	_____	35.	patient	_____
_____	20. energetic	_____	_____	36.	pesty	_____
_____	21. fault-finding	_____	_____	37.	poised	_____
_____	22. reckless	_____	_____	38.	popular	_____

I AM   I WISH I WERE   I AM   I WISH I WERE

	I AM	I WISH I WERE
39. rude	_____	_____
40. sarcastic	_____	_____
41. secure	_____	_____
42. self-centered	_____	_____
43. short-tempered	_____	_____
44. shy	_____	_____
45. silly	_____	_____
46. slow	_____	_____

	I AM	I WISH I WERE
47. sociable	_____	_____
48. stubborn	_____	_____
49. studious	_____	_____
50. tense	_____	_____
51. thoughtful	_____	_____
52. truthful	_____	_____
53. well-organized	_____	_____
54. worrying	_____	_____

PART II

DIRECTIONS:

Below are some statements on which you are asked again to rate yourself. For each of the statements circle the number in Column I, at the LEFT, which you think best describes your characteristics at THE PRESENT TIME. Then, circle the number in Column II, at the RIGHT, which best describes your WISH about each statement.

COLUMN I						ABILITIES	COLUMN II				
MY ABILITY IS AT PRESENT							I WISH MY ABILITY WERE				
VERY GREAT	GREAT	AVER-AGE	NOT TOO GREAT	SOMEWHAT SMALL			VERY GREAT	GREAT	AVER-AGE	NOT TOO GREAT	SOMEWHAT SMALL
1	2	3	4	5		1. to take criticism	1	2	3	4	5
1	2	3	4	5		2. to make decisions	1	2	3	4	5

COLUMN I MY ABILITY IS AT PRESENT					ABILITIES	COLUMN II I WISH MY ABILITY WERE				
VERY GREAT	GREAT	AVER-AGE	NOT TOO GREAT	SOMEWHAT SMALL		VERY GREAT	GREAT	AVER-AGE	NOT TOO GREAT	SOMEWHAT SMALL
1	2	3	4	5	3. to assume leadership	1	2	3	4	5
1	2	3	4	5	4. to work independently	1	2	3	4	5
1	2	3	4	5	5. to solve problems	1	2	3	4	5
1	2	3	4	5	6. to speak before groups	1	2	3	4	5
1	2	3	4	5	7. to express ideas in writing	1	2	3	4	5
1	2	3	4	5	8. to stick to my convictions	1	2	3	4	5
1	2	3	4	5	9. to think clearly	1	2	3	4	5
1	2	3	4	5	10. to carry out responsibility	1	2	3	4	5
1	2	3	4	5	11. my artistic ability	1	2	3	4	5
1	2	3	4	5	12. my athletic ability	1	2	3	4	5
1	2	3	4	5	13. my musical ability	1	2	3	4	5
1	2	3	4	5	14. my dramatic ability	1	2	3	4	5
1	2	3	4	5	15. my mechanical ability	1	2	3	4	5
1	2	3	4	5	16. my intellectual ability	1	2	3	4	5
1	2	3	4	5	17. my social ability	1	2	3	4	5
1	2	3	4	5	18. my self-confidence	1	2	3	4	5
1	2	3	4	5	19. my sense of humor	1	2	3	4	5
1	2	3	4	5	20. my appearance	1	2	3	4	5
1	2	3	4	5	21. my eagerness to learn	1	2	3	4	5
1	2	3	4	5	22. my judgment	1	2	3	4	5
1	2	3	4	5	23. my physical health	1	2	3	4	5
1	2	3	4	5	24. my imagination	1	2	3	4	5
1	2	3	4	5	25. my disposition	1	2	3	4	5

217

PART III

DIRECTIONS:

Below is another list of the same statements on which you rated yourself on the previous pages. For each statement circle the number in Column I at the LEFT, which best describes what OTHER PEOPLE THINK are your abilities. Then, circle the number in Column II at the RIGHT, which you think best describes what MOST OTHER PEOPLE'S ABILITIES ARE.

		COLUMN I					COLUMN II			
	WHAT OTHER PEOPLE THINK OF MY ABILITIES				ABILITIES	MOST OTHER PEOPLE'S ABILITIES				
VERY GREAT	GREAT	AVER-AGE	NOT TOO GREAT	SOMEWHAT SMALL		VERY GREAT	GREAT	AVER-AGE	NOT TOO GREAT	SOMEWHAT SMALL
1	2	3	4	5	1. to take criticism is	1	2	3	4	5
1	2	3	4	5	2. to make decisions is	1	2	3	4	5
1	2	3	4	5	3. to assume leadership is	1	2	3	4	5
1	2	3	4	5	4. to work independently is	1	2	3	4	5
1	2	3	4	5	5. to solve problems is	1	2	3	4	5
1	2	3	4	5	6. to speak before groups is	1	2	3	4	5
1	2	3	4	5	7. to express ideas in writing is	1	2	3	4	5
1	2	3	4	5	8. to stick to my convictions is	1	2	3	4	5
1	2	3	4	5	9. to think clearly is	1	2	3	4	5
1	2	3	4	5	10. to carry out responsibility is	1	2	3	4	5

COLUMN I WHAT OTHER PEOPLE THINK OF MY ABILITIES					ABILITIES	COLUMN II MOST OTHER PEOPLE'S ABILITIES				
VERY GREAT	GREAT	AVER-AGE	NOT TOO GREAT	SOMEWHAT SMALL		VERY GREAT	GREAT	AVER-AGE	NOT TOO GREAT	SOMEWHAT SMALL
1	2	3	4	5	11. artistic ability is	1	2	3	4	5
1	2	3	4	5	12. athletic ability is	1	2	3	4	5
1	2	3	4	5	13. musical ability is	1	2	3	4	5
1	2	3	4	5	14. dramatic ability is	1	2	3	4	5
1	2	3	4	5	15. mechanical ability is	1	2	3	4	5
1	2	3	4	5	16. intellectual ability is	1	2	3	4	5
1	2	3	4	5	17. social ability is	1	2	3	4	5
1	2	3	4	5	18. self-confidence is	1	2	3	4	5
1	2	3	4	5	19. sense of humor is	1	2	3	4	5
1	2	3	4	5	20. appearance is	1	2	3	4	5
1	2	3	4	5	21. eagerness to learn is	1	2	3	4	5
1	2	3	4	5	22. judgment is	1	2	3	4	5
1	2	3	4	5	23. physical health is	1	2	3	4	5
1	2	3	4	5	24. imagination is	1	2	3	4	5
1	2	3	4	5	25. disposition is	1	2	3	4	5

PART IV

DIRECTIONS:

Below is a list of the same adjectives and phrases that you had in an earlier section. At the left of each adjective or phrase is a blank. These blanks are headed MOST PEOPLE THINK I AM. At the right of each adjective or phrase is another blank. These blanks are headed MOST HIGH SCHOOL STUDENTS ARE. Fill in the blanks on the left with the number which best describes how most people think you are. Fill in the blanks on the right with the number which best describes how most high school students are.

Write

5   if the adjective or phrase applies MOST of the time.

4   if the adjective or phrase applies a GOOD DEAL of the time.

3   if the adjective or phrase applies about HALF the time.

2   if the adjective or phrase applies OCCASIONALLY.

1   if the adjective or phrase applies SELDOM.

MOST PEOPLE THINK I AM		MOST HIGH SCHOOL STUDENTS ARE	MOST PEOPLE THINK I AM		MOST HIGH SCHOOL STUDENTS ARE
_____	1. accurate	_____	_____	6. bored	_____
_____	2. agreeable	_____	_____	7. bossy	_____
_____	3. ambitious	_____	_____	8. careless	_____
_____	4. argumentative	_____	_____	9. capable	_____
_____	5. attractive	_____	_____	10. cautious	_____

MOST PEOPLE THINK I AM	MOST HIGH SCHOOL STUDENTS ARE		
_____	_____	11.	cheerful
_____	_____	12.	clear-thinking
_____	_____	13.	clever
_____	_____	14.	cliquish
_____	_____	15.	competitive
_____	_____	16.	considerate
_____	_____	17.	cooperative
_____	_____	18.	dependable
_____	_____	19.	easy-going
_____	_____	20.	energetic
_____	_____	21.	fault-finding
_____	_____	22.	reckless
_____	_____	23.	fearful
_____	_____	24.	friendly
_____	_____	25.	generous
_____	_____	26.	helpful
_____	_____	27.	interesting
_____	_____	28.	irritable
_____	_____	29.	jealous
_____	_____	30.	kind
_____	_____	31.	lazy
_____	_____	32.	likable

MOST PEOPLE THINK I AM	MOST HIGH SCHOOL STUDENTS ARE		
_____	_____	33.	loyal
_____	_____	34.	modest
_____	_____	35.	patient
_____	_____	36.	pesty
_____	_____	37.	poised
_____	_____	38.	popular
_____	_____	39.	rude
_____	_____	40.	sarcastic
_____	_____	41.	secure
_____	_____	42.	self-centered
_____	_____	43.	short-tempered
_____	_____	44.	shy
_____	_____	45.	silly
_____	_____	46.	slow
_____	_____	47.	sociable
_____	_____	48.	stubborn
_____	_____	49.	studious
_____	_____	50.	tense
_____	_____	51.	thoughtful
_____	_____	52.	truthful
_____	_____	53.	well-organized
_____	_____	54.	worrying

Details of Item Selection, Rating Procedures, Pretesting, and Scoring of the Self-Attitudes Inventory

Selection of items

The majority of items was selected from the interviews described in the previous section. Items were grouped into two parts on the inventory. One part contained phrases descriptive of Abilities: *to take criticism, to think clearly, intellectual ability,* etc.; the other part contained adjectives descriptive of personal Characteristics such as *ambitious, cheerful, clever, fearful, secure, well-organized,* etc. The two totals, 25 items referred to hereafter in the discussion as Abilities and 60 items referred to hereafter as Characteristics, were included in the first draft of the Self-Attitudes Inventory.

Rating procedures

The Ability items called for ratings on a five-point scale from "1," "very great," to "5," "somewhat small." The Characteristics called for ratings on a 5-point scale, from "5," designating a response of "most of the time," to "1," corresponding to "seldom." The words "always" and "never" were avoided, as they had been in the Bills Index of Adjustment and Values, in order to increase the probability of occurrence of ratings at the extreme of the scale.

Pretesting the inventory

The initial draft of the instrument was administered to 50 eleventh- and twelfth-grade students selected more or less at random from two homeroom sections. The major purpose of the pretesting was to determine the attitudes of a group of high school students toward completing such an inventory. Toward this end, the participating students were called together after completing the test for a discussion of the problems they had encountered and their feelings about taking such a test. In general, the students found the task relatively simple but wanted to know the purpose of the testing. Students suggested that before the test was administered the student body should be

222

informed of the reasons for it, of how it could help the school work better with the students, understand the students better, etc. In addition, the students suggested that some of the adjectives be removed from the inventory because of ambiguity or difficulty of rating honestly, such as *mature, cynical, disorganized,* etc. Both of these suggestions were followed. The administration procedures included a statement of purpose, and the items viewed as ambiguous by the pilot group of students were eliminated.

The 50 inventories were also analyzed for the negative-positive values assigned to each adjective, and those on which there was no clear cut designation were eliminated. The direction of each item was determined by its mean "I wish" score. Thus, any adjective whose mean "I wish" score fell at or above 4 was considered positive; any whose score fell at or below 2 was considered negative. *Talkative,* with a mean "I wish" score of 2.9, and *curious,* with a mean "I wish" score of 3.4, were eliminated. The remaining adjectives were clearly distinguishable as positive or negative in the pilot sample of 50 papers. After all eliminations, 54 of the original 60 Characteristics items and all 25 of the Abilities items remained in the inventory.

Scoring the inventory

For each of the 250 students in the sample a total score was derived for each of the scales ("My ability is," "I wish my ability were," "Most people think my ability is," "Most high school students' ability is") and the six discrepancy scores (discrepancy between each pair of variables). Separate total scores were derived for the Abilities section and the Characteristics section on the several scales. Thus, each student had 20 total scores.

Since the Characteristics list was composed of both negative and positive traits, it was necessary to reverse the scores on the negative items before adding them into the total. With the direction (negative or positive) of each item determined by the pretesting, the reversals could be made automatically. No such reversals were necessary for the Abilities since all of them dealt with positive aspects of the individual's functioning.

The discrepancy scores were derived by summing (without regard to sign) the item by item differences between an individual's

223

responses on any two scales. Since the discrepancy score was used as a measure of the individual's perceived distance between, for example, his present status and his wished-for status, the direction of the differences was not considered relevant.

The Abilities section was initially rated on a 1 to 5 scale, where 1 was "very great" and 5 was "somewhat small." Thus, the total scores on Abilities went from low to high, the lower score representing the higher assessment.

In order to derive a quantitative score, the 5 points, represented on the Characteristics scales by the letters M (most of the time), G (a good deal of the time), H (about half of the time), O (occasionally) and S (seldom), were translated into the numbers 5, 4, 3, 2, 1 respectively; "1" represented the lowest score, "5," the highest. Negative items which were rated 4 or 5 were given a value of 2 or 1, respectively; those rated 1 or 2 were given a value of 5 and 4 respectively. The 3 rating remained unchanged. Thus the higher the score on the Characteristics items, the higher the assessment.

Table B-1. One-way Analysis of Variance of Scores for Five Groups on Perceived Abilities ("My ability is")

Degree of Variation	Sums of Squares	df	Mean Squares	F	$F_{.95}$
Within groups	27062.46	245	110.46		
Between groups	5244.22	4	1311.05	11.87[a]	2.41
Total	32306.68	249			

[a] Significant at or beyond the .05 level.

Table B-2. One-way Analysis of Variance of Scores for Five Groups on
Perceived Estimates by Others of Own Abilities
("Other people think my abilities are")

Degree of Variation	Sums of Squares	df	Mean Squares	F	$F_{.95}$
Within groups	31406.50	245	128.19		
Between groups	3848.10	4	962.02	7.50[a]	2.41
Total	35254.60	249			

[a] Significant at or beyond the .05 level.

Table B-3. One-way Analysis of Variance of Scores for Five Groups on
Perceived Abilities of Others ("Most other people's abilities are")

Degree of Variation	Sums of Squares	df	Mean Squares	F	$F_{.95}$
Within groups	19145.42	245	78.14		
Between groups	1280.98	4	320.24	4.10[a]	2.41
Total	20426.40	249			

[a] Significant at or beyond the .05 level.

Table B-4. One-way Analysis of Vaiance of Scores for Five Groups on
Wished-for Abilities ("I wish my ability were")

Degree of Variation	Sums of Squares	df	Mean Squares	F	$F_{.95}$
Within groups	29649.48	245	121.02		
Between groups	7449.94	4	1862.48	15.39[a]	2.41
Total	37099.42	249			

[a] Significant at or beyond the .05 level.

Table B-5. One-way Analysis of Variance of Discrepancy Scores for
Five Groups Between Perceived Abilities ("My ability is")
and Wished-for Abilities ("I wish my ability were")

Degree of Variation	Sums of Squares	df	Mean Squares	F	$F_{.95}$
Within groups	22424.30	245	91.53		
Between groups	683.80	4	170.95	1.87	2.41
Total	23108.10	249			

Table B-6. One-way Analysis of Variance of Discrepancy Scores for
Five Groups Between Perceived Abilities ("My ability is")
and Perceived Estimates by Others of Own Abilities
("Other people think my abilities are")

Degree of Variation	Sums of Squares	df	Mean Squares	F	$F_{.95}$
Within groups	7526.38	245	30.72		
Between groups	785.62	4	196.40	6.39[a]	2.41
Total	8312.00	249			

[a] Significant at or beyond the .05 level.

Table B-7. One-way Analysis of Variance of Scores for Five Groups
on Perceived Characteristics ("I am")

Degree of Variation	Sums of Squares	df	Mean Squares	F	$F_{.95}$
Within groups	105403.44	245	430.22		
Between groups	4534.62	4	1133.65	2.365	2.41
Total	109938.06	249			

Table B-8. One-way Analysis of Variance of Scores for Five Groups on
Perceived Estimates of Own Characteristics by Others
("Most people think I am")

Degree of Variation	Sums of Squares	df	Mean Squares	F	$F_{.95}$
Within groups	117770.90	245	480.70		
Between groups	7381.82	4	1845.45	3.84[a]	2.41
Total	125152.72	249			

[a] Significant at or beyond the .05 level.

Table B-9. One-way Analysis of Variance of Scores for Five Groups on
Perceived Characteristics of Others
("Most high school students are")

Degree of Variation	Sums of Squares	df	Mean Squares	F	$F_{.95}$
Within groups	101570.76	245	414.57		
Between groups	10273.10	4	2568.28	6.195[a]	2.41
Total	111843.86	249			

[a] Significant at or beyond the .05 level.

Table B-10. One-way Analysis of Variance of Scores for Five Groups on
Wished-for Characteristics ("I wish I were")

Degree of Variation	Sums of Squares	df	Mean Squares	F	$F_{.95}$
Within groups	101351.46	245	413.68		
Between groups	22582.44	4	5645.61	13.65[a]	2.41
Total	123936.90	249			

[a] Significant at or beyond the .05 level.

Table B-11. One-way Analysis of Variance of Discrepancy Scores for
Five Groups Between Perceived Characteristics ("I am") and
Wished-for Characteristics ("I wish I were")

Degree of Variation	Sums of Squares	df	Mean Squares	F	$F_{.95}$
Within groups	118456.12	245	483.49		
Between groups	3695.06	4	923.77	1.91	2.41
Total	122151.18	249			

Table B-12. One-way Analysis of Variance of Discrepancy Scores for
Five Groups Between Perceived Characteristics ("I am") and
Perceived Estimates of Own Characteristics by Others
("Other people think I am")

Degree of Variation	Sums of Squares	df	Mean Squares	F	$F_{.95}$
Within groups	38468.54	245	151.01		
Between groups	5410.36	4	1352.59	8.61[a]	2.41
Total	43878.90	249			

[a] Significant at or beyond the .05 level.

228

The School-Attitudes Inventory— Evanston Township High School

EVANSTON INTERVIEW STUDY

Horace Mann-Lincoln Institute of School Experimentation
Teachers College, Columbia University

SCHOOL-ATTITUDES INVENTORY

Name _____ Home Room _____ Grade 9 10 11 12
    last name   first name   middle name   (Circle appropriate number)

EVANSTON TOWNSHIP HIGH SCHOOL   Date _____

1. Think over all the courses you now have (or have had) at high school. Then answer the
    following questions:

    A. The subject I like (or have liked) best is _____ (course title)
        because I find (or have found) it . . . . (Check at the left any or all of the following
        that apply.)

        _____ 1. Especially interesting

        _____ 2. Easy

        _____ 3. Challenging

        _____ 4. Satisfying and comfortable in class atmosphere

        _____ 5. Useful in my plans for the future

B. The subject I like (or have liked) <u>second best is</u> _____ (course title) because I find (or have found) it . . . . . (Check at the left any or all of the following that apply.)

_____ 1. Especially interesting

_____ 2. Easy

_____ 3. Challenging

_____ 4. Satisfying and comfortable in class atmosphere

_____ 5. Useful in my plans for the future

C. The subjects I like almost as well as those noted above are . . . . . (List in the space provided below.)

_____

_____

_____

_____

_____

_____

232

D. The subject I like (or have liked) least is _____(course title) because, as compared to the subjects I like (or have liked) best, I find (or have found) it . . . . (Check at the left any or all of the following that apply.)

1. Least interesting

2. Most difficult

3. Least challenging

4. Least satisfying and comfortable in class atmosphere

5. Of least use in my plans for the future

E. The subject I like (or have liked) next to least is_____(course title) because, as compared to the subjects I like (or have liked) best, I find (or have found) it . . . . (Check at the left any or all of the following that apply.)

1. Least interesting

2. Most difficult

3. Least challenging

4. Least satisfying and comfortable in class atmosphere

5. Of least use in my plans for the future

F. Comments:_____

233

2. Students differ in what they expect the high school to provide. Below is a list of pairs of such expectations. From each pair select the one statement which best represents what you yourself think is more important for the high school to provide. Certain choices may be especially hard for you to make. However, even if you think the high school should provide both items, select the one which you feel is more important. Circle the number 1 or 2 at the left of the one statement in each pair that you feel is the MORE IMPORTANT FUNCTION OF THE SCHOOL.

I feel it is more important for the high school to help students . . .

A. 1. Prepare for college
   2. Learn to work better with people

B. 1. Solve their personal problems
   2. Develop new ideas and learn to evaluate ideas critically

C. 1. Acquire knowledge in various subjects
   2. Learn to get along better with members of the same and opposite sex

D. 2. Learn to plan for and participate in school activities and organizations
   1. Become healthy, happy people

E. 2. Develop good attitudes toward learning and toward high scholarship standards
   1. Prepare for a vocation or profession

234

F. 1. Become more friendly, cooperative, fair-minded and tolerant

   2. Learn how to study and how to communicate with others

G. 1. Learn to get along better with members of the same and opposite sex

   2. Prepare for college

H. 1. Develop new ideas and learn to evaluate ideas critically

   2. Become more friendly, cooperative, fair-minded, and tolerant

I. 1. Acquire knowledge in various subjects

   2. Solve their personal problems

J. 1. Develop good attitudes toward learning and toward high scholarship standards

   2. Learn to plan for and participate in school activities and organizations

K. 1. Prepare for a vocation or profession

   2. Become healthy, happy people

L. 1. Learn to work better with other people

   2. Learn how to study and how to communicate with others.

M. 1. Prepare for college

   2. Learn to plan for and participate in school activities and organizations

N. 1. Learn to work better with other people

   2. Develop new ideas and learn to evaluate ideas critically

O. 1. Become more friendly, cooperative, fair-minded, and tolerant

   2. Acquire knowledge in various subjects

P. 1. Learn to get along better with members of the same and opposite sex

   2. Develop good attitudes toward learning and toward high scholarship standards

Q. 1. Solve their personal problems

   2. Prepare for a vocation or profession

R. 1. Become healthy, happy people
   2. Learn how to study and how to communicate with others

S. 1. Become more friendly, cooperative, fair-minded, and tolerant
   2. Prepare for college

T. 1. Develop new ideas and learn to evaluate ideas critically
   2. Become healthy, happy people

U. 1. Learn to work better with other people
   2. Acquire knowledge in various subjects

V. 1. Develop good attitudes toward learning and toward high scholarship standards
   2. Solve their personal problems

W. 1. Learn to plan for and participate in school activities and organizations
   2. Prepare for a vocation or profession

X. 1. Learn how to study and how to communicate with others
   2. Learn to get along better with members of the same and opposite sex

Y. 1. Prepare for college
   2. Become healthy, happy people

Z. 1. Develop new ideas and learn to evaluate ideas critically
   2. Learn to plan for and participate in school activities and organizations

AA. 1. Acquire knowledge in various subjects
    2. Learn to get along better with members of the same and opposite sex

BB. 1. Become more friendly, cooperative, fair-minded, and tolerant
    2. Develop good attitudes toward learning and toward high scholarship standards

CC. 1. Prepare for a vocation or profession
    2. Learn to work better with other people

DD. 1. Learn how to study and how to communicate with others

2. Solve their personal problems

EE. 1. Solve their personal problems

2. Prepare for college

FF. 1. Learn to get along better with members of the same and opposite sex

2. Develop new ideas and learn to evaluate ideas critically

GG. 1. Become healthy, happy people

2. Acquire knowledge in various subjects

HH. 1. Develop good attitudes toward learning and toward high scholarship standards

2. Learn to work better with other people

II. 1. Prepare for a vocation or pro-fession

2. Become more friendly, cooperative, fair-minded, and tolerant

JJ. 1. Learn how to study and how to communicate with others

2. Learn to plan for and participate in school activities and organizations

Comments: _____

237

3. In question 2, you selected from pairs of expectations the ones which you feel are more important for a high school to meet. In this question, you are to indicate HOW WELL you think your school has actually met your expectations.

Read all the statements. Then rank them from 1 - 12. Place the number 1 on the line at the left of the area in which the high school has done the BEST JOB; 2 for the NEXT BEST JOB, etc.; and 12 for the POOREST JOB.

I rank the following (1 - 12) in terms of HOW WELL high school has actually met my expectations in helping students . . .

_____ A. Prepare for college

_____ B. Learn to work better with people

_____ C. Solve their personal problems

_____ D. Develop new ideas and learn to evaluate ideas critically

_____ E. Acquire knowledge in various subjects

_____ F. Learn to plan for and participate in school activities and organizations

_____ G. Develop good attitudes toward learning and toward high scholarship standards

_____ H. Become healthy, happy people

_____ I. Prepare for a vocation or profession

_____ J. Learn to get along better with members of the same and opposite sex

_____ K. Become more friendly, cooperative, fair-minded, and tolerant

_____ L. Learn how to study and how to communicate with others

238

Comments: _____

_____

4. From time to time, students have suggested certain changes which they feel would improve the school. Circle the number at the right which best describes how you feel. Circle the 1 if you think there should be MORE, the 2 if you think that it's o.k. AS IS, the 3 if there should be LESS of the activities and procedures listed. Omit any item with which you have had too little experience on which to make a judgment.

I feel as follows about changes suggested in activities listed below . . .

	more	as is	less	comments or suggestions
A. Time spent in official class	1	2	3	
B. Time spent in home room period	1	2	3	
C. Special interest clubs (Latin Club, Chess Club, International Round Table, etc.)	1	2	3	

239

		more	as is	less	comments or suggestions
D.	Music activities	1	2	3	
E.	Dramatics activities	1	2	3	
F.	Art activities	1	2	3	
G.	Scholarship awards and special recognition	1	2	3	
H.	Extra-curricular activities	1	2	3	
I.	College counseling	1	2	3	
J.	Course selection counseling	1	2	3	
K.	Vocational Guidance	1	2	3	
L.	Personal guidance	1	2	3	
M.	Required courses	1	2	3	
N.	Homework	1	2	3	
O.	Teacher assistance and interest in students' academic work	1	2	3	
P.	Teachers' interest in students as persons	1	2	3	
Q.	Discipline	1	2	3	

240

	more	as is	less	comments or suggestions
R. Special interest courses (Music, Art, Science Seminar)	1	2	3	
S. Athletics	1	2	3	
T. Guidance testing	1	2	3	
U. Subject matter tests	1	2	3	
V. Competition (in class, activities, etc.)	1	2	3	
W. Opportunities for independent rather than assigned projects	1	2	3	
X. Advanced and honors courses	1	2	3	
Y. Elective courses	1	2	3	
Z. School parties, open houses, and dances	1	2	3	

5. No student can share in all of the experiences which a school provides. Because of interest, abilities, and time each person becomes more involved in some areas than others. However, students looking back at what has happened in school sometimes wish they had had more experiences in some areas than they actually did.

Below is a list of such school experiences. Read each one and circle the number on the right which best describes your feelings about that particular area.

		WANT NO MORE			WANT MORE			Comments and Suggestions
		Had Many	Had Some	Had Few or None	Had Many	Had Some	Had Few or None	
A.	Experiences in school athletics (varsity and intramural)	1	2	3	4	5	6	
B.	Opportunities for membership in clubs	1	2	3	4	5	6	
C.	Experiences in student government	1	2	3	4	5	6	
D.	Experiences in orchestra, band, chorus	1	2	3	4	5	6	
E.	Experiences in dramatics	1	2	3	4	5	6	
F.	Experiences in cheerleading	1	2	3	4	5	6	
G.	Opportunities for dating	1	2	3	4	5	6	
H.	Friendships	1	2	3	4	5	6	
I.	Scholastic honors	1	2	3	4	5	6	

	WANT NO MORE			WANT MORE			Comments and Suggestions
	Had Many	Had Some	Had Few or None	Had Many	Had Some	Had Few or None	
J. Awards for special abilities other than academic	1	2	3	4	5	6	
K. Offices	1	2	3	4	5	6	
L. Opportunities to choose courses	1	2	3	4	5	6	
M. School responsibilities	1	2	3	4	5	6	
N. Interesting courses	1	2	3	4	5	6	
O. Opportunities to develop good study habits	1	2	3	4	5	6	
P. Opportunities for teacher assistance	1	2	3	4	5	6	
Q. Opportunities for leadership (other than offices)	1	2	3	4	5	6	

243

6. There are always a number of factors which help a person to become a recognized leader. Some of these factors are listed below. Circle the number under the statement which best describes how important you think each factor is in making a person a recognized leader in your school. Circle the 1 if you think the factor is of GREAT IMPORTANCE, the 2 if of CONSIDERABLE IMPORTANCE, etc.

Factors	Of Great Importance	Of Considerable Importance	Of Some Importance	Of Little Importance	Of No Importance
A. Personal qualities of the leader himself	1	2	3	4	5
B. Home room director's influence	1	2	3	4	5
C. Help of student cliques	1	2	3	4	5
D. Academic standing of leader	1	2	3	4	5
E. Teacher's influence	1	2	3	4	5
F. Athletic ability of the leader	1	2	3	4	5
G. Family position of the leader	1	2	3	4	5

Factors	Of Great Importance	Of Considerable Importance	Of Some Importance	Of Little Importance	Of No Importance
	1	2	3	4	5
H. Appearance of the leader					
I. Others (specify)					

Comments: _____

_____

_____

_____

_____

_____

_____

_____

_____

7. Below is a list of in-school extra-curricular organizations to which students frequently belong. In Column I check the ones YOU NOW BELONG TO; in Column II, the ones you have BELONGED TO IN THE PAST; in Column III name the OFFICES YOU ARE NOW HOLDING; in Column IV, the OFFICES YOU HAVE HELD IN THE PAST in each of the organizations of which you are (or were) a member.

In-School Organizations	I Belong Now	II Offices Now Holding	III Belonged in Past	IV Offices Held in Past
A. Student government				
B. Trireme, Quadrangle, Pentangle				
C. Athletics				
D. Art clubs				
E. Music clubs, or band, orchestra or glee club				
F. Journalism staff				
G. Radio, audio-visual, and drama clubs				
H. Others (specify)				

8. Below is a list of out-of-school organizations to which students frequently belong. In Column I check the ones YOU NOW BELONG TO; in Column II, the ones you have BELONGED TO IN THE PAST; in Column III name the OFFICES YOU ARE NOW HOLDING; in Column IV, the OFFICES YOU HAVE HELD IN THE PAST in each of the organizations of which you are (or were) a member.

	I	II	III	IV
Out-of-School Organizations	Belong Now	Offices Now Holding	Belonged in Past	Offices Held in Past
A. 'Y' Club				
B. YWCA				
C. Junior Achievement				
D. Church youth group				
E. Scouts				
F. Others (specify)				

247

9. The following activities take up the out-of-school time of many high school students. AT THE RIGHT indicate approximately HOW OFTEN you engage in each pursuit during a week. CIRCLE the number under the statement which best describes your participation.

On the line AT THE LEFT of each item write the approximate number of HOURS PER WEEK that you spend on each activity.

Hours Per Week		Almost Daily	2-3 Times a Week	Once a Week	Occasion-ally	Not at All
_____	A. I watch television	1	2	3	4	5
_____	B. I listen to radio and record player	1	2	3	4	5
_____	C. I practice musical instruments	1	2	3	4	5
_____	D. I read for pleasure	1	2	3	4	5
_____	E. I attend scouts	1	2	3	4	5
_____	F. I attend other club meetings of one kind or another	1	2	3	4	5
_____	G. I participate in sports	1	2	3	4	5
_____	H. I work at hobbies	1	2	3	4	5
_____	I. I go to church services or church school (excluding club-type activities)	1	2	3	4	5

Hours Per Week		Almost Daily	2-3 Times a Week	Once a Week	Occasionally	Not at All
_____	J. I go out on a date	1	2	3	4	5
_____	K. I get together or go out with one or more friends of my sex	1	2	3	4	5
_____	L. I go out alone	1	2	3	4	5
_____	M. I go out with a crowd	1	2	3	4	5
_____	N. I do homework	1	2	3	4	5
_____	O. I work for pay	1	2	3	4	5
_____	P. I work on jobs at home	1	2	3	4	5
_____	Q. I do things with my family	1	2	3	4	5
_____	R. I go to the movies	1	2	3	4	5
_____	S. I study things not assigned for homework	1	2	3	4	5

Comments: _____

_____

249

10. Students usually discuss their problems at some time or another with someone. Circle the number at the right which best tells how often you yourself discuss your problems with the various people listed below. Circle the 1 if you discuss your problems with the person FREQUENTLY, the 2 if OCCASIONALLY, and the 3 if SELDOM.

I discuss my . . .

		Frequently	Occasionally	Seldom
A.	Educational problems with my mother	1	2	3
B.	Educational problems with my father	1	2	3
C.	Educational problems with some other member of my family	1	2	3
D.	Educational problems with a close friend of the same sex	1	2	3
E.	Educational problems with my friend of the opposite sex	1	2	3
F.	Educational problems with some teachers	1	2	3
G.	Educational problems with my guidance counselors	1	2	3
H.	Educational problems with my minister	1	2	3
I.	Educational problems with my doctor	1	2	3
J.	Educational problems with my neighbors	1	2	3
K.	Personal problems with my mother	1	2	3

		Frequently	Occasionally	Seldom
L.	Personal problems with my father	1	2	3
M.	Personal problems with some other member of my family	1	2	3
N.	Personal problems with a close friend of the same sex	1	2	3
O.	Personal problems with my friend of the opposite sex	1	2	3
P.	Personal problems with some teachers	1	2	3
Q.	Personal problems with my guidance counselors	1	2	3
R.	Personal problems with my minister	1	2	3
S.	Personal problems with my doctor	1	2	3
T.	Personal problems with my neighbors	1	2	3

Comments: _____

_____

_____

_____

11. Parents have a variety of attitudes and opinions toward their son's and daughter's school life. Below are a number of statements representing parental attitudes. For each item circle the number at the LEFT of the one statement which you think best describes the attitudes of your parents.

A. To my parents, my school life is of
   1. Great interest
   2. Some interest
   3. Little interest

B. My parents feel that the program (school subjects) offered at ETHS is
   1. Full and varied
   2. Limited in some important areas
   3. Inadequate in many areas

C. My parents feel that in general ETHS is offering me
   1. The best possible school experience
   2. A good school experience
   3. Only a fair school experience

D. My parents feel that the amount of social activity I take part in at ETHS is
   1. Just about right
   2. Too great
   3. Too little

E. My parents feel that ETHS's academic standards
   1. Are too high for me
   2. Are fair and right for me
   3. Are too low for me

252

F. My parents' attitude toward what the school expects of me is best described as
   1. Wholehearted approval
   2. Considerable approval
   3. Considerable disapproval

G. My parents' attitude toward my school achievement is one of
   1. Complete satisfaction
   2. Considerable satisfaction
   3. Little or no satisfaction

H. My parents feel that my choice of elective subjects should be
   1. Largely guided by their decisions
   2. Determined by decisions made jointly by them and me
   3. Largely left to my own decision

I. My parents feel that whether I should complete high school or not should be
   1. Decided by them
   2. Decided jointly by them and me
   3. Decided by me

J. My parents feel that my post-high school plans should be guided by
   1. Their judgment of what is best for me
   2. Joint decisions made by them and me
   3. My own best judgment

K. My parents feel that, if I go to college, that college should be selected
   1. Largely on the basis of their preferences
   2. On the basis of joint discussion of the matter
   3. On the basis of my own preferences

253

L. In regard to homework, my parents
   1. Put a great deal of pressure on me
   2. Put some pressure on me
   3. Put little or no pressure on me

M. My parents feel that my going to college is
   1. Essential
   2. Desirable, but not essential
   3. Of little importance

Comments: _____

_____

_____

_____

_____

_____

_____

_____

_____

_____

254

12. Students find that they learn better under some circumstances than under others. In each of the questions below, select the one choice which best describes the circumstances which are most effective for you. Circle the number at the left of the choice you select.

A. I work harder when assignments are
   1. Required daily
   2. Required weekly
   3. Required for the semester
   4. Not required but left up to student's initiative

B. I learn more when assignments are
   1. Required daily
   2. Required weekly
   3. Required for the semester
   4. Not required but left up to student's initiative

C. I work harder for a course when tests or quizzes are
   1. Sprung at any time
   2. Given regularly every week
   3. Given at announced intervals
   4. Not given

D. I learn better when
   1. Each piece of work is evaluated and graded by the teacher
   2. Students grade their own work
   3. Study is recognized by grades at marking periods only
   4. There is no marking or evaluation at all

E. I am more likely to expend greater effort on courses which
   1. Will have practical value in my chosen profession
   2. Are related to, but not essential in my chosen profession
   3. I enjoy even if they are not related to my chosen profession

F. I get more out of a class when
   1. The teacher lectures
   2. The teacher directs a question and answer period
   3. There is a student-led discussion
   4. I am working with a small group on individual projects

Comments: _____

256

13. As you look over your high school experiences as a whole, which one of the following best describes your feeling?

_____ A. It has been almost entirely happy and enjoyable

_____ B. It has been generally happy and enjoyable

_____ C. It has been all right

_____ D. It has not been generally happy and enjoyable

_____ E. It has almost never been happy and enjoyable

Comments: _____

Details of Rating Procedures, Pretesting, and Scoring of the School-Attitudes Inventory

Rating procedures

The rating procedures varied with each section of the instrument. The scales included ranking (Sections 1 and 3); paired comparisons (Section 2); ratings (Sections 4 through 6 and 9 through 13); and tallying and enumerating (Sections 7 and 8).

Pretesting the instrument

A preliminary form of the School-Attitudes Inventory was pretested using the same population and within a few days of the Self-Attitudes Inventory. As a result of student responses on the inventory and their remarks and suggestions following administration of the preliminary forms, a few changes were made. For instance, an additional item was introduced in each section for open-ended comments. A section (8) specifying out-of-school organizations was added. The section (10) pertaining to confidants was revised to include ten items dealing with confidants used for educational problems and ten items dealing with confidants used for personal problems. The section (11) on parental reactions was revised from a form calling for "yes" and "no" responses to one eliciting ratings on a 3-point scale.

Table C-1. Frequency of Choices for Subjects Liked Best and
Subjects Liked Least by Each of Five Groups

Subject Area	H Liked Best	H Liked Least	U Liked Best	U Liked Least	O Liked Best	O Liked Least	L Liked Best	L Liked Least	R Liked Best	R Liked Least
Language and literature	11	14	6	10	11	15	10	13	9	15
Social studies	8	12	7	11	9	9	7	18	4	8
Mathematics	16	6	14	14	8	10	9	6	9	9
Sciences	7	8	12	4	7	4	4	5	12	3
Foreign languages	5	8	3	10	5	8	0	1	5	9
Art	1	0	2	0	5	0	2	2	4	1
Physical Education	0	2	1	0	0	3	2	1	2	1
Business, vocational, miscellaneous	1	0	4	1	3	1	16	4	4	4
No response	1	0	1	0	2	0	0	0	1	0
Total	50	50	50	50	50	50	50	50	50	50

Table C-2. Frequency of Choices for Subjects Liked Best and
Subjects Liked Least by Each of Five Groups by Categories

Subject Area	H Liked Best	H Liked Least	U Liked Best	U Liked Least	O Liked Best	O Liked Least	L Liked Best	L Liked Least	R Liked Best	R Liked Least
Humanities	19	26	13	21	20	24	17	31	13	23
Foreign languages	5	8	3	10	5	8	0	1	5	9
Mathematics and science	23	14	26	18	15	14	13	11	21	12
Art	1	0	2	0	5	0	2	2	4	1
Business, vocational, etc.	1	2	5	1	3	4	18	5	6	5
No response	1	0	1	0	2	0	0	0	1	0
Total	50	50	50	50	50	50	50	50	50	50

Table C-3. Frequency Distribution and Rank Order of Reasons for Selecting School Subjects as Best Liked by Each of Five Groups

Reason	H		U		O		L		R		Total	
	f	Rank	f	Rank	f	Rank	f	Rank	f	Rank	f	Rank
Interesting	43	1	43	1	41	1	32	1	38	1	197	5
Easy	7	5	11	5	11	5	10	5	10	5	49	25
Challenging	35	2	21	3	29	2	13	4	18	4	116	15
Satisfying and comfortable	27	3	18	4	22	4	21	3	21	3	109	17
Useful	24	4	24	2	30	3	23	2	27	2	128	13

Table C-4. Frequency Distribution and Rank Order of Reasons for Selecting School Subjects as Least Liked by Each of Five Groups

Reason	H		U		O		L		R		Total	
	f	Rank	f	Rank	f	Rank	f	Rank	f	Rank	f	Rank
Least interesting	28	1	27	2	24	1	20	2	23	2	122	8
Most difficult	18	4	30	1	20	2	30	1	29	1	127	9
Least challenging	19	3	8	5	10	5	4	5	4	5	45	23
Least satisfying	21	2	20	3	12	4	13	4	12	4	78	17
Least useful	15	5	14	4	17	3	16	3	14	3	76	18

260

Table C-5. Rank Order of School's Adequacy in Fulfilling Academic and Personal-Social Functions for Each of Five Groups

School Function	H	U	O	L	R
Academic:					
Prepare for college	1	1	1	1	1
Develop new ideas and learn to evaluate ideas critically	3	4	5	7	6
Acquire knowledge in various subjects	2	2	2	6	2
Develop good attitudes toward learning and toward high scholarship standards	4	7	4	2	5
Prepare for a vocation or profession	7	3	6	8	4
Learn how to study and how to communicate with others	6	6	7	5	7
Mean Rank for Academic Functions	3.9	3.0	4.2	4.9	4.2
Personal-Social:					
Learn to work better with other people	5	5	3	4	3
Solve personal problems	12	12	12	11	12
Learn to plan for and participate in school activities and organizations	8	8	8	3	8
Become healthy, happy people	11	11	10	10	11
Learn to get along better with members of same and opposite sex	10	10	11	12	10
Become friendly, cooperative, fair-minded, and tolerant	9	9	9	9	9
Mean rank for Personal-Social Functions	9.2	9.2	8.8	8.0	8.8

Table C-6. Frequency Distribution and Rank Order for Satisfaction on
Twenty-six School Provisions for Each of Five Groups

Item	H f	H Rank	U f	U Rank	O f	O Rank	L f	L Rank	R f	R Rank
Time spent in official class	43	1	36	2	44	1.5	38	1	46	1
Time spent in homeroom period	34	7	30	6.5	42	3	29	10	34	6.5
Special interest clubs	32	8	22	20	34	9	28	12.5	28	14
Music activities	27	15	27	11.5	29	16.5	25	17	28	14
Dramatic activities	27	15	28	10	29	16.5	31	7	32	10.5
Art activities	27	15	32	4	20	20	29	10	35	5
Scholarship awards and special recognition	22	22	22	20	19	21	20	22.5	20	22
Extracurricular activities	30	10	29	8.5	35	8.5	33	3	33	8.5
College counseling	12	26	16	25	15	26	14	26	20	22
Course selection counseling	21	24.5	19	24	16	24	17	24	15	26
Vocational guidance	23	20	24	14.5	16	24	20	22.5	17	24
Personal guidance	26	17.5	23	17.5	31	14	22	20	20	22
Required courses	40	2	37	1	44	1.5	32	5	36	4
Homework	30	10	24	14.5	32	12.5	24	18.5	25	18.5
Teacher assistance and interest in students' academic work	28	12.5	24	14.5	33	11	26	15.5	27	16
Teacher interest in students as persons	24	19	15	26	28	18	21	21	16	25
Discipline	36	4.5	31	5	40	4	32	5	34	6.5
Special interest courses	22	22	27	11.5	18	22	26	15.5	28	14
Athletics	37	3	29	8.5	39	6	28	12.5	38	2.5
Guidance testing	21	24.5	24	14.5	32	12.5	32	5	32	10.5
Subject matter tests	28	12.5	33	3	39	6	36	2	31	12
Competition	36	4.5	30	6.5	39	6	27	14	38	2.5
Opportunities for independent rather than assigned projects	26	17.5	21	22.5	16	24	29	10	26	17
Advances and honors courses	22	22	22	20	23	19	30	8	33	8.5
Elective courses	30	10	23	17.5	30	15	24	18.5	25	18.5
School parties, open houses, and dances	35	6	21	22.5	35	8.5	16	25	24	20

262

Table C-7. Group Frequencies and Means Per Student for Belonging to
In-School and Out-of-School Organizations during the School
Year 1955–56 and in the Past for Each of Five Groups

Organizations	H		U		O		L		R	
	f	M	f	M	f	M	f	M	f	M
In-school, 1955–56	112	2.2	94	1.9	122	2.4	52	1.0	70	1.4
In-school, past	99	2.0	77	1.5	81	1.6	39	0.8	61	1.2
Out-of-school, 1955–56	74	1.5	65	1.3	74	1.5	56	1.1	72	1.4
Out-of-school, past	85	1.7	67	1.3	85	1.7	39	0.8	74	1.5
Total	370	1.8	303	1.5	362	1.8	186	0.9	277	1.8

Table C-8. Group Frequencies and Means Per Student for Leadership
Positions Held in In-School and Out-of-School Organizations during
the School Year 1955–56 and in the Past for Each of Five Groups

Leadership Positions Held	H		U		O		L		R	
	f	M	f	M	f	M	f	M	f	M
In-school organizations, 1955–56	35	0.7	17	0.3	40	0.8	19	0.4	5	0.1
In-school organizations, past	38	0.8	21	0.4	45	0.9	9	0.2	15	0.3
Out-of-school organizations, 1955–56	32	0.7	20	0.4	27	0.5	15	0.3	28	0.6
Out-of-school organizations, past	59	1.2	39	0.8	50	1.0	20	0.4	48	1.0
Total	164	0.8	97	0.5	162	0.8	49	0.2	110	0.6

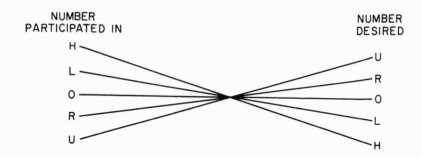

NUMBER
PARTICIPATED IN

NUMBER
DESIRED

H
L
O
R
U

U
R
O
L
H

Figure C-1. Rank order of groups on number of school experiences participated in and number desired.

Table C-9. Approximate Median Number of Hours per Week Spent in
Out-of-School Activities for Each of Five Groups

Activities	H	U	O	L	R
Watching television	5.5	6.5	5.0	4.5	6.5
Listening to radio and records	5.5	7.5	4.0	4.0	5.0
Practicing musical instruments	1.5	0.7	1.0	0.8	0.8
Reading (not for school)	4.0	4.0	3.5	2.5	3.0
Scouts	0.5	0.6	0.6	0.5	0.5
Other clubs	2.5	2.5	2.5	2.2	2.2
Sports	3.7	3.5	2.5	2.5	4.0
Hobbies	1.5	2.5	2.0	1.0	2.5
Church attendance	2.5	2.0	2.5	3.0	3.5
Dates	3.0	4.5	3.2	4.5	4.5
Get together with friend of same sex	5.5	6.0	4.0	3.7	6.0
Go out alone	1.5	2.5	1.5	2.5	1.3
Go out with crowd	2.5	3.2	2.5	3.3	4.3
Do homework	11.0	8.0	14.0	4.5	9.5
Work for pay	2.5	2.0	2.0	3.7	4.0
Do chores at home	2.7	3.0	3.0	2.5	3.0
Do things with family	3.0	3.0	3.0	3.0	3.5
Movies	2.5	3.0	3.0	4.0	3.5
Study (not homework)	2.5	2.0	2.0	1.7	1.5
All going out items (J, K, L, M)	3.1	4.0	2.8	3.5	4.0

264

References

Alter, H. M. A study of high school students with scores of 130 and above on the California Test of Mental Maturity. Unpublished paper. 1953.

Altus, W. D. A college achiever and non-achiever scale for the Minnesota Multiphasic Personality Inventory. *J. appl. Psychol.*, 1948, **32**, 385–397.

Applbaum, M. J. A special guidance program for gifted underachievers of the tenth grade. *Bull. Natl Ass. Sec. Sch. Princ.*, 1961, **45**, 20–33.

Armstrong, Marion E. A comparison of the interests and social adjustment of underachievers and normal achievers at the secondary school level. *Diss. Abstr.*, 1955, **15**(12), 1349–1350.

Assum, A. L., and Levy, S. J. A comparative study of the academic ability and achievement of two groups of college students. *J. educ. Psychol.*, 1947, **38**, 307–310.

Atkinson, J. W. Motivational determinants of risk-taking behavior. *Psychol. Rev.*, 1957, **64**, 359–372.

Atkinson, J. W. *Motives in fantasy, action, and society: a method of assessment and study.* New York: Van Nostrand, 1958.

Atkinson, J. W. Personality dynamics. *Ann. Rev. Psychol.*, 1960, **11**, 255–290.

Barrett, H. O. Underachievement, a pressing problem. *The Bull.*, 1956, **36**(3), 111.

Barrett, H. O. An intensive study of thirty-two children. *Personnel guid. J.*, 1957, **36**, 192–194.

Barzun, J. *The house of intellect.* New York: Harper, 1959.

Battle, H. J. Relation between personal values and scholastic achievement. *J. exp. Educ.*, 1957, **26**, 27–41.

Bayley, Nancy. On the growth of intelligence. *Amer. Psychologist*, 1955, **10**, 805–818.

Berger, I. L., and Sutker, A. R. The relationship of emotional adjustment and intellectual capacity to academic underachievement of college students. *Ment. Hyg., N.Y.*, 1956, **40**, 65–77.

Bills, R. E., Vance, E. L., and McLean, O. S. An index of adjustment and values. *J. consult. Psychol.*, 1951, **15**, 257–261.

265

Bishton, R. C. A study of some factors related to achievement of intellectually superior eighth-grade children. *J. educ. Res.*, 1957, **51**, 203–207.

Blackman, G. J. A clinical study of the personal structures and adjustments of pupils underachieving and overachieving in reading. *Diss. Abstr.*, 1955, **15**(10), 1199–1200.

Bonney, A. A. A study of characteristics of selected eighth grade pupils in relation to differences between educational achievement as measured by standardized tests and academic success as indicated by school marks. *Coll. educ. Rec.* (Univer. of Washington), 1959, **25**(3), 31–32.

Borislow, B. Self-evaluation and academic achievement. *J. counsel. Psychol.*, 1962, **9**(3), 246–254.

Borow, H. A. A psychometric study of non-intellectual factors in college achievement. Unpublished doctoral dissertation, Pennsylvania State Col., 1945.

Boyce, E. M. A comparative study of overachieving and underachieving college students on factors other than scholastic aptitude. *Diss. Abstr.*, 1956, **16**(3), 2088–2089.

Brameld, T. Anti-intellectualism in education. *J. soc. Issues*, 1955, **40**(3), 35–40.

Bresee, C. W. Affective factors associated with academic underachievement in high school students. *Diss. Abstr.*, 1957, **17**(1), 90–91.

Bridgman, D. S. Where the loss of talent occurs and why. In *College Admissions*, vol. 7, *The search for talent*. New York: College Entrance Examination Board, 1960, pp. 30–45.

Bronfenbrenner, U. Freudian theories of identification and their derivatives. *Child Develpm.*, 1960, **31**(1), 15–40.

Brookover, W. B., Paterson, Ann, and Thomas, S. Self-concept of ability and school achievement. Final report of Cooperative Research Project, No. 845. East Lansing: Office of Research and Publications of Michigan State Univer., 1962.

Brown, H. S. An investigation of the validity of the Minnesota Multiphasic Personality Inventory for a college population and the relationship of certain personality traits to achievement. Unpublished doctoral dissertation, Univer. of Minnesota, 1947.

Bruner, J. S., and Caron, A. J. Cognition, anxiety, and achievement in the pre-adolescent. Unpublished report, Harvard Univer., November 1959.

Burgess, Elva. Personality factors in over- and underachievers in engineering. *Abstr. of Diss.*, 1953, **16**, 536–543 (Pennsylvania State Univer.).

Caldwell, E. Short-term effect of intensive vocational counseling upon talented students with inferior school marks. California Test Bureau, unpublished paper, Title V, NDEA research through the State Department of Education, Tallahassee, Fla., March 1962 (mimeographed).

Calhoun, S. R. The effect of counseling on a group of eighth grade underachievers. *Diss. Abstr.*, 1956, **16**(2), 1397–1398.

Caron, A. J. Variables on knowledge-seeking behavior. In M. J. Aschner and C. E. Bish (Eds.), *Productive thinking in education.* Washington, D.C.: Natl Educ. Ass., 1965, pp. 131–151.

Carter, H. D. Overachievers and underachievers in the junior high school. *Calif. J. educ. Res.,* 1961, **12,** 51–56.

Carter, H. L. J., and McGinnis, Dorothy. Some factors which differentiate college freshmen having lowest and highest point-hour ratios. *J. educ. Res.,* 1952, **46,** 219–226.

Centi, O. Personality factors related to college success. *J. educ. Res.,* 1962, **55**(4), 187–188

Chance June E. Independence training and first graders' achievement. *J. counsel. Psychol.,* 1961, **25**(2), 149–154.

Clark, J. H., Grade achievement of female college students in relation to non-intellective factors: MMPI items. *J. soc. Psychol.,* 1953, **37,** 275–281.

Clark, K. B. The most valuable hidden resource. *Coll. Bd Rev.,* 1956, **29,** 23–26.

Clarks, E. C. Factors relating to underachievement. *Sch. and Community,* November 1962, **49,** 22–23.

Cohn, B. A school report on group counseling. *Personnel guid. J.,* 1962, **41**(2), 133–138.

Coleman, J. S. *The adolescent society.* New York: Free Press, 1961.

Conklin, Agnes M. A study of the personalities of gifted students by means of the control group. *Amer. J. Orthopsychiat.,* 1931, **1,** 178–183.

Conklin, Agnes M. Failures of highly intelligent pupils. *Teach. Coll. Contr. Educ.,* 1940, No. 792.

Cooley, W. Predicting choice of a career in scientific research. Paper presented to Amer. Psychol. Ass., September 1962.

Cronbach, L. J. Studies of the group Rorschach in relation to success in the college of the University of Chicago. *J. educ. Psychol.,* 1950, **41,** 65–82.

Crowne, D. P., and Stephens, M. W. Self-acceptance and self-evaluative behavior: a critique of methodology. *Psychol. Bull.,* 1961, **58,** 104–121.

Curry, R. L. The effect of socioeconomic status on the scholastic achievement of sixth-grade children. Part I. *Brit. J. educ. Psychol.,* 1962, **32,** 46–49.

Darley, J. G. Scholastic achievement and measured maladjustment. *J. appl. Psychol.,* 1937, **21,** 485–493.

Davie, J. S. Some observations on superior students. *J. educ. Sociol.,* 1961, **35**(4), 172–177.

Dearborn, W. F. The student's background in relation to school success. In Wilma T. Donahue (Ed.), *Guidance conference on the measurement of student adjustment and achievement.* Ann Arbor: Univer. of Mich. Press, 1949, pp. 191–200.

de Hirsch, Katrina. Two categories of learning difficulties in adolescents. *Amer. J. Orthopsychiat.,* 1963, **33**(1), 87–91.

D'Heurle, Edna A., Mellinger, Jeanne C., and Haggard, E. A. Personality, intellectual and achievement patterns in gifted children. *Psychol. Monogr.*, 1959, **73** No. 13 (Whole No. 483).

Diener, C. L. Similarities and differences between overachieving and underachieving students. *Personnel guid. J.*, 1960, **38**(5), 396–400.

Doppelt, J. E. The organization of mental abilities. *Teach. Coll. Contr. Educ.*, 1950, No. 962.

Dowd, R. J. Under-achieving students of high capacity. *J. Higher Educ.*, 1952, **23**, 327–330.

Drasgow, J. Underachievers. *J. counsel. Psychol.*, 1957, **4**(3), 210–211.

Drews, Elizabeth M. A four-year study of 150 gifted adolescents. Report presented to the Amer. Psychol. Ass., December 1957 (mimeographed).

Drews, Elizabeth M., and Teahan, J. E. Parental attitudes and academic achievers. *J. clin. Psychol.*, 1957, **13**, 328–332.

Duff, O. L., and Siegel, L. Biographical factors associated with academic over- and underachievement. *J. educ. Psychol.*, 1960, **51**(1), 43–46.

Eckert, Ruth F. Analyzing the superior college student. *Sch. & Soc.*, 1935, **41**, 69–72.

Edelston, H. Educational failure with high intelligence quotient: a clinical study. *J. genet. Psychol.*, 1950, **77**, 85–116.

Farquhar, W. W., and Payne, D. A. Factors in the academic-occupational motivations of eleventh grade under- and over-achievers. Mimeographed Report Project No. 846. East Lansing: Mich. State Univer., 1963.

Fink, M. B. Self-concept as it relates to academic underachievement. *Calif. J. educ. Res.*, 1962, **13**, 57–62.

Fliegler, L. A. Understanding the underachieving gifted child. *Psychol. Rep.*, 1957, **3**, 533–536.

Ford, T. R. Social factors affecting academic performance: further evidence. *Sch. Rev.*, 1956, **4**, 415–422.

Fox, Mildred. Providing for the gifted. *Natl Ass. Sec. Sch. Princ.*, 1953, **37**, 78–81.

Frankel, E. A comparative study of achieving and underachieving high school boys of high intellectual ability. *J. educ. Res.*, 1960, **53**, 172–180.

Fund for the Advancement of Education. *They went to college early.* Evaluation Report No. 2, New York: Author, 1957.

Gardner, J. W. *Excellence: can we be equal and excellent too?* New York: Harper, 1961.

Gebhart, G. G., and Hoyt, D. P. Personality needs of under- and over-achieving freshmen. *J. appl. Psychol.*, 1958, **42**, 125–128.

Getzels, J. W., and Jackson, P. W. *Creativity and intelligence.* New York: Wiley, 1962.

Gilmore, J. V. A new venture in the testing of motivation. *Coll. Bd Rev.*, 1952, **15**, 221–226.

Goldberg, Miriam L. Early identification of potential underachievers. Unpublished report of the Talented Youth Project, Horace Mann–Lincoln Inst. of Sch. Experimentation, Teachers Coll., Columbia Univer., 1957.

Goldberg, Miriam L. Studies in underachievement among the academically talented. In A. Frazier (Ed.), *Freeing the capacity to learn*. Washington, D.C.: Ass. Supervis. and Curriculum Develpm., 1960, pp. 56–73.

Goldberg, Miriam L., *et al.* A three-year experimental program at DeWitt Clinton High School to help bright underachievers. *High Points* (Board of Education of the City of New York), 1959, 4, 5–35.

Gough, H. G. The relationship of socio-economic status to personality inventory and achievement test scores. *J. educ. psychol.*, 1946, 37, 527–540.

Gough, H. G. Factors relating to the academic achievement of high school students. *J. educ. Psychol.*, 1949, 40, 65–78.

Gough, H. G. The construction of a personality scale to predict scholastic achievement. *J. appl. Psychol.*, 1953, 37, 361–366. (a)

Gough, H. G. What determines the academic achievement of high school students? *J. educ. Res.*, 1953, 46, 321–331. (b)

Gough, H. G. Factors related to differential achievement among gifted persons. Paper presented at Amer. Psychol. Ass., 1955 (mimeographed).

Gowan, J. C. The under-achieving gifted child. A problem for everyone. *Except. Child.*, 1955, 21, 247–249.

Gowan, J. C. Dynamics of the underachievement of gifted students. *Except. Child.*, 1957, 24, 98–102.

Gowan, J. C. Factors of achievement in high school and college. *J. counsel. Psychol.*, 1960, 7, 91–95.

Gowan, J. C., and Scheibel, R. W. The improvement of reading in gifted children. *Educ. Admin. Superv.*, January 1960, 35–40.

Graff, F. A. Occupational choice factors in normally achieving and underachieving intellectually superior twelfth grade boys. *Diss. Abstr.*, 1957, 17(3), 2207–2208.

Granzow, K. R. A comparative study of underachievers, normal achievers, and overachievers in reading. *Diss. Abstr.*, 1954, 14(1), 631–632.

Griffiths, G. R. The relationship between scholastic achievement and personality adjustment of men college students. *J. appl. Psychol.*, 1945, 29, 360–367.

Guilford, J. P. The three faces of intellect. *Amer. Psychologist*, August 1959, 14(8), 469–479.

Haggard, E. A. Socialization, personality and academic achievement in gifted children. *Sch. Rev.*, 1957, 65, 388–414.

Hall, W. E., and Gaeddert, W. Social skills and their relationship to scholastic achievement. *J. genet. Psychol.*, 1960, 96, 269–273.

Harris, C., and Trolta, F. An experiment with underachievers. *Educ.*, 1962, 82, 347–349.

Hausdorff, H., and Kowitz, G. An exploratory study of tenth grade achievement. Unpublished report, Univer. of Pittsburgh, 1964 (mimeographed).

Herron, E. W. Intellectual achievement-motivation: a study in construct clarification. *Diss. Abstr.*, 1962, 23(1), 298.

Holland, J. L. The prediction of college grades from the California Psychological Inventory and the Scholastic Aptitude Test. *J. educ. Psychol.*, 1959, **50**(4), 135–142.

Holland, J. L. The prediction of college grades from personality and aptitude variables. *J. educ. Psychol.*, 1960, **51**, 245–254.

Holland, J. L. Creative and academic performance among talented adolescents. *J. educ. Psychol.*, 1961, **52**(3), 136–147.

Holland, J. L., and Austin, A. W. The need for redefining "talent" and "talent loss." *J. Higher Educ.*, 1962, **33**(2), 77–82.

Holland, J. L., and Stalnaker, Ruth C. A descriptive study of talented high school seniors: National Merit Scholars. *Bull. Natl Ass. Sec. Sch. Princ.*, 1958, **42**, 9–21.

Hollingworth, Leta M. *Gifted children: their nature and nurture.* New York: Macmillan, 1926.

Holmes, Frances B. A study of the psychological, emotional, and intellectual factors associated with academic underachievement. *Indep. Sch. Bull.*, 1962, **1**, 54–59.

Hopkins, J., Mallenson, N., and Sarnoff, I. Some non-intellective correlates of success and failure among university students. *Brit. J. educ. Psychol.*, 1958, **28**, 25–36.

Horrall, Bernice M. Academic performance and personality adjustments of highly intelligent college students. *Genet. Psychol. Monogr.*, 1957, **55**, 3–83.

Hoyt, D. P., and Norman, W. T. Adjustment and academic predictability. *J. counsel. Psychol.*, 1954, **1**, 96–99.

Hunt, J. McV. *Intelligence and experience.* New York: Ronald, 1961.

Iscoe, I. Probationers and honor students. *Univer. Texas Arts and Sciences*, 1959, **3**(2), 1–5.

Jackson, P. W., and Getzels, J. W. Psychological health and classroom functioning: a study of dissatisfaction with school among adolescents. *J. educ. Psychol.*, 1959, **50**(6), 295–300.

Jonietz, Alice K. A study of achieving and non-achieving students of superior ability. Unpublished report, Univer. of Illinois, 1959 (mimeographed).

Kagan, J., and Moss H. *Birth to maturity: A study in psychological development.* New York: Wiley, 1962.

Kagan, J., Moss, H. A., and Sigel, I. Psychological significance of styles of conceptualization. *Monogr. of the Soc. for Res. in Child. Develpm.*, 1963, **28**, 73–112.

Kahl, J. A. Educational aspirations of 'common man' boys. *Harvard Educ. Rev.*, 1953, **23**, 186–203.

Karnes, Merle B. The efficacy of two organizational plans for underachieving gifted children. *Except. Child.*, 1963, **29**, 438–446.

Karnes, Merle B., McCoy, G. F., Zerbach, R. R., Wollersheim, Janet, Clarizio, H. F., Gostin, Lela, and Stanley, Lola. Factors associated with underachievement and overachievement of intellectually gifted children. *Except. Child.*, 1961, **27**, 167–175.

Kehas, C. D. Underachievement as a function of self-concept. Paper presented at Amer. Personnel and Guid. Ass., Washington, D.C., 1963.

Keppers, G. L., and Caplan, S. W. Group counseling with academically able underachieving students. *New Mexico Studies in Educ.*, *Educ. Res. Bull.*, 1962, 1, 12–17.

Kimball, Barbara. The sentence completion technique in a study of scholastic underachievement. *J. consult. Psychol.*, 1952, 16, 353–358.

Kimball, Barbara. Case studies in educational failure during adolescence. *Amer. J. Orthopsychiat.*, 1953, 23, 406–415.

Kirk, Barbara. Test versus academic performance in malfunctioning students. *J. consult. Psychol.*, 1952, 16, 213–216.

Knaak, Nancy K. A study of the characteristics of academically successful and unsuccessful freshman women who entered Northwestern University in the fall of 1954. *Diss. Abstr.*, 1957, 17(1), 304–305.

Kreuter, G. Vanishing genius: Lewis Terman and the Stanford study. *Hist. Educ. Quart.*, March 1962, 2, 6–18.

Krippner, S. The vocational preference of high-achieving and low-achieving junior high school students. *Gifted child Quart.*, 1961, 5, 88–90.

Krugman, M. Identification and preservation of talent. *Teach. Coll. Rec.*, 1960, 51, 459–463.

Kurtz, J. J., and Swenson, Esther J. Factors related to overachievement and underachievement in school. *Sch. Rev.*, 1951, 59, 472–480.

Layton, Edna T. A study of the factors associated with failure in the ninth grade of the Hempstead High School. *Microfilm Abstr.*, 1951, 11(11), 924–925 (New York Univer.).

Leibman, O. B. The relationship of personal and social adjustment to academic achievement in the elementary school. *Diss. Abstr.*, 1954, 14 (1), 67.

Lewis, W. D. A study of superior children in the elementary school. *Contri. to Educ.*, No. 266, 1940. (George Peabody College for Teachers).

Lewis, W. D. Comparative study of the personalities, interests, and home backgrounds of gifted children of superior and inferior intellectual achievement. *Pedag. Seminary* and *J. genet. Psychol.*, 1941, 59, 207–218.

Little, K. J., Donaldson, A., Fenske, R. H., and Fintel, N. O. *Exploration into the college plans and experiences of high school graduates: a statewide inquiry.* Madis Sch. of Educ., Univer. of Wisconsin, 1959.

Lum, Mabel K. A comparison of under- and overachieving female college students. *J. educ. Psychol.*, 1960, 51(3), 109–114.

McCarthy, Sister May Peterbo. The effectiveness of a modified counseling procedure in promoting learning among bright underachieving adolescents. Final summary of research supported under the terms of Public Law 531, Project 052. Weston, Mass.: Regis Coll., 1957 (mimeographed).

McClelland, D. C., Atkinson, J. W., Clark, R. A., and Lowell, E. L. *The achievement motive.* New York: Appleton-Century-Crofts, 1953.

McClelland, D. C., Baldwin, A. L., Bronfenbrenner, U., and Strodtbeck, F. L. *Talent and society: new perspectives in the identification of talent.* New York: Van Nostrand, 1958.

McCracken, R. A. Accelerating the reading speed of sixth grade gifted children. *Except. Child.*, 1960, **27**, 27–28.

McGuire, C. The prediction of talented behavior in the junior high school. In Educational Testing Service, *Proceedings: Invitational Conference on Testing Problems.* Princeton, N.J.: Author, 1960, pp. 46–73.

McGuire, C. Creativity emotionality. Report 12, Austin: Laboratory of Human Behavior, Univer. of Texas, 1962.

McKeachie, W. J. Motivation, teaching methods, and college learning. In M. R. Jones (Ed.), *Nebraska Symposium on Motivation.* Lincoln, Neb.: Univer. of Nebraska Press, 1961, pp. 11–146.

McKenzie, J. D., Jr. An attempt to develop Minnesota Multiphasic Personality Inventory scales predictive of academic over- and under-achievement. *Diss. Abstr.*, 1961, **22**(1), 632.

McQuary, J. P. Some relationships between non-intellectual characteristics and academic achievement. *J. educ. Psychol.*, 1953, **44**, 215–228.

McQuary, J. P. Some differences between under- and over-achievers in college. *Educ. Admin. Supervis.*, 1954, **40**, 117–120.

Malpass, L. F. Some relationships between students' perception of school and their achievement. *J. educ. Psychol.*, 1953, **44**, 475–482.

Marx, G. L. A comparison of the effectiveness of two methods of counseling with academic underachievers. *Diss. Abstr.*, 1959, **20**(6), 2144–2145.

Matire, J. G. Relationships between the self-concept and differences in the strength and generality of achievement motivation. *J. Pers.*, 1956, **24**, 364–375.

Mead, Margaret. The gifted child in the American culture of today. *J. Teach. Educ.*, 1954, **5**, 211–214.

Michael, W. B., Jones, R. A., and Trembly, W. A. The factored dimensions of a measure of motivation for college students. *Educ. psychol. Measmt*, 1959, **19**(4), 667–671.

Middleton, G., Jr., and Guthrie, G. M. Personality syndromes and academic achievement. *J. educ. Psychol.*, 1959, **50**(2), 66–69.

Miles, Catherine C. Gifted children. In L. Carmichael (Ed.), *Manual of child psychology* (2nd ed.). New York: Wiley, 1954, pp. 984–1063.

Miller, D. R., and Swanson, G. E. *Inner conflict and defense.* New York: Holt, 1960.

Miller, L. M. (Ed.) *Guidance for the underachiever with superior ability.* Bull. EO 25021, U.S. Dept. of Health, Educ., and Welfare, Washington, D.C., 1961.

Miller, Vera V. The early identification and treatment of underachieving primary school pupils. Evanston, Ill.: Community Consolidated Schools, 1962 (mimeographed).

Mitchell, Blythe. *The underachiever: a new approach.* New York: Test Department, Harcourt, Brace and World, 1963.

Mitchell, J. V., Jr. Goal-setting behavior as a function of self-acceptance, over- and underachievement and related personality variables. *J. educ. Psychol.,* 1959, **50**(3), 93–104.

Monroe, Ruth L. Prediction of the adjustment and academic performance of college students by a modification of the Rorschach method. *Appl. Psychol. Monogr.,* 1945, No. 7.

Montalto, Fannie D. An application of the group Rorschach technique to the problem of achievement in college. *J. clin. Psychol.,* 1946, **2**, 254–260.

Morgan, H. H. A psychometric comparison of achieving and non-achieving college students of high ability. *J. consult. Psychol.,* 1952, **16**, 292–298.

Morrow, W. R., and Wilson, R. C. Family relationships of bright high-achieving and underachieving high school boys. *Child Develpm.,* 1961, **32**(3), 501–510. (a)

Morrow, W. R., and Wilson, R. C. The self-reported personal and social adjustment of bright high-achieving and underachieving high school boys. *J. child Psychol. Psychiat.,* 1961, **2**, 203–209. (b)

Motto, J. J. A reply to Drasgow on underachievers. *J. counsel. Psychol.,* 1959, **6**(3), 245–247.

Musselman, J. W. Factors associated with the achievement of high school pupils of superior intelligence. *J. exp. Educ.,* 1942, **11**, 53–68.

Nash, R. A study of particular self-perceptions as related to scholastic achievement of junior high school age pupils in a middle class community. *Diss. Abstr.,* 1964, **24**(9), 3837.

Nason, L. J. Academic achievement of gifted high school students. *Univer. S. Calif. Educ. Monogr. Ser.,* 1958, No. 17.

National Merit Scholarship Corporation. *Annual report for the year ending June 30, 1956.* Evanston, Ill.: Author, 1956.

Norman, R. D., Clark, Betty P., and Bossemer, D. W. Age, sex, IQ, and achievement patterns in achieving and nonachieving gifted children. *Except. Child.,* 1962, **29**(3), 116–123.

Ohlsen, Merle M., and Proff, F. C. The extent to which group counseling improves the academic and personal adjustment of the underachieving gifted adolescents. Urbana, Ill.: Univer. of Illinois, 1960. Cooperative Research Project No. 623 (mimeographed).

O'Leary, M. U. The measurement and evaluation of the work habits of overachievers and underachievers to determine the relationship of these habits to achievement. *Diss. Abstr.,* 1955, **15**(3), 2104–2105.

Owens, W. A., and Johnson, Wilma C. Some measured personality traits of collegiate underachievers. *J. educ. Psychol.,* 1949, **40**, 41–46.

Payne, D. A., and Farquhar, W. W. The dimensions of an objective measure of academic self-concept. *J. educ. Psychol.,* 1962, **53**(4), 187–192.

Pearlman, S. An investigation of the problems of academic under-achievement among intellectually superior college students. *Diss. Abstr.*, 1952, **12**(1), 599.

Phelps, M. O. An analysis of certain factors associated with underachievement among high school students. *Diss. Abstr.*, 1957, **17**(1), 306–307.

Pierce, J. V. Personality and achievement among able high school boys. *J. Indiv. Psychol.*, 1961, **17**, 102–107. (a)

Pierce, J. V. *Sex differences in achievement motivation of able high school students.* Quincy, Ill.: Univer. of Chicago Quincy Youth Development Project, December 1961 (mimeographed). (b)

Pierce, J. V., and Bowman, P. H. Motivation patterns of superior high school students. In *The gifted student*. Cooperative Res. Monogr., No. 2, Washington, D.C.: Superintendent of Documents, U.S. Government Printing Office, 1960, pp. 33–66.

Pimsleur, P., Stockwell, R. P., and Comrey, A. L. Foreign language learning ability. *J. educ. Psychol.*, 1962, **53**, 15–26.

Portland Public Schools. The gifted child in Portland: a report of five years of experience in developing a program for children of exceptional endowment, Portland public schools. *The School System.* Portland, Oreg.: Author, 1959, Chap. IX.

Powell, W. J., and Jourard, S. M. Some objective evidence of immaturity in underachieving college students. *J. Counsel. Psychol.*, 1963, **10**(3), 276–282.

Quinn, S. B. Relationships of certain personality characteristics to college achievement. *Diss. Abstr.*, 1957, **17**(1), 809.

Ratchick, I. Achievement and capacity: a comparative study of pupils with low achievement and high intelligence quotients with pupils of high achievement and high intelligence quotients in a selected New York City high school. *Diss. Abstr.*, 1953, **13**, 1049–1050.

Reed, C. E. A study of three groups of college preparatory students who differ in relative achievement. *Diss. Abstr.*, 1955, **15**(3), 2106.

Regensburg, Jeanette. Studies of educational success and failure in supernormal children. In R. S. Woodworth (Ed.), *Archives of Psychology*, No. 129. New York: Columbia Univer. Press, 1931.

Ritter, E., and Thome, L. The gifted aren't delivering. *Calif. J. sec. Educ.*, 1954, **29**, 480–482.

Roache, Miriam H. Counseling underachievers: does it help? *The Exchange*, March 1963, 3.

Robinowitz, R. Attributes of pupils achieving beyond their level of expectancy. *J. Pers.*, 1956, **24**, 308–317.

Rockefeller Panel Reports. *The pursuit of excellence: education and the future of America.* Special Studies Project Report V. Garden City, N.Y.: Doubleday, 1958.

Roe, Anne. *The making of a scientist.* New York: Dodd, Mead, 1952.

Rogers, C. R. A theory of therapy, personality, and interpersonal relationships, as developed in the client-centered framework. In S. Koch (Ed.), *Psychology: a study of a science.* Study I. *Conceptual and Systematic.* Vol. 3. *Formulations of the person and the social context.* New York: McGraw-Hill, 1959, pp. 184–256.

Rosen, B. C. The achievement syndrome: a psychocultural dimension of social stratification. *Amer. sociol. Rev.,* 1956, **21,** 203–211.

Rosen, B. C., and D'Andrade, R. The psychosocial origins of achievement motivation. *Sociometry,* 1959, **22,** 185–195; 215–218.

Rust, R. M., and Ryan, F. J. The relationship of some Rorschach variables to academic behavior. *J. Pers.,* 1953, **21,** 441–456.

Rust, R. M., and Ryan, F. J. The Strong Vocational Interest Blank and college achievement. *J. appl. Psychol.,* 1954, **38,** 341–345.

Ryan, F. J. Personality differences between under- and overachievers in college. *Diss. Abstr.,* 1951, **11,** 967–968.

Sarason, S. R., Davidson, K. S., Lighthall, F. F., Waite, R. R., and Ruebush, B. K. *Anxiety in elementary school children.* New York: Wiley, 1960.

Saunders, D. R. Moderator variables in prediction. *Educ. Psychol. Measmt,* 1956, **16,** 209–222.

Sharpe, Susie M. The relation of personality factors to intellectual functioning and achievement in nine- and ten-year-old children. *Diss. Abstr.,* 1954, **14**(2), 2278–2279.

Shaw, M. C. Need achievement scales as predictors of academic success. *J. educ. Psychol.,* 1961, **52**(6), 282–285.

Shaw, M. C., and Black, M. D. The reaction to frustration of bright high school underachievers. *Calif. J. educ. Res.,* 1960, **11**(3), 120–124.

Shaw, M. C., and Brown, D. J. Scholastic underachievement of bright college students. *Pers. guid. J.,* 1957, **36,** 195–199.

Shaw, M. C., and Dulton, B. E. The use of the Parent Attitude Research Inventory with the parents of bright academic underachievers. *J. educ. Psychol.,* 1962, **53**(5), 203–208.

Shaw, M. C., Edson, K., and Bell, H. M. The self-concepts of bright underachieving high school students as revealed by an adjective check list. *Pers. guid. J.,* 1960, **39,** 193–196.

Shaw, M. C., and Grubb, J. Hostility and able high school underachievers. *J. counsel. Psychol.,* 1958, **5**(4), 263–266.

Shaw, M. C., and McCuen, J. T. The onset of academic underachievement in bright children. *J. educ. Psychol.,* 1960, **51**(3), 103–108.

Siss, R. N. Expectations of mothers and teachers for independence and reading and their influence upon reading achievement and personality attributes of third grade boys. *Diss. Abstr.,* 1963, **23**(11), 4230.

Spence, K. W. A theory of emotionally based drive (D) and its relation to performance in simple learning situations. *Amer. Psychologist.,* 1958, **13,** 131–141.

REFERENCES

Stagner, R. The relation of personality to academic aptitude and achievement. *J. educ. Res.*, 1933, **26**, 648–660.

Stamatakos, L. C., and Shaffer, R. H. Effects of special attention upon potentially superior freshman students. *Pers. guid. J.*, 1959, **38**, 106–111.

Steinzor, B. Rorschach responses of achieving and nonachieving college students of high ability. *Amer. J. Orthopsychiat.*, 1944, **14**, 494–504.

Stephenson, W. *The study of behavior: Q-technique and its methodology.* Chicago: Univer. of Chicago Press, 1953.

Stoner, W. G. Factors related to the underachievement of high school students. *Diss. Abstr.*, 1957, **17**(1), 96–97.

Strodtbeck, F. L. Family interaction, values and achievement. In D. C. McClelland, *et al.* (Eds.), *Talent and society: new perspectives in the identification of talent,* Princeton, N.J.: Van Nostrand, 1958.

Strong, D. J., and Feder, D. D. Measurement of the self-concept: a critique of the literature. *J. counsel. Psychol.*, 1961, **8**, 170–178.

Super, D. E., and Overstreet, Phoebe L. *The vocational maturity of ninth grade boys.* New York: Teachers College Press, Teach. Coll., Columbia Univer., 1960.

Sutcliffe, C. E. Factors related to low achievement by high school pupils of high mental ability. Unpublished doctoral dissertation, Univer. of Southern California, 1958.

Sutton, Rachel S. An analysis of factors related to educational achievement. *J. genet. Psychol.*, 1961, **98**, 193–201.

Svensson, N. Ability grouping and scholastic achievement. *Educ. Res.*, 1962, **5**(1), 53–56 (abstract).

Swanson, E. O. A follow-up study of college trained versus non-college trained high school graduates of high ability. *Diss. Abstr.*, 1954, **14**(1), 499–500.

Sweet, L. F. The measurement of personal attitudes of younger boys. YMCA National Council. *Occasional Studies,* No. 9. New York: Association Press, 1929.

Tannenbaum, A. *Adolescent attitudes toward academic brilliance.* New York: Teachers College Press, Teach. Coll., Columbia Univer., 1962.

Taylor, J. A. Drive theory and manifest anxiety. *Psychol. Bull.*, 1956, **53**, 303–320.

Terman, L. M., and Oden, Melita. The gifted child grows up. *Genetic studies of genius,* **14**. Stanford: Stanford Univer. Press, 1947.

Terman, L. M. *et al. Mental and physical traits of a thousand gifted children.* Vol. 1. *Genetic Studies of Genius.* Stanford: Stanford Univer. Press, 1925.

Thelen, H. A. Teachability grouping. Unpublished report, Univer. of Chicago, 1961 (mimeographed).

Thistlethwaite, D. L. Scholarships and the college-going behavior of talented students. *Coll. and Univer.*, 1958, **34**(1), 65–73.

Thistlethwaite, D. L. Effects of social recognition upon the educational motivation of talented youth. *J. educ. Psychol.*, 1959, **50**, 111–116.

Thorndike, R. L. Review of California Psychological Inventory. In O. K. Buros (Ed.), *Fifth ment. measmt ybk.* Highland Park, N.J.: Gryphon Press, 1959, p. 37.

Thorndike, R. L. Methodological issues in relation to the definition and appraisal of underachievement. Paper presented to Amer. Psychol. Ass., September 1961 (mimeographed).

Thorndike, R. L. *The concepts of over- and underachievement.* New York: Teachers College Press, Teach. Coll., Columbia Univer., 1963.

Todd, F. J., Terrell, G., and Frank, C. E. Differences between normal and underachievers of superior ability. *J. appl. Psychol.*, 1962, **46**(3), 183–190.

Uhlinger, Carolyn A., and Stephens, M. A. Relation of achievement motivation to academic achievement in students of superior ability. *J. educ. Psychol.*, 1960, **51**, 259–266.

Walsh, Ann M. *Self-concepts of bright boys with learning difficulties.* New York: Teachers College Press, Teach. Coll., Columbia Univer., 1956.

Warren, Sue A., and Iannaccone, L. L. Normal children who just don't try. *Sch. Exec.*, 1959, **78**(11), 40–41.

Wedemeyer, C. A. Gifted achievers and non-achievers. *J. Higher Educ.*, 1953, **24**, 25–30.

Weigand, G. Adaptiveness and the role of parents in academic success. *Pers. guid. J.*, 1957, **35**, 518–522.

Weitz, H., Clarke, Mary, and Jones, Ora. The relationship between choice of a major field of study and academic preparation and performance. *Educ. psychol. Measmt*, 1955, **15**, 28–38.

Westfall, F. W. Selected variables in the achievement or non-achievement of the academically talented high school students. *Diss. Abstr.* (Univer. of Southern California), 1957–1958, 389–392.

White, R. W. Motivation reconsidered: the concept of competence. *Psychol. Rev.*, 1959, **66**, 297–333.

White, R. W. Competence and psychosexual stages of development. In M. Jones (Ed.), *Nebraska Symposium on Motivation.* Lincoln, Neb.: Univer. of Nebraska Press, 1960, pp. 97–144.

Whitla, D. K. Effect of tutoring on scholastic aptitude test scores. *Pers. guid. J.*, 1962, **41**(1), 32–37.

Williams, Elizabeth H. Selected cultural factors in scholastic achievement of a group of fifth grade children in Scranton public schools. *Diss. Abstr.*, 1957, **17**(1), 288.

Williams, Meta S. Acceptance and performance among gifted elementary school children. *Educ. res. Bull.* (Ohio State Univer.), 1958, **37**(8), 216–220.

Williamson, E. G. Scholastic motivation and the choice of a vocation. *Sch. and Soc.*, 1937, **46**, 353–357.

Wilson, A. B. Residential segregation of social classes and aspirations of high school boys. *Amer. soc. Rev.*, 1959, **24**(6), 836–845.

Wilson, J. A. A study of the effect of special work for gifted nonmotivated students at the eighth grade level. Paper presented to the Calif. Educ. Res. Ass., Spring, 1956.

Wilson, R. C., and Morrow, W. R. School and career adjustment of bright high-achieving and under-achieving high school boys. *J. genet. Psychol.*, 1962, **101**, 91–103.

Winborn, B., and Schmidt, L. The effectiveness of short-term group counseling upon the academic achievement of potentially superior but under-achieving college freshmen. *J. educ. Res.*, 1962, **55**, 169–173.

Winkelman, Sidra L. California Psychological Inventory profile patterns of underachievers, average achievers and overachievers. *Diss. Abstr.*, 1963, **23**(3), 2988–2989.

Winterbottom, Marian R. The relation of need for achievement to learning experiences in independence and mastery. In J. W. Atkinson (Ed.), *Motives in fantasy, action and society.* Princeton, N.J.: Van Nostrand, 1958, pp. 453–478.

Witkin H. A. *Psychological differentiation: studies of development.* New York: Wiley, 1962.

Wolfle, Dael. Diversity of talent. *Amer. Psychologist*, 1960, **15**(8), 534–545.

Young, C. W., and Estabrooks, G. W. Non-intellective factors related to scholastic achievement. *Psychol. Bull.*, 1934, **31**, 735–736.

Zorbaugh, G. S., and Kuder, G. T. College grades and the vocational motive. *Sch. and Soc.*, 1937, **46**, 62–64.

Author index

279

Subject index